DISCARD

VESTAL 940.5412 OGBU
Ogburn, Charlton,
The marauders /

FEB 2 0 2007			
DEC 3 0 2008			
NOV 0 4 2010			
APR 1 4 2011			
JUN 2 7 2011			
DEC 1 3 2011			
AUG 0 2 2019 APR 2 7 2016			

JUN 2 4 2003

DISCARD

VESTAL PUBLIC LIBRARY

0 00 10 0258840 6

Vestal Public Library
Vestal, New York 13850

The Marauders

Charlton Ogburn, Jr.

THE OVERLOOK PRESS
WOODSTOCK & NEW YORK

To those who fought there

This edition first published in paperback in the United States in 2002 by
The Overlook Press, Peter Mayer Publishers, Inc.
Woodstock & New York

Woodstock:
One Overlook Drive
Woodstock, NY 12498
www.overlookpress.com
[for individual orders, bulk and special sales, contact our Woodstock office]

New York:
141 Wooster Street
New York, NY 10012

Copyright © 1956, 1959 by Charlton Ogburn, Jr.

All rights reserved. No part of this publication may be reproduced or
transmitted in any form or by any means, electronic or mechanical,
including photocopy, recording, or any information storage and
retrieval system now known to be invented, without permission in
writing from the publisher, except by a reviewer who wishes to quote
brief passages in connection with a review written for
inclusion in a magazine, newspaper, or broadcast.

Library of Congress Cataloging-in-Publication Data

Obgurn, Charlton, Jr.
The marauders / Charlton Ogburn, Jr.
p. cm.
1. United States. Army. Composite Unit (Provisional), 5307th—History.
2. World War, 1939-1945—Regimental histories—United States.
3. World War, 1939-1945—Campaigns—Burma. I. Title
D767.6 .O4 2002   940.54'1273–dc21   2002020614

Printed in Canada
ISBN: 1-58567-234-3
1 3 5 7 9 0 8 6 4 2

MAPS

An eight-page section of photographs follows page 116

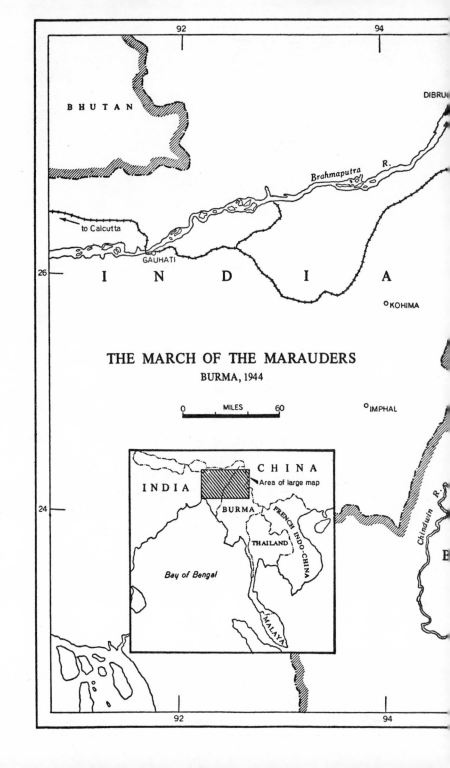

THE MARCH OF THE MARAUDERS
BURMA, 1944

0   MILES   60

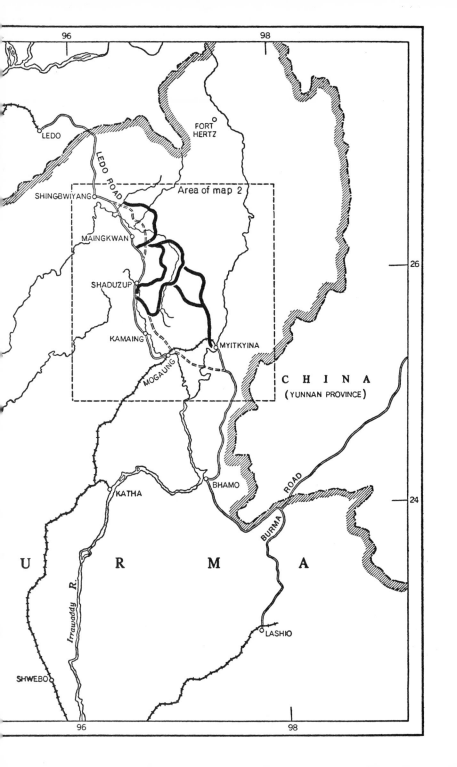

ACKNOWLEDGMENTS

It is hardly necessary to point out how much this excursion into the past owes to others. To anyone who reads it, the magnitude of their contribution will be apparent.

Two histories of the organization known originally as "Galahad" had fortunately been compiled under official direction, one during and one immediately after the period of its operations, and these were indispensable. One was a day-by-day account of those operations from January 15 to May 17, 1944, maintained by Major John M. Jones of the Public Relations Office of the China-Burma-India Theater, which, under the designation *War Diary of the 5307th Composite Unit (Provisional)*, constituted Annex 16 to the official history of the theater. Major Jones was attached to the headquarters of the organization and managed to get on paper a wealth of detail of the kind which, if not recorded at the time, can never be recaptured. For the discovery of the diary, which was buried in the Army's files and had never been printed, I am greatly indebted to Dr. A. Lewis Kolodny, formerly a captain in 2nd Battalion.

The other history was the 113-page account entitled *Merrill's Marauders* which was put out as part of the American Forces in Action Series by the Historical Branch of the Army. Based on interviews and the limited records the unit accumulated, it is a professional and readable presentation of Galahad's organization and the campaign it fought.

Other publications illuminating various episodes in Galahad's career of which I have had the advantage include an article in the *Infantry Journal* on 1st Battalion's action at Shaduzup, by Lieutenant Colonel William Lloyd Osborne; articles by Sergeant Dave Richardson in *Yank; Merrill's Marauders—What Really Happened,* by Captain Fred O. Lyons as told to Paul Wilder, which appeared in *Cosmopolitan;* and *The "Fightin' Preacher,"* by Captain Logan E. Weston.

For background, I am indebted even more than the footnotes indicate to *Stilwell's Command Problems,* by Charles F. Romanus and Riley Sunderland, an impressive and informative study which forms a volume of the vast series on the *U.S. Army in World War II* produced by the Office of the Chief of Military History, Department of the Army.

Officials of three agencies of the Government to whom I became only too familiar a figure deserve my thanks for their patience and helpfulness. The agencies are:

Magazine and Book Branch, Public Information Division, Office of the Chief of Information, Department of the Army, Office of the Chief of Military History, Department of the Army, and Reference Branch, National Archives and Reference Service, World War II Division, General Services Administration.

My thanks are also owing to the Department of the Army's Kansas City Records Center, which went to the trouble of shipping several boxes of files to the National Archives and Reference Service in Alexandria, Va., for me to examine, and to Mr. Franklin T. Orth, Deputy Assistant Secretary of the Army for Manpower and Reserves (formerly American Liaison Officer with the Chinese 150th Regiment at Myitkyina) for his part in arranging for this special service. The files were particularly valuable in that they contained a special order issued by the 475th Infantry listing those in the 5307th entitled to the Combat Infantry Badge, which is the nearest thing to a roster of the organization that has ever come to light.

I might say that this account of the Marauders would probably have done more justice to its subject had the Department of the Army's spirit of co-operation been equaled by the flow of documents it provided. For the most part such documents appear simply not to exist. As the American Forces in Action Series pamphlet explains, "the Marauders restricted their files in order to maintain mobility while they were operating behind Japanese lines. During the second mission a Japanese artillery shell scored a direct hit on the mule carrying the limited quantity of records and maps kept by the unit headquarters. During the third mission the heavy rains made preservation of papers impossible for more than a day or two. The unit's intelligence officer [Captain William A. Laffin] was killed at Myitkyina, and his records were washed away before they could be located."

For the photographs included in the book and for permission to use them, I should like to express my gratitude to the United States Army Signal Corps; Dr. A. Lewis Kolodny of Baltimore, Maryland; and Lieutenant Edward Siever, formerly of 1st Battalion. In Lieutenant Siever's case, permission has had to be assumed since I have been unable to find him.

Of my debt to former members of the organization for other contributions, I shall have something to say at the conclusion.

CHARLTON OGBURN, JR.

Oakton, Virginia
1959

TO BEGIN WITH . . .

In May, 1944, the Inspector General of the China-Burma-India Theater conducted an investigation of an American infantry regiment known to the War Department as Galahad. The investigation, undertaken in response to conditions approaching the rebellious, disclosed "an almost complete breakdown of morale in the major portion of the unit."[1] * What had happened caused a good deal of public stir when it became known and led to a Congressional hearing. Under the appellation of "Merrill's Marauders" the regiment had touched the imagination of the American people by the character of its operations, which were reminiscent of those that had given the War Between the States much of its drama. The most recent of these had been what *Time* called a "23-day mountain march that was one of the epic infantry advances of the war."

According to the *New York Times,* "the tough Marauders cracked up when by somebody's blunder their convalescents were ordered back to the flooded slit trenches." Under the heading "The Bitter Tea of General Joe"—the reference being to Joseph W. Stilwell—*Time* reported that "in the long history of warfare good outfits have disintegrated before, but seldom has their commander swallowed his pride enough to tell the whole story."

What was given out was far from being the whole story, however, even assuming that a "whole story" can ever be told.

* Superior figures refer to notes in a reference section beginning on page 297.

Unusual precautions were taken to delay the time when much of the story would even reach official ears in Washington. At a time when enlisted men in large numbers were being sent back for leave in the United States by air, the officer who had just been relieved from command of Galahad received orders from the Commanding General of the theater directing him to report to the port of embarkation "for first available water transportation to the United States." Colonel Charles N. Hunter had been with Galahad from the start as its ranking or second ranking officer, had commanded it during its times of greatest trial, and was more responsible than any other individual for its record of achievement. He also knew better than anyone else why events at the end had taken the turn they did. Sending him home by ship was calculated to postpone his arrival by a month.

In its summing up, *Time* offered a forecast that proved to be accurate: "Now that the story was out, Army men wondered what would be done. The answer was: very little."

Galahad had already been given the Distinguished Unit Award, the equivalent of a citation for outstanding performance of duty for every man in its ranks. Its accomplishments in marching 600 or 700 miles through the forests and over the hills of northern Burma and in fighting five major and seventeen minor engagements (by the War Department's tally) in a campaign that saw the Japanese driven from an area the size of Connecticut had thus been officially recognized. For the rest, there were large numbers in the hospitals to bring back to health. There were those who had served two years abroad (accounting for two thirds of the whole) to be returned to the United States for leave and reassignment. There were those who were scattered in guardhouses all across India to be dealt with in accordance with the magnitude of their offenses. There was the residue to be incorporated in a new infantry regiment for another campaign in the next dry season. There were the dead to be remembered. Other than that, there was nothing to do.

2

There was one possible exception: there was the story of Galahad to be told.

That the story was to remain untold, outside the official histories, for fourteen years seemed to me surprising, for surely it was one of the remarkable stories of the war. Nevertheless, in considering whether I should undertake to try to tell it, in default of anyone else's having done so, I had to ask myself whether it would have much to say to us today.

Would anything be accomplished by stirring up the coals of old controversies? Injustices, it seemed to me, had been done, but even if anyone cared after all these years, I doubted that I could ever come into sufficient possession of the facts to render a judgment. Beyond that I could see little purpose to be served by an account of Japan's defeat on a remote sector of the front, unless it were a study by a professional for professionals. We have new enemies today, enemies so menacing we can only wonder how the Empire of Japan, with a steel production below 20 million tons a year, could ever have seemed as dangerous as it did. Warfare, too, has changed. The weapons of World War II are archaic—certainly the ones Galahad carried. Time had moved on to an age we hardly dreamed of. It is true that some of those with whom I talked, who had been with Galahad, argued that Galahad was one kind of unit produced by the last war that had a lesson for the future, even the kind of future our world faces today. "I can't see two ways about it," said Major Samuel Vaughan Wilson, who had been the leader of of an intelligence and reconnaissance platoon. "It was guerrilla units that defeated the French in Indochina and the Dutch in Indonesia. In the next world war, if there is one, we are going to have to rely on Galahad-type forces—small, free-ranging units unhampered by fixed ties with their bases. The massing of armies is out in an era of atomic weapons. And if the giants cut loose and pummel each other into fragments with missiles, what's there going to be left to fight with but small forces able to wage war without benefit of big industrial bases?" It may well be that Sam is right. Major General Orde C. Wingate, a renowned practitioner of the art, went further when he said, "It is time to realize that most modern war is guerrilla in character." But the kind of study Sam felt was due would, again, be a matter for a professional writing for professionals.

I had to recognize, too, that if I attempted to tell the human story of Galahad I should have none of the fiction writer's privileges (even if I had his talents) but should be confined to what actually happened to identifiable individuals and—more restrictive still—to what could be discovered to have happened from such records as had been preserved and from accessible survivors of the organization, whose memories, I feared, would prove to be as unretentive as my own. I could not make up characters and incidents and revealing remarks. And because I could not get into the heads of others, there would be a disproportionate and embarrassing amount of me.

While turning these matters over in my mind I remembered how in Burma we used to sit and talk sometimes in the evening when things were slack and tell one another that it wasn't the hardship and the danger that signified most, but something beyond that. We thought maybe it had to do with our isolation, so deep in another world, the only American infantry between Italy and New Guinea, as if we were off fighting on Mars with only the supply planes overhead to connect us with the earth. But we were never able to say what it was. And this uncertainty had remained with me. What had it all proved? Galahad's brief career was in some respects a sensational one, and certainly its demonstration of courage and endurance was impressive, but I knew it had a meaning beyond that, at least for me, though I was not sure what it was.

I had a chance to ask two veterans of Galahad what, at this distance of time, the experience chiefly signified to them. Sam Wilson was one, John B. George, formerly the intelligence officer of 2nd Battalion, the other. The conviction and unanimity with which they replied struck me forcefully. What it signified was that they would never take comforts and security for granted again. No matter how grim the outlook

4

might be otherwise, they would never fail to appreciate what it meant to have a cover against the rain, to have enough to eat, to be not under fire. They had learned what was important and they would never forget it.

Well, I could subscribe to that. In a batch of letters my parents had saved was one I had written the day after I got out of Burma, sitting up in bed in an improvised hospital ward. In it I read:

"I don't know how to convey the effect of the past three months' experience. It would be easy to overdo its nightmarish aspects, for we had much to be grateful for—a temperate climate, generally fair weather, and hazards rather less than American troops had to endure in Africa and Italy. And of course one adjusts to almost any way of life and can come to derive really tremendous pleasure from the occasional opportunity to spend the night on the bamboo floor of a basha instead of on a wet hillside, and from a situation that permits one to have fires after dark, or from those rare times when one can actually eat one's fill and when enough coffee has been provided so that one can make three cups of it a day if one wishes without having to do without it later. Then there were those times when we laid up for a day alongside a beautiful clear river and we could swim and shave and wash our filthy uniforms. There were great compensations, and I think one laughed and joked about as much as one does normally. And yet it would not be enough to say that it was the worst experience I have ever been through. It was so incomparably the worst that at the time I could hardly believe in the rest of my life at all."

What was it that made it so bad? There was the hunger, the exhaustion, the drenchings, the disease, the sores, the denial of every comfort and amenity. There was the danger—above everything. All that was reason enough for most of the organization to feel that life could hold little worse than what they were going through. But that alone, I felt, did not account fully for the impress those months had made. On the other hand, it was perhaps not for me to say. I had been lucky. I was one of the few who had never had a day's illness the whole time. Until, at the end, I was injured ignominiously—and fittingly—like Achilles, in the heel. I never had any trouble keeping going. That I should have felt so well was ironical, for I had an assignment in the battalion that exposed me to much less danger than most of the others had to face.

Yet I believe others would agree with me that the major enemy was not the Japanese themselves but your own apprehensions. "The worst thing," I wrote, "was the suspense. You never knew from one moment to the next when you'd run into the Japs. Of course in the jungle you could never see a thing except a small stretch of the trail ahead." Not just when it happened but a hundred times a day you lived in anticipation through the sudden *pup-pup-pup . . . pup-pup-pup-pup* of a machine gun opening up on the column. "They say," wrote General Joseph W. Stilwell, "the coward dies a thousand deaths, the valiant dies but once. But possibly the valiant dies a thousand deaths too, if he is cursed with imagination." There was always the knowledge that we had no one on our flanks. The unit was all alone.

Then there was the consuming sense of being unready, ill-equipped for what was demanded of you. Your soul rose up in protest against the terms of trial. This was not what you were meant for! Maybe others were meant for it, but not you. Not at this time, at this place, in this way. You were not prepared. . . . Perhaps again what I say must be discounted because my case was exceptional. To make up for being spared dysentery and the fevers-of-unknown-origin, I had a piece of bad luck. I had a job I had had no training for and had no competence in.

I say bad luck. But in looking back on it I found myself wondering. For nothing could have been better calculated than that experience to bring home to me a lesson that has to be learned. It was one I could wish had been imparted to me early in life. It was one I believe must have been understood in advance by those who gave Galahad its record of heroism.

6

It is this. Being unready and ill-equipped is what you have to expect in life. It is the universal predicament. It is your lot as a human being to lack what it takes. Circumstances are seldom right. You never have the capacities, the strength, the wisdom, the virtue you ought to have. You must always make do with less than you need in a situation vastly different from what you would have chosen as appropriate for your special endowments.

In one of the old letters I came upon a clue to what had been puzzling me. It was in a passage about the sensation of being under artillery fire. "Unless you've got something to keep you occupied while it's going on," I wrote, "you're a gone goose." Nothing had ever impressed me more with the importance of work. But it was the remark that "being shelled is like normal living with the film speeded up" that opened my eyes to what I had so long been groping for. It was not as an exception to life as it is ordinarily lived that the story of Galahad had its significance. The exotic properties were deceptive; I had been looking in the wrong direction. The experience of Galahad was in fact the common experience of mankind, compressed and intensified—with the film speeded up. That was why it mattered.

What was Galahad? It was 3,000 infantrymen so recruited as to ensure that they would exhibit the extremities of human character, the worst as well as the best, the best as well as the worst. It was a band of men who were unready and ill-prepared for the mission they had and who lived with fear. It was an organization that was never given time to organize, that was caught up in historical currents and crosscurrents far beyond its control or even understanding, that was mismanaged, that was driven until the accumulation of hardships and strain and the seeds of corruption it contained brought about its undoing.

The past, when we look back upon it, is apt to move us with a special quality it has for us, and we are told that this is a trick time plays upon us, that in fact the past was as humdrum and pointless as the present: but perhaps the truth is otherwise,

7

and the adventures we have had seem after the passage of years to have been fresh and brave and poignant because—cast as it is against odds that must in the end always prove hopeless—that is what life itself truly is.

Seen in relation to all that had to be overcome, the march of Galahad's three battalions retains, I venture to believe, an enduring luster. Knowing what the combat soldiers of Galahad had to go through, you cannot but wonder how it was done. How are men equal to this?

It is a good question. It is the crucial question. Is there anyone who in the course of his life has not had reason to ask it of himself: how can I make it? This is where Galahad has, I think, the relevance I spoke of. It is why I decided to try to write the story of what happened. As far as an answer can be supplied to the question of how it is possible to keep on going, Galahad seems to me to supply it.

I On August 31, 1943, a telegram went out from the Operations Division (OPD) of the War Department General Staff in Washington to the Commanding General, United States Army Forces, China-Burma-India Theater, Forward Echelon, Chungking, marked "For personal attention Stilwell from Marshall." Its subject was "Information Pertaining to Three American Long-Range Penetration Groups," and it read in part:

Total of approximately 2,830 officers and men organized into casual detachments will arrive in India in early November. They will all be volunteers. 950 will be battle-tested troops in jungle fighting from the South and Southwest Pacific. 1900 will be from jungle-trained troops from the Caribbean Defense Command and the Continental United States. All will be of a high state of physical ruggedness.

Above volunteers have been called for with requisite qualifications and commensurate grades and ratings to form three Independent Battalions after their arrival in the theater. They must be intensively trained in jungle warfare, animal transportation and air supply in a suitable jungle area in preparation for combat in February. These units should be supplemented by such native guides and interpreters and either British, Indian, or Chinese Liaison groups as may be necessary. . . .

This telegram was an outcome of a conference held earlier in the month between President Roosevelt and Prime Minister

9

Churchill at Quebec. By then it had been well over a year since the Japanese had completed the conquests that with stunning rapidity had given them an immense empire in Eastern Asia and the Western Pacific—though they did not regard their conquests as complete. Intense and bloody fighting was in progress in the Pacific, but on the continent of Asia the two fronts, one in China and the other along the border between Burma and India, were relatively static. One of the purposes of the Quebec Conference had been to prepare for offensive action against the Japanese on the mainland. To this end, the conference established a United Nations Southeast Asia Command under an aggressive and able Britisher, Admiral Lord Louis Mountbatten, who had gained fame as a Commando leader. As soon as he had heard of his projected appointment, Admiral Mountbatten had planned to seek a more active American contribution to the theater, and this he urged with success at Quebec.

In the total picture of the war, the allocation of a regimental-sized American unit to the Burma front was a minor detail. However, this was to be the first American combat ground force to be sent to the continent of Asia in World War II and the first to go into action there since the Boxer rebellion in China at the turn of the century, and the significance of the decision went beyond the numbers involved. Among other things, it represented a success and a hopeful augury for two very singular, controversial, nonconformist, stubborn military leaders, one British and the other American, each given to making enemies or winning exasperated admiration by their coruscating bluntness of speech, intractable idiosyncrasies and single-mindedness in pursuit of their purposes. They were Major General Orde C. Wingate and Lieutenant General Joseph W. Stilwell, and their purposes, as it happened, were complementary. This was fortunate since the men themselves were antithetical in some ways as well as similar in others. Both were to leave the impress of their ideas on Galahad and, in their separate departments, to shape its destinies.

10

Wingate was the originator of the Long-Range Penetration Group. He was a fanatic—an emotional, brilliant, intellectual, sensitive, eccentric and somberly religious man. His deepest affinities were with the Old Testament, on which he had been brought up by a widowed mother. In 1936 Wingate as a young officer had been sent to Palestine to serve with British intelligence. There he had discovered in himself a burning attachment to the Zionist cause and an unusual talent for irregular warfare of the kind known in America as Indian fighting. More ardent than the Jewish leaders themselves, he had infused the Zionist movement with a militarily offensive spirit and rehearsed the illegal Jewish troops in his special brand of combat. General Dayan, Chief of Staff of the Israeli Army, has said of him, "He taught me and many another Israeli soldier everything we know." [1] In defiance of his government's express policy, he repeatedly led Jewish patrols on raids against the Arabs. It is hard not to view his conduct as having verged upon treason, as when, addressing a Jewish patriot group, he said, "Members of Hagana, the White Paper has turned you down. There will be no Jewish state unless you fight for it, and it is the English you will have to fight. The time has come to declare war on the English. I have come to ask you to make that declaration tonight." He even proposed to lead a raid on the British oil refinery at Haifa, and it was the Zionists who balked at such a blow against Great Britain in the year 1939.

Official action was taken against Wingate, but the upshot was that he was found guilty of disloyalty "only in Palestine."

There is little doubt that Wingate, as his biographer, Leonard O. Mosley, suggests, looked on himself as a modern Gideon, to whom the Lord had said, "Go in this thy might, and thou shalt save Israel." Gideon was the name Wingate gave to his first long-range penetration group, which he formed when in 1940 he was sent to the Anglo-Egyptian Sudan (with a passport stamped "Not Valid for Palestine") to take charge of rebel Ethiopian activities against Italian rule.

The force that Wingate organized, consisting of 70 British

11

officers and noncoms and 1,000 Ethiopians and Sudanese, played a part far out of proportion to its strength in Ethiopia's liberation, although Wingate had complained that the officers he was given were "escapists and make-weights," that some of the noncoms were "the scum of the Army" and that the natives were "an ill-trained, ill-armed, ill-equipped and demoralized rabble." (Had Wingate been in the original Gideon's place and been given an army of 230,000 he would doubtless have done as Gideon did and have rejected all but the 300 most zealous— only Wingate would not have waited for the Lord to propose that he do so.)

"The war for the liberation of Ethiopia," said Wingate, "is the war for all down-trodden nations—just like the war for the Jews." He threw himself into it with his usual unsparing fervor. His route of march was marked by the bones of no less than 25,000 camels, the last of which, after crossing 600 miles of some of the hardest country in Africa, died on a hill overlooking Addis Ababa. When in traversing the Sudanese desert the overloaded beasts had lain down and refused to move, he had fires built under them, and it is told how the whole country smelled of burning camel flesh. At the end, leading his Patriot Army, Wingate escorted Emperor Haile Selassie into Addis Ababa. His small army had killed almost 1,500 of the enemy and wounded over 2,000 and, largely through maneuver and bluff, had captured over 1,000 Italian officers and noncoms and 14,500 colonial troops. It had also established the conception of the Long-Range Penetration Group: a force organized for guerrilla operations deep inside enemy-occupied territory without fixed attachment to its base and relying upon radio and aircraft for communications and supply. Those who brought Galahad into being were all unquestionably acquainted with Gideon, a name of which "Galahad" was obviously reminiscent, being also dactylic in meter, inspirational in intent. It is less certain that they were aware of the aftermath of Gideon.

"After the Ethiopian campaign was over," wrote General Sir

12

Archibald P. Wavell, Commander of British Forces in the Middle East, "Wingate sent my headquarters a vehement memorandum of protest at the grievances suffered by him and his officers." In his Appreciation, as he called it, Wingate indicted his superiors for failing to give Gideon even a minimum of support and charged that "Cynicism in this war will defeat us, but it is very prevalent in our councils." Wavell, who had become a sort of protector of Wingate's, was not unduly upset, but his staff, exploding with anger, rounded up all the copies it could lay hands on of the more than 250 Wingate had had mimeographed and burned them. Taking a room in a Cairo hotel, Wingate cut his throat in an attempt at suicide that very nearly succeeded.

After Field Marshal Wavell was transferred to the command of British troops in India, he sent for Wingate. If Wingate had found the atmosphere stultifying at the Middle Eastern headquarters, he must have been appalled indeed by New Delhi, which at that time—April, 1942—and for a time thereafter had a reputation for inertia even among those less demanding of action than Wingate. However, he soon set to work upon a new application of his principles. In preparation for a long-range penetration of Burma, he organized and trained the 77th Brigade, better known as the Chindits—again complaining of the quality of the men he was given. With this force, consisting of 3,000 British and Gurkhas accompanied by 1,000 mules and bullocks and a few elephants, he set out for Burma in February, 1943. Organized in separate columns, the Chindits pushed 200 miles into Japanese-occupied territory, blowing up bridges and cuts on the railroad supplying the Japanese northern front and interrupting other Japanese communications. After three months, two thirds of the original force succeeded in getting back to India. The lessons learned, declared Wingate, could "if properly used . . . be worth the loss of many brigades."

A different appraisal was written by Lieutenant General William Slim, Commander of the British Fourteenth Army. Said

13

Slim: "As a military operation, the raid had been an expensive failure. It gave little tangible return for the losses it had suffered and the resources it had absorbed. The damage it did to Japanese communications was repaired in a few days, the casualties it inflicted were negligible, and it had no immediate effect on Japanese dispositions or plans. . . . If anything was learnt of air supply or jungle fighting, it was a costly schooling. These are hard things to say of an effort that required such stark courage and endurance as was demanded of and given by Wingate and his men." Wavell's decision to send the Chindits in, Slim argued, "was justified, not on military but on psychological grounds. . . . There was a dramatic quality about the raid which . . . lent itself to presentation as a triumph of British jungle fighting over the Japanese. Skilfully handled, the press of the Allied world took up the tale, and everywhere the story ran that we had beaten the Japanese at their own game. . . . Whatever the actual facts, to the troops in Burma it seemed the first ripple showing the turning of the tide. For this reason alone, Wingate's raid was worth all the hardship and sacrifice his men endured." [2]

One of those impressed by the exploit was Winston Churchill, who wrote of Wingate: "He is a man of genius and audacity, and has rightly been discerned by all eyes as a figure quite above the ordinary level. The expression 'The Clive of Burma' has already gained currency. There is no doubt that in the welter of inefficiency and lassitude which has characterized our operations on the Indian front, his force and achievements stand out."

The British Prime Minister had Wingate sent for and brought him to the Quebec Conference, presumably as the most effective rebuttal available of the view widely held in the United States that the British military in India were entirely too passive. He also thought Roosevelt would take to Wingate, who, though "a strange, excitable, moody creature," as Slim expressed it, "had fire in him" that "could ignite other men." ("The most persuasive talker I have ever met," General Dayan

14

called him.) The two did not hit it off, however; it may have been a clash of messiahs. But Wingate made a decided impression on other Americans at the conference. General H. H. ("Hap") Arnold, Commander of the United States Army Air Force, wrote of him: "You took one look at that face, like the face of a pale Indian chieftain, topping the uniform still smelling of jungle and sweat and war and you thought, 'Hell, this man is serious.' When he began to talk, you found out just how serious."

General Arnold agreed at Quebec to provide Admiral Mountbatten, the new Supreme Commander, Southeast Asia, with a special Air Force unit which he named Number 1 Air Commando in honor of the famous raiders Mountbatten commanded. This unit was to fly a second and much larger Chindit force into central Burma in the spring of 1944, putting it in position to disrupt Japanese communications. The Americans also agreed at Quebec to contribute a volunteer force modeled on the original Chindit brigade and of the same size, to serve in Burma and help open the way to China. The training and organization of the American force, to be known as Galahad, was to be supervised by Wingate. The original plan was for Wingate to command it too, but a later decision was to place it under Stilwell. The drawbacks to the kind of operation Wingate had conducted a few months earlier were brought out in the discussions. General Brooke, Chief of the Imperial General Staff, "expressed the thought that the long-range penetration groups should be worked in close co-operation with the units in contact with the principal Japanese forces, rather than for dramatic penetrations deep into Burma." [3] This was also to be the view of Stilwell, the practitioner of the progressive series of short hooks to the enemy's rear area, and the way in which Galahad was to be used.

Wingate had reason to be pleased by the outcome of Quebec. He could now look forward to a larger-scale effort during the next dry season to undermine the defenses of the Japanese on the front in Burma by methods that would demonstrate the

15

validity of his idea of how to win the war—an idea which he considered applicable to Europe as well as Asia and which possessed him.

Joseph W. Stilwell too was possessed by an idea for winning the war—a strategy to which, as it happened, Wingate's tactics were well adapted. He also had a right to be pleased by the decision taken at Quebec. The entry in his diary for September 2, 1943, reads: "Radio from George Marshall on US units. . . . Only 3,000, but the entering wedge. Can we use them! And how!" [4]

Stilwell, who divided his time between China and India, had several functions. He had been sent to Chungking when Roosevelt and Churchill had proposed that Generalissimo Chiang Kai-shek become commander of a United Nations "China Theater" and Chiang in acceding had asked to be provided with an officer of the United States Army to serve as his chief of staff for the theater. General Stilwell, whose background in China went back to 1921, had been proposed and accepted. He arrived in China on March 4, 1942, just before the Japanese captured Rangoon, the port through which supplies had been moving north to the so-called Burma Road, leading to Kunming. A week later he departed to take command of the Chinese troops fighting in Burma, two division-sized units. With the debacle of the Allied defenses in May, he escaped by walking 140 miles from the Chindwin River over the Chin Hills into Manipur State, in India. Upon arriving by plane in New Delhi, he was quoted by the Associated Press as making a statement that was to become the best known of his career. Observing that he regarded Burma as a vitally important area for re-entry into China, he declared, "I claim we got a hell of a beating. We got run out of Burma and it is humiliating as hell. I think we ought to find out what caused it, go back and retake it."

With the Japanese capture of Burma, China was cut off from all overland communication with its allies. The problems Stilwell had come out to help solve were now, to say the least,

16

vastly compounded. He had been given by General Marshall, United States Chief of Staff, the mission of "supporting China" and of improving the combat efficiency of the Chinese armed forces. Certainly the efficiency of those forces could stand improving. The Chinese Army consisted of over 300 divisions, which, as Stilwell wrote later, "looks formidable on paper, till you go into it closely. Then you find: that the average strength per division instead of 10,000 is not more than 5,000; that the troops are unpaid, unfed, shot with sickness and malnutrition; that equipment is old, inadequate, and unserviceable; that training is non-existent; that the officers are job-holders; that there is no artillery, transport, medical service, etc., etc.; that conscription is so-and-so; that business is the principal occupation." [4] Of the 300 divisions, such as they were, "about 30 . . . were commanded by officers whose loyalties were principally to the Generalissimo; the others were loyal to local war lords or provincial governors." [3] Many of these divisions had never even been in combat—after nine years of war with Japan! Moreover, when Stilwell arrived in China an undeclared truce prevailed generally over the front, and this truce the Chinese felt no strong incentive to break.

Stilwell's aim, to which he was committed both by intense personal conviction and by the mission he had been given, was to bring an effective Chinese fighting force into being. This force was to consist of a relatively small number of elite divisions trained and supplied by the Americans and would be used to capture one or more ports, which would make possible the launching of devastating air assaults from the mainland upon the Japanese home islands. Despite all that was unpromising, Stilwell went to work with a consuming dedication to achieve that goal.

The first task was to get through to China again. In June, 1943, a month after the fall of Burma, the India-China Wing of the United States Air Transport Command was organized and the famous flights began over the Hump of the Himalayas —the "oxygen run"—from Assam in Northeast India to Kun-

17

ming in China. Within a year airplanes were ferrying 6,000 tons of cargo a month into China over the Hump. It was a magnificent and heroic performance, but even though the tonnage carried was to continue to grow, it clearly could not begin to meet the minimum needs of China's armed forces. Only ground supply could do that "and therefore the reconquest of Burma became an obsession, a primitive, single-minded passion at Stilwell's headquarters."

At this time Stilwell assumed command of the United States Army Forces (which included air forces) of the China-Burma-India Theater—an American organization. This gave him a headquarters in New Delhi as well as one in Chungking. The former grew steadily in importance in comparison with the latter. It was to India that Lend-Lease supplies for both the British and the Chinese came. India was the base from which the Hump flights were made. It was from India that the American Tenth Air Force was flying ever more numerous sallies against the Japanese in Burma and beyond—although there was another American Air Force in China, the 14th under Major General Claire L. Chennault. It was also in India, at Ramgarh, that an American training center for Chinese troops was opened in August, 1942. Here four divisions, comprising the Chinese Army in India, as it was called, were to be created by 1944 out of 9,000 Chinese soldiers who had escaped into India from Burma and 45,000 others who were flown into India from China. This new army Stilwell planned to employ as part of a concerted Allied drive to recapture Burma.

If Stilwell was to achieve his purposes, a great deal was clearly required of others. From his own country Stilwell needed generous supplies if not also American divisions—for which he longed. From the British he needed a general offensive against the Japanese in Burma. From Chiang Kai-shek he needed unstinting co-operation in building up the projected elite force and in opening a supply line from India across northern Burma into China—this being the only possible route until Burma as a whole should have been retaken. This would mean a determined drive by the Chinese Army in India moving eastward and by the Chinese American-trained divisions in Yunnan moving westward to effect a juncture. In anticipation, Stilwell had in November, 1942, directed that a road be begun at Ledo, in Assam, to cross the mountains into upper Burma and eventually traverse Burma and connect with the so-called Burma Road into China. The road, to be built behind the advancing Chinese Army in India, would supply that army and when completed carry supplies to China. "There was no possible way of delivering the goods to Chiang Kai-shek unless he made an effort on his part to help break the blockade," Stilwell wrote later, adding that also "It seemed reasonable to expect Great Britain to use the huge Indian Army for the purpose."

None of those whose co-operation Stilwell required, however, gave very strong indication of coming through as he had hoped. His diary reveals his frustration, resentment and bitterness. "It is no fun," he complained, "bucking two nationalities to get at the Japs." Of General Wavell, Viceroy and Commander of British Forces in India, he wrote, " 'Can't' is his best word. Everything is so goddam 'difficult' it's practically impossible." He charged that "the Limeys" were "looking for an easy way, a short-cut for England" and were "not interested in the war in the Pacific." Chiang Kai-shek—"Peanut," as he generally called him—he considered "a grasping, bigoted, ungrateful little rattlesnake" and the Chinese government "a gang of thugs with the one idea of perpetuating themselves and their machine," with "money, influence, and position the only considerations of the leaders." He went on: "Intriguing, double-crossing, lying reports. Hands out for anything they can get; their only idea to let someone else do the fighting; false propaganda on their 'heroic struggle'; indifference of 'leaders' to their men. . . . The 'intellectuals' and the rich send their precious brats to the [United] States and the farmer boys go out and get killed—without care, training, or leadership. And we are maneuvered into the position of having to support this

19

rotten regime and glorify its figurehead, the all-wise great patriot and soldier—Peanut. My God!"

His own government he regarded as a sucker. "Churchill has Roosevelt in his pocket," he declared. He was convinced that nothing should be given Chiang without ensuring that Chiang would do his part by taking commensurate measures within his power to improve the quality and performance of the Chinese armed forces. Accordingly, it was with evident sarcasm that he quoted the judgment expressed by Roosevelt in a letter to Marshall that Chiang "came up the hard way to accomplish in a few years what it took *us* 200 years to attain. . . . One cannot speak sternly or exact commitments from a man like that, as if he were a tribal chieftain."

In his efforts to make something of the Chinese Army, Stilwell also found himself having to contend with General Chennault. Chennault maintained that with 105 fighter planes, 35 medium bombers and 12 heavy bombers he could open the way for the defeat of Japan.[3] He dismissed Stilwell's contention that "any increased air offensive that stung the Japanese enough would bring a strong reaction that would wreck everything and put China out of the war." At the Washington Conference between Roosevelt and Churchill, Stilwell urged "that the first essential step was to get a ground force capable of seizing and holding airbases, and opening communications to China from the outside world." But, as he reported, "Nobody was interested in the humdrum work of building a ground force but me. Chennault promised to drive the Japs right out of China in six months, so why not give him the stuff to do it?" From then on, with Chiang's hearty concurrence, Chennault's Fourteenth Air Force rather than the Chinese Army received the lion's share of the supplies ferried over the Hump.

There was a period of several months, however—a period including the Quebec Conference—when things looked up for Stilwell. An American-British proposal for an offensive in Burma, called "Saucy," had been sent to Chiang Kai-shek, and on July 12, 1943, Stilwell was able to write in his diary, "RED-

20

LETTER DAY. The answer came from Peanut to the Combined Chiefs-of-Staff Saucy proposals. In *writing*. And *signed*. After a year of constant struggle, we have finally nailed him down. He is committed, in writing, to the attack on Burma. What corruption, intrigue, obstruction, delay, double-crossing, hate, jealousy, and skulduggery we have had to wade through. . . . Holy Christ, I was just about at the end of my rope."

For his part, Chiang at this time seems to have come to appreciate what Stilwell was trying to do. There was a period almost of cordiality in his attitude toward his American chief of staff, interrupted though it was by a move on Chiang's part—reconsidered upon Admiral Mountbatten's intervention—to have Stilwell recalled. At the time of the Quebec Conference, Chiang had caused Stilwell to head an entry in his diary *"Victory!"* by agreeing to put up 30 divisions for training in East China, near Kweilin, in addition to the 30 committed for training in Yunnan. Then, three months after Quebec, at the Cairo Conference of November, 1943, where Chiang had his initial meeting with Roosevelt and Churchill (neither of whom had he seen before), Marshall was able to report that for the first time since the war began Chiang showed an active interest in the improvement and employment of his army.[3] This was ironical, for Cairo represented the high-water mark of China's importance as a battlefront of the war in the eyes of her allies, who were thereafter to be progressively more concerned with other fronts.

The appointment of Admiral Mountbatten to the new Southeast Asia Command at Quebec was another favorable augury, for by placing an officer of such standing at the head of the command the British demonstrated that they meant business. General Stilwell was appointed Admiral Mountbatten's deputy. Both men, it is true, had reason to regard the arrangement as less than ideal. Mountbatten is said to have felt that no one serving as his deputy should have had such other high-level posts as Stilwell held. Stilwell was already chief of staff for the China Theater and commanding general of the United States

Army Forces, China-Burma-India Theater, as well as Lend-Lease Administrator for the theater; his new appointment meant that Kandy, Ceylon, was added to his other headquarters in Chungking and New Delhi, and the confusion was not much improved by the fact that he was to absent himself most of the time from all three of them in favor of commanding operations on the northern front in Burma. "Only the Trinity could carry out his duties," Mountbatten later observed.[3] But he had given in on the issue upon Roosevelt's urging the desirability of liaison at the top between Kandy and Chungking.

For his part, Stilwell, who was sixty years old and held the permanent rank of lieutenant general, now found himself junior to a man of forty-three whose permanent rank was only that of captain in the Navy, three rungs below him. Nevertheless, Stilwell was pleased with the appointment of Mountbatten, whom he called "a good egg, full of enthusiasm and also of disgust with inertia and conservatism," and he was to accept without demur and loyally carry out the orders he received from the young Supreme Commander. His satisfaction was enhanced when his new superior undertook successfully to dissuade Chiang Kai-shek from seeking his recall. Moreover, as a result of Quebec, Stilwell had received his promise of American combat troops—Galahad—which he had hailed as "the entering wedge," little knowing how much that wedge represented of all he was ever going to see.

The portents were that Galahad would be in on the beginning of a major Allied effort against the Japanese in Southeast Asia and of a new era of good feeling and co-operation among the Allies in the theater. It was soon evident, however, that this was not to be the case. What happened was, first, that the Combined Chiefs of Staff decided that an island-to-island advance upon Japan across the Pacific promised faster progress toward ultimate victory at less expense than operations in China and, second, that the shipping to have been used by Mountbatten's command in amphibious operations was recalled for the use of the Allies in their offensives in the Mediterranean.

The real character that Stilwell's mission seems to have had is not stated in the published official record. By "supporting China" what must actually have been meant was keeping something called "China" in the war. This had some bearing upon Japan's military position on the mainland, but it was chiefly significant in relation to Allied morale. After the disasters beginning with Pearl Harbor it was very important for our side to believe there was a great power called China which was committed to an all-out war against Japan. The fact that the Joint Chiefs of Staff considered that the means were lacking to endow the illusion of a powerful China with much reality ensured that Stilwell would find himself constantly thwarted and that Chiang would be aggrieved and angered—and would take it out on Stilwell. Stilwell's secondary mission, one would judge, was to promote as much trouble for Japan on the mainland as he could without involving the United States in any very considerable outlays in his theater. Our Joint Chiefs of Staff appear to have believed that more of the military potential of the Chinese and British Indian armies could have been used against the Japanese. Chiang Kai-shek was restrained by what he considered to be the necessity of maintaining himself in power in China; the British were restrained by the military requirements of their role in India and by their reluctance to commit their only imperial reserve while the issues in Western Europe were still unsettled. It was inevitable, therefore, that Stilwell and the United States would be dissatisfied with whatever the Chinese or the British in India elected to do because it was never enough. The consequences were bound to be friction, suspicion and acrimony.

Churchill wrote: "I disliked intensely the prospect of a large-scale campaign in North Burma. One could not choose a worse place for fighting the Japanese. Making a road from Ledo to China was also an immense, laborious task, unlikely to be finished until the need for it had passed. Even if it were done in time to replenish the Chinese armies while they were still engaged it would make little difference to their fighting capacity. . . . We of course wanted to recapture Burma, but we did not want to have to do it across the most forbidding fighting country imaginable. The South of Burma, with its port of Rangoon, was far more valuable than the north." [5]

Churchill's reservations about a campaign in northern Burma were undeniably well taken. In the upshot, the first convoy from Ledo was to roll into China over six months before Japan's surrender and over three months before the British Fourteenth Army, driving through Burma from India, reached Rangoon. But while the opening of the supply line doubtless made the handwriting on the wall clearer to Japan, the war would probably have ended much as it did had it not occurred. So, too, the logic of the United States Joint Chiefs of Staff decision to concentrate on operations in the Pacific was incontrovertible. Nevertheless, there must remain a question whether, if China had been made a major theater of the war and object of American effort, the Chinese government might not have been inspired, assisted and jockeyed into establishing a more enlightened and effective rule, and the subsequent history of the country have been different. It hardly matters now. What does matter is that it was not done. The China-Burma-India Theater, which started out with a priority lower than that of the Caribbean Command, remained, as General Marshall phrased it, "out at the end of the thinnest supply line of all; the demands of the war in Europe and the Pacific campaign, which were clearly the most vital to final victory, exceeded our resources. General Stilwell could have only what was left." [6]

Stilwell's spirit was undampened by the setbacks to his hopes. He kept hammering away. He was sustained by his Yankee dedication to getting a job done. And, as Wingate was spurred by the conviction that small nations could learn to fight their own battles, so was Stilwell by the conviction that the Chinese soldier when adequately trained and supplied would prove "as good as anybody." In a broadcast he said, "To me the Chinese soldier best exemplifies the greatness of the Chinese people— their indomitable spirit, their uncompromising loyalty, their honesty of purpose, their steadfast perseverance."

24

Those were conspicuously Stilwell's own qualities. But among them there seems to have been one which, while giving him much of his drive, was perhaps also his greatest weakness. His writing reveals him to us as constitutionally eaten at by a desire to "show them"—"them" being the British and everyone Stilwell could suspect of a superior attitude. ("If we get Kamaing, we tell the Limeys to go to hell.") He appears always to have been anticipating and seeking to discount to himself the disdain of the urbane by making a great point of his unaffected plainness and earthiness and by ridiculing those from whom condescension might be expected. His trademark was a battered campaign hat, and Field Marshal Slim said that he was always struck by "how unnecessarily primitive" his headquarters were. Stilwell, Slim wrote, "delighted in an exhibition of rough living which, like his omission of rank badges and the rest, was designed to foster the idea of the tough, hard-bitten, plain, fighting general. Goodness knows he was tough and wiry enough to be recognized as such without the play acting, for it was as much a bit of stage management as Mountbatten's meticulous turn-out under any conditions." Stage management it may have been, but it bespoke the way Stilwell saw himself, which comes out repeatedly in his diary, as when he wrote: "Mountbatten has left temporarily, and as heir to the throne, Little Willie, the Country Boy, had to come down and take over. This is a laugh. A goddam American in the driver's seat, etc., etc., etc." The motto he devised for himself, while amusing, is also revealing: *Illegitimati non Carborundum,* or "Don't let the bastards grind you down." He seems always to have been preoccupied with the bastards. His favorite passage from Shakespeare was Hotspur's eloquent speech beginning:

> But I remember, when the fight was done,
> When I was dry with rage and extreme toil,
> Breathless and faint, leaning upon my sword,
> Came there a certain lord, neat, trimly dressed,
> Fresh as a bridegroom . . .

25

The choice seems to indicate that a prime motive of Stilwell's in his wishing to be a plain, fighting soldier was to have a legitimate grievance against trimly dressed lords, whose position and polish would otherwise have made him unsure of himself. A lack of self-assurance deep within would perhaps also explain why Stilwell added to his problems (and the problems of others) by giving important positions to second-raters—officers he could not, or at any rate evidently did not, trust.

Corresponding to Stilwell's irreverent old campaign hat, Wingate affected a tropical helmet that Mountbatten deduced had been acquired from a museum or an ancestor, since its vintage was pre-1914. (It was to provide one of the few marks of identification of his body after the airplane crash in which he was killed.) In addition, Wingate at times wore a patriarchal beard. The trademarks of both men may be interpreted as a defiance of those who maintained the conventions. If Wingate did not eschew badges of rank, he achieved the same effect, as when he reported for duty to headquarters in Khartoum with a fly-whisk dangling from a finger of one hand and an alarm clock from a finger of the other. He had, moreover, according to Leonard Mosley, "a special grease-stained uniform to wear when meeting important personages, as a mark of his indifference to them." There is certainly a suggestion of Stilwell in his having as "one of his most persistent and damaging faults an inability to delegate his authority, a temptation to doubt the ability of any subordinate and do everything for himself."

The Soviet Russians, who have no nonsense about them and had set a model for dealing with snobs by exterminating everyone in reach with social status or pretensions, are among the few recipients of praise in Stilwell's published diary. America's other allies come off badly. At Mountbatten's headquarters the conviction was general that Stilwell had a violent anti-British bias and had communicated it to the younger officers on his staff.

In his diary Stilwell's sideswipes at his superior in Kandy grew ever more unrestrained. Comparing Mountbatten with

Chiang Kai-shek, he wrote in a letter to his wife, "I don't know which is worse."

It was, perhaps, difficult for Stilwell to admit to himself that a carefully groomed and titled Britisher could be a good soldier. But he was an honest man, too. He is reported to have told Mountbatten, "Admiral, I like working with you; you are the only Britisher I have met who wants to fight." There is other evidence too that Stilwell privately had very considerable regard for Mountbatten and that the published record, incorporating sarcastic digs at his handsome chief, who seemed to have all the human endowments, reflects more the pettiness of his entourage than his own considered judgment.

Mountbatten, for his part, it is said, could not help liking Stilwell despite Stilwell's evident anti-British feelings. On the occasion when Stilwell actually had to deputize for Mountbatten in Kandy for 22 days—the time "Little Willie . . . had to come down"—it was said that the senior staff, American as well as British, were dismayed to find him at sea in high-level administration and to be incapable of taking charge or giving any useful directions. The view was that the requirements of an army command were entirely beyond Stilwell's scope, and perhaps even of a corps command, but that he would have been first-rate as a divisional commander, the job he liked best as well as the one he knew best. Mountbatten himself is quoted as having said that as a general in the field one could not have had a better man. As General Slim wrote: "He was not a great soldier in the highest sense, but he was a real leader in the field; no one else I knew could have made his Chinese do what they did. He was undoubtedly the most colorful character in South-East Asia—and I liked him." [2]

It remains only to add what General Marshall said of General Stilwell's mission: that it "was one of the most difficult of the war. . . . He faced an extremely difficult political problem and his purely military problem of opposing large numbers of the enemy with few resources was unmatched in any theater." [6]

II While the world speculated on the results to be anticipated of the Quebec Conference, I had more immediate concerns. I had discovered that even in Mississippi you can begin to be chilly at night early in September. At least you can if you are on maneuvers and are sleeping on the ground. Standing in the mess line, I dropped the remark that I wished I could make sure of doing my fighting in a warm climate. As it happened, my neighbor in the line, another lieutenant, was in the Adjutant General's section.

"Do you?" he said. "I think we've got just the thing for you—orders from Washington asking for volunteers with jungle training. I don't know what for. Probably for a training center in Panama or some place. Why don't I send your name in?"

"I don't see how I could claim to have had jungle training."

"Oh, well. You could say that Mississippi is like a jungle in spots. In fact, isn't life itself a jungle?"

You do not have to spend much time in the Army to discover that when something desirable is coming up there is no need to ask for volunteers. And I had been in almost two and a half years. I said I'd think it over.

Unpleasant rumors began to circulate almost at once about those orders from Washington—rumors doubtless started by someone who had actually read the orders, which my informant obviously had not. As far as I knew they were only rumors, however, and it was cold again the next night. Also the night after that.

"You remember that jungle-training thing?" I said to the Adjutant General's lieutenant. "How about putting me down for it?"

I had not even composed myself for the inevitable long period of waiting for something to happen when I was handed Special Orders 218, 10 Sep 43, of which paragraph 8 stated that I was "reld of asgmt and dy with the 99th Sig Co, 99th Inf Div, Camp Van Dorn, Miss, and asgd P/E Camp Stoneman, San Francisco, Calif, reporting to the CO, Cas Det 1688-A not later than 17 Sep 43. . . ." P/E meant port of embarkation.

The sensation of having been caught up in the war was a novel one to most soldiers at that time. I felt as if I had stepped backward onto a high-speed conveyer belt.

The 99th Division must have been the only organization to have contributed a single recruit, no more and no less. I journeyed across the continent by train all by myself, feeling very much surrounded by emptiness.

Quite unknown to me, a widespread convergence upon San Francisco was taking place. At important commands all across the country and at posts in the Caribbean the directive from Washington had been read aloud at formations, including the specific statement that what volunteers were wanted for was "a dangerous and hazardous mission." It had also been read to the troops in the South and Southwest Pacific. The response was such as was indicated in a Memorandum for General Handy that someone back in Washington was now writing (OPD 320.2, dated 18 September 1943):

1. The following personnel for the American Long-Range Penetration Units for employment in Burma are being satisfactorily assembled at the San Francisco Port of Embarkation:
     960 jungle-trained officers and men from the Caribbean Defense Command.
     970 jungle-trained officers and men from the Army Ground Forces.

29

2. . . .

3. A total of 674 battle-tested jungle troops from the South Pacific area are being assembled at Noumea and will be ready for embarkation on the *Lurline* 1st October.

4. General MacArthur was directed to furnish 274 battle-tested troops. He was able to secure only 55 volunteers meeting our specifications. He was accordingly authorized to secure volunteers from trained combat troops that have not been battle-tested. These troops will be picked up by the *Lurline* at Brisbane.

The only one of our number who knew even as much as was set forth in the Memorandum for General Handy was Lieutenant Colonel Charles N. Hunter, who had been selected to organize the shipment and command it en route. Colonel Hunter, a native of Oneida, New York, and a graduate of West Point, Class of 1929, was in all ways a professional soldier. He had a mouth that was a straight line across a firm jaw, the gaze of command in a countenance that sometimes surprised you with its boyish look, a sinewy build, and a bearing that made you unaware of his being of only average height. He had been three years in the Philippines and two and a half in the Canal Zone. The reputation he had acquired there for ability, efficiency and precision had been enhanced during the past year, when he had run a combat training course in the infantry school at Fort Benning, Georgia. Earlier in the month, Colonel Hunter had spent several days in Washington being enlightened in the Operations Division of the General Staff as to what was planned for the Long-Range Penetration Group he was to shepherd. Nothing much had yet been decided with respect to the organization of the group other than that it would comprise three battalions, which at that time were expected to operate more or less independently and hence were not considered as constituting a regiment.

Among those Colonel Hunter brought with him from Fort Benning was William Lloyd Osborne, who had been lecturing there on the fighting in the Philippines. Major Osborne was to command 1st Battalion. A reserve officer, he had been a battalion commander in the Philippine Army when Pearl Harbor and Manila were bombed, had been through the defeat at Bataan, had evaded capture, and for three months had kept a jump ahead of the Japanese. Then he and another fugitive American officer had sailed a 22-foot launch to Australia in a 56-day voyage. When I first saw Major Osborne, who had a kind of birdlike slightness and weighed perhaps 115 pounds, he reminded me more of a young assistant professor of mathematics than anything else. It finally came out that, disguised by his seemingly frail physique and a mild manner, there was a characteristic that must be rare among those who have actually been through war; he liked battle. Months later in Burma, during a period of tranquillity unusual at the time, he was to make a lasting impression on me by observing plaintively, "I don't see much chance of any contact with the Japs, but of course we *could* cross the ridge and have a fight with 2nd Battalion." He gave a half-laugh, and of course he was joking, but all the same . . . the idea *had* occurred to him.

Major Osborne came across the continent by car in a four-day dash. Sharing the driving with him was Caifson Johnson, who was to be next in rank in the battalion. He was a Swedish-American with a studious mien accentuated by glasses, a deliberate, gentle manner, and what could have passed in any vestry (though he would be greatly surprised to hear it) as an air of moral dedication. He could well have been the headmaster of a boys' school. I found it difficult to believe that he had been a professional wrestler until I saw him lift a grown man over his head with one hand, though even then his pedagogical appearance made the performance look like an optical illusion.

While the troops for 1st Battalion, all from posts in the United States, moved on San Francisco on their own, those for 2nd Battalion were sped across the country in a guarded train as virtual prisoners. Among the unfortunates—many of whom had volunteered chiefly for the sake of the home leave they counted on being granted—were some who had to look out the window helplessly while the train stopped in their home towns.

While many had been stationed in Puerto Rico, the majority had come from the 33rd Infantry Regiment in Trinidad, whole companies of which, officers and men, had volunteered, and with them the future battalion commander, Major George A. McGee, Jr., a young West Pointer. For that reason 2nd Battalion, alone of the three, was to have a semblance of previous organization.

Camp Stoneman, the port of embarkation for San Francisco, situated at a place called Pittsburg, had a depressing aspect. You felt you had always known it—or perhaps what you felt was a premonition of inevitably coming to know it. With its dreary barracks, its air of improvisation made permanent, its anonymous and transient population queued up for clothing issue, physical and dental inspection and inoculations, its background of low hills covered with sere and tawny grass, it could have been a way station through which departing souls were processed for their final embarkation. Maybe in other circumstances its charms would have been more apparent. The evening before, in San Francisco, the other occupant of the room the desk clerk at the hotel had found for me had turned out, by an unlikely coincidence, to have orders identical with mine. He turned out to be Sam Wilson, one of the youngest first lieutenants in the Army and until recently an instructor in Colonel Hunter's school at Fort Benning. It struck me that the name Samuel did not suit him and that neither, particularly, did Wilson; he made you think rather of the anointed of Samuel, David, "a youth ruddy and of fair countenance." From Sam I learned that I had volunteered for that "dangerous and hazardous mission." It is indicative of the effect on me that at the time I scarcely noticed the characteristic military redundancy. (How the hell could a mission be dangerous without being hazardous?)

Worse followed at Stoneman itself. There I was not only given Special Orders 227 of Headquarters Army Ground Forces, Washington, D.C., of which paragraph 4 stated that by Presidential Directive I had been detailed in Infantry (det

32

in INF), but was greeted with the inside dope that those who had put in for this job should not expect to return. This was the sort of pronouncement that anyone with experience in the service should have been prepared to discount, but by then my detachment was not all it could have been. Some such dark appraisal of prospects, moreover, was required to explain why the War Department, instead of taking an already existing regiment trained in jungle combat—say the 33rd Infantry from Trinidad in its entirety—felt it had to ask for volunteers, who would have to be organized on the dock in the mere hope that they would acquire the necessary cohesion before it was too late.

Anyway, now that we were there, no time was lost in getting us organized. The first evening ten or a dozen of us, including some sergeants, were handed close to a thousand qualification cards and told to construct the semblance of a battalion out of them by reveille.

I had my final and worst blow of the day. The communications platoon, which I was to command, contained, according to the table of organization we were given, only radio specialists, other than a few code clerks and messengers. Signal Corps officers, unlike communications officers in the infantry, are usually specialists. I had had a good deal of experience in field wire and telephone but none in radio. (I had gone into the Signal Corps in the first place as a photographer but had yet to see an Army camera.)

Before dawn we had created the paper edifice of a battalion—1st Battalion—out of Casual Detachment 1688-A, as we were known. Down the line, 2nd Battalion had similarly been created out of 1688-B. Later in the morning we held a formation of the men who went with the cards. In any body of troops, I suppose, it is the ones who are likely to give trouble that stand out. I remember that the word "pirates" crossed my mind. An assemblage of less tractable-looking soldiers I had never seen.

I glanced at the young captain beside me. "The only thing stupider than volunteering is asking for volunteers," he allowed amiably in a Southern accent. "We've got the misfits of half the divisions in the country." Tom Senff, a member of the Fort Benning contingent and a former law student from Kentucky, had a face as round, eyes as quick, and a disposition as chirpy as a plover's. His appraisal did not seem to bother him. Very little, I found, did.

The next day, during our last evening, I had a chance to meet some of our live-now-pay-later types individually. During a two-hour stint I had in charge of the orderly room my main job was receiving Casual Detachment 1688ers from the MPs. Since we were confined to the post, the charge was being AWOL as well as drunk and disorderly. Wrongdoing on this scale was utterly unknown in the prim, conventional division I had come from, and I felt much like a Sunday-school teacher in a reformatory. After a while I grew tired of visiting a stream of high-toned scorn and wrath on transgressors of such dreamy imperturbability and thereafter contented myself with taking down names in anticipation of finding myself chief witness in a prolonged series of courts-martial. In fact, nothing was ever said about the delinquencies I reported. This was an organization that was never to have a chance to catch up on the important things, let alone on the niceties.

The next day we were marched down to a wharf on the San Joaquin River and into a small steamer which took us down-river to our transport, waiting in San Francisco.

Watching the battalion move up the gangplank, Major Osborne turned to Caifson Johnson. "They look pretty good," he said. Wartime embarkations could be sorry affairs, with a mass of reluctant, half-evolved mechanics, farmers and office workers, of unweaned sons and husbands producing a high quota of ship-jumping, tear-shedding and psychopathic breakdowns. This was different. Those who were boarding the transport had asked for it. They seemed to Osborne to be on the whole an adventurous-minded lot, if appearances counted for anything, with a spirit of readiness that troops generally take a long time to develop, if they develop it at all.

34

We lay in the harbor overnight and stole out at dawn, when the gray haze merging water and land was beginning to show pink and azure, as if with iridescence. Going under the Golden Gate Bridge we passed two destroyers. The vessel picked up motion and soon there was nothing left of the land but small, brown albatrosses that swung on stiff wings into the troughs of the seas and paid no attention to us.

On closer acquaintance, which a voyage across the Pacific did not fail to promote, Casual Detachment 1688 seemed a soberer and less unruly body of men than it had at first sight, differing from the usual military outfit chiefly in encompassing even more variety.

We had a considerable sprinkling of Regular Army in 1st Battalion. Two of the five officers with whom I shared a stateroom had been noncoms in the Regular Army. One, Lieutenant Morgan, was a peppery little gamecock whose lurid anecdotes of life in the pre-war Philippines were delivered in staccato bursts, like machine-gun fire, with a startlingly incongruous air of astonished innocence. The other, Thomas Dalton, a warrant officer with Irish good looks and the suavity of one familiar with the ropes, had been taking glider training, for which he had volunteered, and had just about decided, he said, that after all an infantryman's place to die is on the ground when the call for men with jungle training opportunely came in.

One of the others in the stateroom, a first cousin of the governor of Massachusetts, had been a reporter and a writer on the foreign desk of *The Chicago Daily News* before joining the Army. Philip S. Weld's last name was familiar to me as the name of the boathouse at Harvard, which a member of his family had given. Phil was a lean, muscular 6-foot-2er with an enthusiastic nature and the omnivorous interests of a good newspaperman. An animated talker whose long arms were generally in motion, he was in striking ways the antithesis of the stereotype of the New Englander, but it was as difficult to imagine him as anything else as to imagine anyone not liking him. What had caused him to volunteer for this mission after having previously

35

volunteered first for the Army and then for the infantry, despite his having a wife and two little children who obviously were of tremendous importance to him, was, I felt sure, the same sense of obligation that had sent his ancestors across the Atlantic to a hostile wilderness. His account of the circumstances, however, was calculated to give a different impression. He had been in a camp in Oregon as one of a number of unassigned new second lieutenants known as "fillers," whose futile days were occupied with housecleaning and yardwork, such as cutting the grass around the barracks with bayonets. One week the Saturday inspection party was headed by a fat, sadistic colonel with a Polish name who, during the tour of the latrine, made a show of rubbing the inside of one of the soap receptacles and finding dirt on his finger. "Unsgrew all dem dishes," he ordered, "and get dem glean." For four hours, while Phil's wife waited at the gate to the post, they worked on the latrine hardware. It was at the next formation that a way out of Camp Adair was offered to those with jungle training. Phil, who had been on an expedition to the Jívaro country of the upper Amazon, said he did not think twice.

It was considered remarkable that the three most prominent sets of ears in the ship should have been assigned to the same stateroom. One was Phil's, another—I was told—was mine, the third was Charles Scott's. Scotty, who with his sharp gray eyes, long jaw and wicked grin looked rather like a frontiersman, had been a fire marshal in Ohio before the war and a member of many rescue squads whose grisly undertakings he liked to recall with a sardonic relish of the effect on his listeners. Equally he liked to inveigh against the English, for whom his animus seemed to compound Midwestern isolationism, an early American revolutionism, and an unexpected outcropping of Scottish nationalism. It was perhaps partly to take the war out of the hands of our ally, as far as he could, that he had volunteered for this mission, though it was chiefly, I suspect, because as a passionate hunter he was drawn to the opportunity to match skills with what has always been known as the most challenging game of all.

Whether bona fide or not, Meredith Caldwell's explanation of how he came to volunteer was certainly the most original. Lieutenant Caldwell, who was quartered down the corridor, was an angular young Tennessean with a thin nose and what Phil called a thick, night-club voice. His deliberation in speech and manner and the care with which he disposed his limbs when sitting down suggested that he considered energy a commodity not lightly to be dissipated. Tom Senff said he had the true, long loping gait of a Tennessee walking horse and on foot could wear out a mule. Meredith had devoted himself since his twelfth year to dealing in cotton futures and he regarded all other human pursuits with a tolerant skepticism.

Meredith had been at Fort Benning, taking a refresher course, and his class, as he recalled in his dry drawl, "had had an exercise in weapons placement out in some ol' piney hills." Young Caldwell—his friends were not surprised to learn—had taken the occasion to catch up on his sleep and was somewhat at a loss when the members of the class were called upon to submit written terrain evaluations.

"So Ah just put down, 'About ten dollars an acre.' They gave me the choice of joining up with you all or taking a court-martial. And so, ol' gallant Caldwell—here he is."

Sam Wilson said it was true about the paper Caldwell had handed in; he had heard about it as an instructor at Benning. The gulf between instructor and student was of course a wide one and was still yawning when the two found themselves cabin mates in our transport. It was narrowed rapidly, however. Sam had an anthology of poetry he used to take with him into his bunk and Meredith liked to have him read aloud from it— especially "The Congo," which he would pour out with a Negro preacher's intonation. When he turned in at the end of the day, Meredith would roll over in his bunk, open one eye and say, "Young Sam, let's have some more of them *boomlay-boomlays.*"

Lieutenant Wilson, who was twice to receive the Silver Star

for bravery in addition to the Bronze Star, was a Virginian. From the house in which he grew up, situated half a mile from Sayler's Creek near its junction with the Appomattox River, it was little more than two miles to the historic ground on which, on April 6, 1865, there took place, in Douglas Southall Freeman's phrase, "the last rally of the great Army of Northern Virginia." Another house that had been in Sam's family still bore the marks of cannon and small-arms fire it had received before it was declared neutral ground and used as a hospital for the wounded of both sides. Exploring on his pony the area where the battle of Sayler's Creek was fought and listening to the reminiscences of his great-aunt, who as a girl of ten had been in hiding in the cellar while the fighting raged around the house, Sam grew up with an imagination nourished on the imagery of the war—except that the process of his growing up was interrupted by another war. Having already composed an epic poem pledging support of Britain in her hour of crisis and sent it off to Winston Churchill (from whom a handsome acknowledgment was received), Sam found one stormy night at the age of sixteen that he could stand idly by no longer. He walked seven miles through the rain to the town of Farmville (where General Grant had drafted his proposal for the surrender of Lee's army) and enlisted in the National Guard, adding two years to his age to qualify. Sometime after he had received his commission at Benning, Colonel Hunter had reached down through sixty or seventy junior officers to pick Sam to conduct a course on raiding operations. Sam must have fairly killed himself to prove that Hunter had not made a mistake, for the Commanding General of the Replacement and School Command, General Hazlett, said of him: "The energy and enthusiasm of this young officer were contagious. . . . His personal attitude before the class constituted a splendid picture of the trained leader, mentally and physically alert, vigorous, aggressive and supremely confident."

That was a remarkable tribute to a 19-year-old, but Sam, as you came very soon to see, was a remarkable youngster, ardent and idealistic, yet unfailingly self-possessed, self-disciplined and coolly analytical—and articulate; he must have been born speaking in fully formed periods of precise and graphic English. After Colonel Hunter had received his appointment to Galahad he had asked his precocious young lieutenant if he would not like to put into practice what he had been teaching. For Sam, though he was about to be transferred to the glamorous Office of Strategic Services, there could be but one answer.

Of the 3rd Battalion, then being assembled on the other side of the Pacific, the one I came to know best was Captain John B. George, a figure, I thought, who might have been encountered in a tavern in 1775 arguing, with brow furrowed, the difficult questions of the day. His air of early Americanism had to do, I suppose, with his lean build, the quality of his gray eyes and of his nearly black hair, which looked as if it ought to be worn long and drawn back to a knot, and his lifelong habituation to the rifle, with which he was undoubtedly the best marksman in our organization and one of the best in the Army —perhaps especially to his way of puzzling things out for himself. Like many others in the battalion, he was with the Americal Division in Fiji when the call from the War Department came through. Weary with the combination of stagnation and chronic uncertainty that was their lot, he seized on the promise of a change and of something conclusive that it offered. Perhaps that was how it was with others too. There were some, though, that John said seemed to be positively seduced by combat. One of those who had been in his platoon in Guadalcanal was an example. A handsome youngster of about twenty, nervous and restless, Sergeant Russell Hill would rub his hands together when firing sounded and a glow would come into his eyes. "Oh, y'know it, y'know it!" he would mutter, getting up and pacing around until finally he could hold out no longer and would slip away to the spot whence the sound came.

Among those in 3rd Battalion was a lieutenant whose reputation as a combat leader was to spread far beyond our organization. Logan E. Weston had already, by September, 1943, been

39

through a year of Guadalcanal and New Georgia and through some of the most brutal fighting in the Pacific. This included what must have been one of the most terrible ordeals any unit had to suffer when his battalion (part of the 148th Infantry of the 37th Division) was surrounded by the Japanese for thirty-one days with nothing to eat but five days' rations and what rice could be taken by stealth from the decaying bodies of the enemy that lay in windrows beyond the perimeter. A divinity student at the Transylvania Bible School, in Pennsylvania, before the war, he had been aware since adolescence of an overwhelming religious vocation, and later, while turning in case-book performances as an infantry platoon leader, thought of himself not so much as a fighting man but as a witness of God. After his induction into the Army, he had been recommended for Officer Candidate School by his company commander, but, as he was to recall, "the inspecting board rejected me when they found out my religious background. To them I was a psychic case and the psychiatrist expressed regret that I was being shipped out, as he wanted to make a more thorough study of my case." He was subsequently commissioned in the field, and from then on, in whatever unit he was assigned to, he served both as infantry officer and as chaplain. The combination, considering how wholeheartedly and effectively he fulfilled both roles, seemed an unlikely one, and it seemed no less so after you came to know Logan. He had the large, dark, gentle, down-sloping eyes and dark, sweeping lashes of a llama, but at the very moment you were forming a picture of an unworldly, soft, almost feminine nature, an impression of a physically stalwart fighting man with nerves of steel supervened, without there having been any visible change in his appearance. It was disconcerting.

Shortly before the request for volunteers for the dangerous mission came through, Logan had heard from his family that his home had been broken up and sold and from his fiancée that she had changed her mind. It was generally believed in his outfit, he said, that the mission would be a landing on Bougainville and many volunteered out of recklessness or because they were too sick or depressed to care much about the future. (The bitterness or cynicism of many of the volunteers struck John George too.) Logan later wrote for the Transylvania Bible School an account of his life and vocation, basing it on his letters (it was printed under the title *The "Fightin' Preacher"*), and in it he told how, undecided about what to do, he opened his Bible and read " 'What doth the Lord require of thee but to do justly, and to love mercy, and to walk humbly with thy God?' This verse contained my answer. . . . The men who needed help were asking for danger. The only 'just' thing to do was to help them in any way possible. 'Mercy and peace' could not come to the world by sitting back and waiting for it. We had to go after it by driving the intruder out of the land."

There was in my battalion one other junior officer who was a born infantryman, like Logan Weston, to whom in every other respect he was the direct antithesis. At this stage I was aware of his existence chiefly in connection with the soft, reverential sounds, such as might have tempered the silence of a chapel or an expensive men's haberdashery, that could be heard from across the corridor when the talk in our stateroom subsided, which was seldom for long. Sometimes the sounds could be likened to the fluttering of a bird's wings, sometimes they were human voices: "I'll see your ten and raise you ten." The stateroom was the domain of John P. McElmurray, a very tall, very spare, taciturn, profane Oklahoman with pale-red hair and pale, thin skin, legs that seemed rather to hang down from his hips than to support him, and a predilection—as I learned—for facing life's vicissitudes with the butt of a cigar sticking out in front, the butt of a pearl-handled revolver sticking out from behind, and the prospect of a not-necessarily-friendly little game to look forward to. He was as fearless of danger as Logan, if for different reasons—disdainful would probably have better described McElmurray's attitude—and the careers of the two men were to parallel each other, until they came to opposite ends.

41

Among all those who formed Casual Detachment 1688, however various an assortment they composed, it seemed to me there must be a common denominator. In the course of a 42-day voyage I formed an idea of what it might be. Whatever else they were—adventurers, musicians, drunkards, journalists, delivery boys, wealthy ne'er-do-wells, old Army hands, investment brokers, small-town Midwesterners, farm boys from the South, offspring of Eastern slums, Saltonstalls and Gomezes, Cudahys and Matsumotos (our dozen Nisei were a prime asset), Rothchilds and Indians (our Sioux and our Cherokee particularly distinguished themselves), idealists and murderers (and there was no doubt we had the latter as well as the former), each of them had something egging him on. In some it was the wildness of the hunting male or the nomadic instinct that is never reconciled to the settlement. In some it was a sense of what was owing a cause in which so many hundreds of thousands were having to die. Whatever it was in the unit's supply officer, a sporty-looking major in the Regular Army, it was to lead after the war to a term in Leavenworth for passing bad checks. In the younger members of my platoon—Eve, a blond youngster who had the gift of a way with mules, and Passanisi, an intent New Yorker on whose precocious skill in radio repair so much would have to depend—it was perhaps the simple high-mindedness of youth. In the oldest member—a quiet, steady, slow-smiling New Englander who was to outlast many of his juniors, a housebuilder by trade—it seemed to be the conscience of craftsmanship. With Lew Kolodny, a young doctor whose turn to fight was to come when he had been through the battle with the enemy, it could perhaps best be defined as sheer vitality of spirit. With Winnie Steinfield, another young doctor, it was perhaps an incentive to enlarge the realm of experience, stimulated by a playful love of life and a scientist's restless curiosity —an incentive one follows ultimately to one's peril. It was a collection of individualists, holdouts against assimilation.

The junior officers with whom I was thrown impressed me with few exceptions as having more character than any others

I had ever been with. They also impressed me as being very competent, and this made me feel more than ever an impostor. The question of my military background came up a few days out of San Francisco. A headquarters had been set up in one of the saloons of our transport, which we soon identified as the S.S. *Lurline,* her elegance concealed under the designation SF 1260, a coat of gray paint, and board walls over her interior gilt-work. A small staff was installed in the saloon headed by Colonel Hunter and including Master Sergeant Doyer. Thanks to Doyer, the organization seemed a little less rootless than it otherwise would have. A veteran of the Canadian Black Watch Highlanders who had served with distinction in World War I, he was the oldest one of us, probably twenty years above the average. He was to come through the worst of what lay ahead but not to survive it by long.

Colonel Hunter, when in my turn I was presented to him, looked at me objectively. "Quite a distinction for us," he commented, "having a Signal Corps officer for a communications platoon leader."

I took the occasion to summon up my courage and confess knowing next to nothing about radio.

Colonel Hunter received this intelligence without wincing. "Then, Lieutenant," he said, "you had better learn something about it."

There was nothing I would rather have done, especially after I had seen the table of organization for my platoon, which listed not a single switchboard, telephone or reel of wire. Although semaphore flags and signal lamps appeared on it, interestingly enough (I thought they had gone out with the Spanish-American War), the items that counted were radios. But in the time likely to be available, and with a platoon of 30-odd men to look after, I could not hope to master the to-me-incomprehensible principles of electronics or even become an operator; mine was the kind of mind that could not transpose Morse code without repeating it as *dahs* and *dits* and visualizing

it, which put a ceiling on my speed of eight groups a minute—
baby talk. Fortunately we had some first-class operators and
repairmen. But that was not the same as having the qualifications oneself, and in the months ahead I felt as if I were doing
penance for all my sins and some others' too that had got mixed
up in my file.

On its way across the Pacific and for better than two months
thereafter the 1688th Casual Detachment lacked even a proper
designation. It was not the Such-and-suchth Infantry Regiment.
It was just two (soon to be three) tentative, nameless battalions
of something or other. This was a little unsettling even to a
contingent of soldiers who had in common chiefly an antipathy
to conformity.

"You get up in the morning," said Morgan—or if not Morgan, then another Regular Army veteran—"and what the hell
are you?"

We had a stiff training schedule which was not suspended
even when the wind was so strong it crooned in the neck of an
empty canteen, as the saying was, and the work gave you the
feeling of the platoon's identity, but for the rest it was as if our
organization did not fully exist. Presumably because it would
have indicated that we did exist, the name "Galahad" was
classified secret along with everything else. We in the ranks, at
least, had never heard of it—and when finally we did, it only
added uncertainty to the question of our identity. (Galahad!
They sure as hell couldn't mean us!)

Our organization was never to have any contact with any
other in the Army. Its isolation, which was to affect its psy-
chology, had already begun. The SF 1260 had no convoy, no
escorts. She was all by herself, depending for her safety on the
small cannon and antiaircraft guns mounted fore and aft and
more on her swiftness, which would enable her to outrun a
submarine.

On the twelfth day we made our first landfall, New Caledonia. At Noumea, where we lay overnight in the broad harbor
ringed with bare green hills, we picked up the 670 combat

44

veterans of the South Pacific Theater. They came alongside on flat, iron barges and shocked us by their yellow color, which came from the Atabrine they had been dosed with. Their uniforms and shoes were dusty, and the dust was yellow too. As Phil Weld observed, it intensified the impression they gave of men from another world—the world of the war in Asia.

The 3rd Battalion was completed by the 270 officers and men from the Southwest Pacific Command we picked up in Brisbane. The members of the battalion regarded themselves as a separate species. They declined to don the ignoble fatigues in which the rest of us trained and disported themselves about the ship in haughty cotton suntans, eating like wolves at mess and stealing the fruit from the staterooms between meals. They had been living on C rations so old the cans had no labels on them, John George said, and the *Lurline* seemed magnificent beyond belief. (She seemed hardly less so to the rest of us, for she was a naval transport, and provisioned as no Army transport ever was.) "We were full of bragadoccio because we had been in combat," said John, "and we looked down on the other battalions. Among ourselves we talked constantly of our experiences. The kind of fighting we had done—palm-grove-and-jungle fighting —was pretty much the same, and that tended to weld the battalion together." Most of the newcomers had a somewhat feverish look, which was probably part physical and part psychological in origin.

Those officers in 3rd Battalion who already knew the former railroad policeman who was to command them heard of his appointment with sinking hearts; they regarded him as slow-thinking and crude although without fear—which they ascribed to his being also without imagination—and rather touching in his desire to be liked. He was one of those curious cases of a commander who while little respected by his officers is very popular with the enlisted men.

South of Brisbane, the weather grew steadily colder, and while we were rounding the Great Australian Bight, followed by giant white albatrosses that hung above the afterdeck, it was bitter, gray and blustery. The Dutch destroyer that had picked us up as we neared Australia seesawed heavily. None of us had woolen clothes and the enlisted men quartered on the boarded-in promenade deck suffered. ("If Australia's bark is worse than its Bight, I don't want to hear it.")

In Fremantle, where we put in for supplies, we were allowed ashore for the first time, albeit in formation—such being our commanders' estimate of our dependability. It turned out to be an English market town pitched at the end of the earth, whence it looked out across an empty ocean. Through its narrow streets our organization held the one public parade of its existence. You could feel a good deal of sentiment on both sides. Fremantle looked like home to us, and we perhaps looked to Fremantle like what it had lost. There were no young men on the streets. Even the men in uniform were middle-aged. It was like a town in the Confederacy. As the procession wound among the streets, the Fremantlese poured out of their houses with mugs and pitchers of beer, and many a happy 1688er achieved an amelioration of pain without once breaking ranks.

The most significant event of the 40-day voyage was the issuance of several hundred copies of a pamphlet on Long-Range Penetration Units prepared by the infantry school at Benning specifically for Galahad on the basis of General Wingate's experience. Our inflammable patriots denounced the British for having appropriated and gained credit for originating what they maintained was a traditional backwoods American school of fighting. But whatever the national origin of what we were in for, all of us now knew pretty well what it was.

We also learned that our destination was India. Because Calcutta could not handle a ship of her draft, the *Lurline* made port in Bombay. After a night alongside, we streamed out of her across the dock to the wooden coaches drawn up on the railroad tracks on the other side. We stared at the porters with their turbans, their sticklike limbs, their resentful, reproachful eyes that flashed white at the corners, at the uniforms of the British Indian Army we saw on all sides, at the Union Jack on

46

a building farther down the quay. Reality here was Indian reality. Its strangeness came to us in the mingled scents of curry, open drains, and aromatic wood smoke that—if I am right about the ingredients—is the breath of tropical Asia.

Across the floors of the railway cars, smelling of dust and dirt and heat, cockroaches like animated cigar butts scurried awkwardly and maliciously; they were not accustomed to aerosol bombs or to getting out of the way of anything, I should think.

"Don't run from him! What the hell, are you scared of an insect?"

The retreating soldier swore resoundingly and the car roared with laughter.

After 125 miles we spilled out of our coaches at a town near Nasik and were marched across a treeless plain to a tent city erected for the enlisted men. Officers were quartered in the town itself, in brick barracks. Here we were to remain for a couple of weeks, until our training area was ready.

The town was Deolali, and unknown as it was to us until that hour it was astonishingly familiar. There were the parade grounds we shared with the neatly bekhakied, shorts-clad, arm-swinging Indian troops marching behind bagpipes and drums: Rajputs, Punjabis, Mahrattas, perhaps. There was the bazaar, at once sordid and mysterious, spattered with the gory expectorations of the betel nut chewers, dusty and tawdry by day and at night twinkling with little flames and murmurous with the padding of naked feet. There was the tree-shaded British quarter and the colonel's lady buying a book from a little shop. There were banyan trees, small forests in themselves, the roads quiet in the evening, and a small snake wriggling in the dust of a gutter. Cobra-and-mongoose fights were advertised by itinerants. Tea broke into drill in the afternoon and tea was brought to us at dawn by our Moslem bearers, who crouched most of the day at the entrance to our quarters awaiting our return and plotting new peculations.

An American colonel on the staff of the Southeast Asia Command arrived to take charge of our training. We failed to understand why our own commander, Colonel Hunter, needed any direction in this, but the new officer had a reputation as an expert in jungle warfare and presumably represented the highest command and we looked forward to the lecture it was announced that he would give the assembled officers. The secrecy of the proceedings was stressed, which strengthened our hope that now at last we should be told something specific about what lay ahead of us. Nothing was said about that, however. The lecturer appeared to be less concerned about our contacts with the Japanese than about our contacts with the British. The danger that effete Albion would corrupt our simple American manliness was explained to us and we were warned against carrying swagger sticks and taking portable bathtubs to the field.

Against Colonel Hunter's advice, but with General Wingate's backing the new colonel decreed that in order to spread the combat experience of the Pacific veterans more widely there would be exchanges of personnel between 3rd Battalion and the other two battalions. Because it broke up long-standing associations, the order caused a good deal of unhappiness.

The Operations Division of the War Department General Staff (OPD) had in the meantime—unknown to us, of course —sent an urgent telegram to General Wedemeyer of the United States contingent at Admiral Mountbatten's headquarters saying it understood "that Stilwell's Rear Echelon Headquarters had arrangements prepared for immediate housing and training of Galahad upon arrival in Assam, that these arrangements were declined by South-East Asia Command . . . that under present arrangements at least two weeks delay will be occasioned in the start of training for Galahad." It went on to point out that "over-riding priority here was assigned and maximum effort directed toward the assembly and movement of this force to permit longest time for training in India. The Chief of Staff gave his personal attention to this matter throughout this period. *Lurline* was obtained from the Navy only by General

Marshall's direct action. . . . In view above, the report of a delay in India of two weeks, which apparently could have been avoided, is disturbing."

The record is silent on the dissension suggested by the telegram, but the probability is that it reflected the continuing conflict over who was to control Galahad. Brigadier Wingate, according to a War Department report, had "stated categorically that if the American group was to operate as part of his plan they must be under his command during such operations and they must be placed under his supervision for training not later than December 1, 1943. He feels very strongly that the operations of groups must be co-ordinated and that any plan calling for various groups [to operate] separately in front of different forces is doomed to failure and that he will not be a part of it. He desires that General Marshall be informed of his point of view." In any event, General Wedemeyer replied placatingly to the Operations Division on November 6 that "everything regarding Galahad training is under control."

In point of fact, Deolali was no sort of training area for us but we did the best we could, proceeding in ignorance of the Olympian interest in us. Schedules of instruction were prepared in our headquarters but the actual training was left pretty much to the platoon leaders. That was as it should be. A platoon must learn to function as an organism, and it cannot be told how; it must function as one until it is one. A communications platoon is a separate case. With us it was individual technical skills that counted; we were always broken up for operations anyway. Even more than the others we were left to our own devices. The biggest difference was that we had no devices —not a single item of radio equipment. I tramped around the country until I located a British signals unit from which I was able to borrow some telegraph keys and dry cells. For signal flags I went into the commercial market and had six sets made at my own expense through the agency of my bearer, whose percentage on the transaction was, I was sure, the talk of his profession throughout the Bombay Presidency. Signal lamps, I found, could be improvised out of flashlights by fitting them with levers to operate the button switches. This training went for nought, I am sorry to have to say, visibility in the Burmese forest proving to be virtually nil, and the only good we got out of the handsome visual communications equipment we ultimately were issued was in lightening a mule's load when we ditched it during the campaign.

The combat platoons held schools of one kind or another between the brick barracks, and there were sessions of close-order drill daily for all of us. The ritual of the drill field never seemed to sit naturally upon our organization, least of all upon the communications platoon, whose members went through the paces with the aloof and martyred dignity of a faculty of scientists and philosophers bullied by a sadistic Storm Trooper. Meredith Caldwell, I recollect, did not make one's task any easier. He had by this time acquired a broad-brimmed, plantation-style hat, and while he naturally did not wear it on the drill field, its ineffable presence clung to him as he stood before his platoon in an odd, willowy kind of way that suggested an elegant parody of the dread Tac Officer of OCS and also a parody of elegance itself.

We went on conditioning marches from Deolali out across the plains. They were long and they were wearisome, and because I had a callus on the ball of my foot that had to be cut out every week or so with a razor blade, I did not enjoy every moment of them. But I would not have missed them. On the other side of the flat expanse surrounding the town were bare hills. These hills stood up steeply, seamed by erosion, like lofty battlements crumbling with age. As the column wound its way across that worn and ancient country, beneath the craggy summits recalling the pictures you had seen of the Khyber Pass, you had a powerful sense of identity with all the columns that had marched by such hills as these since the land was young. In the 10-minute breaks when you cast your eye over the men in your command, fallen out beside the dusty road in poses of fatigue and repose, you were no longer an American lieutenant solely.

You stood with the same nostalgia for home, the same wonder over the strange sights you had seen, the same concern over the training and abilities of those for whom you were responsible, the same nagging awareness of your own shortcomings, the same anxiety about the unknown that lay ahead, the same haziness of comprehension of what went on beyond your regiment, the same tantalizing taste in your imagination of the rich pastry of luxury and indulgence that was to be had somewhere, the same weariness, the same reminiscent smile over someone's wisecrack, the same love of your comrades with which you looked around from the head of your platoon in the army of Clive, of Nadir Shah, of Akbar and Baber, and before them of Asoka and Alexander.

I never ceased to give thanks that life, whatever else it might have in store for me, had brought me not as a mere traveler but as a soldier to that country which represents for us perhaps more than any other the splendor and squalor, the color and pageantry and cruelty of the past. Wherever we went in India we encountered hostility. The eyes that met ours were sullen with a consciousness of grievance and hurt. Even the vendors, the porters and the tonga drivers who cheated us and the beggars who harried us resented us—more than any, perhaps. But none of it bothered us. It did not make us feel out of place or ill at ease. It was not we but they who were the newcomers, the interlopers, the transients. We knew it and they knew it. We belonged to that which was older than any nation. We were the British, we were the Moguls, we were the Aryans, we were the Dravidians. We went back to the beginning of history. We *were* the beginning of history. We were the soldiery.

The training area for which we headed when we left Deolali turned out to be near the geographical center of India. For two days and three nights on the Great Indian Peninsula Railway we ambled across the flat, grassy plains of Central India. At Jahklann, which was as far as you could get from anything without beginning to draw nearer something else, we left the train. The announcement was made that the march to the camp

51

itself would be conducted as a tactical exercise—as in combat, that is.

Major Osborne looked around and his eye alighted on me. "You take the point," said he.

I wondered if his sense of the proprieties had been so affected by the irregularities of the Philippines fighting that he thought the way to use a communications officer was to have him lead the battalion column into action. But it was just that having an ex-book-reviewer among his lieutenants tended to stimulate his whimsicality.

The march took us across a thinly-populated country of thorn scrub and low, tangled woods with occasional gullies where in the damper soil the vegetation was more luxuriant. Our camp, which we were all afternoon in reaching, had been set up close to the Betwa River, which formed the border of Gwalior, and near a village of a few thatched hovels and culti-vated plots called Deogarh. The name was said by some to mean House of God. As applied to our camp, it would have been a little extravagant, if not sacrilegious. Yet what we saw looked better to us than anything we had dared hope for. From a distance it appeared as tidy as a camp for toy soldiers. There were rows of single-man tents for the officers, batteries of squad tents for the men, and circus-sized tents for the offices and stores, and each tent had a fly over it, blue-lined beneath, to give protection from the sun. The area was fresh, clean and uncontaminated. The 1688th was like a bride being set down at last in her own establishment. The only trouble was that this arid area, freezing cold at night and turning hot as soon as the sun cleared the stunted woods, had nothing in common with the kind of country in which we were going to have to operate.

We went to work the morning after we arrived at Deogarh and we scarcely stopped thereafter except to sleep; we knew we were working against time. "I have a uniform for every day of the week," one of the company commanders remarked, "and this is it. Including Sunday." It was often noon before you had a chance even to wash your face or brush your teeth. Our meals we ate without sitting down, standing before tables constructed of red sandstone slabs on posts, while pariah kites perched about waiting to pounce on any unguarded morsel. After dark we had critiques on the exercises he had held during the day—until these were extended to last overnight. We shot off quantities of ammunition, mostly at informal or pop-up targets; 3rd Battalion had brought back from the Pacific a conviction of the uselessness of conventional firing ranges. There was scouting and patrolling, squad and platoon attacks upon entrenchments, pillboxes, roadblocks, bivouacs, practice booby-trapping, taking airdrops, evacuating wounded, trailing and trail concealment, demolition, and approaching, withdrawing from and crossing rivers. There were attacks under varying conditions by half the battalion against the other half. (Said the training schedule nervously: "This attack to be without ammunition.") And there were marches. "Marches," wrote Phil Weld in a notebook, "across endless bullock-plowed grain fields, clods turning ankles, skirting mud and thatch villages rimmed by maze of thorn hedges fencing plot gardens against jackals and monkeys. . . . Moonlight march through villages deep in sleep. Biblical primitiveness of lightless mud houses, narrow streets. . . . Night march to Mungaoli in moonlight. Camel looming in dusk."

In the battalion communications school we had classes with a homemade blackboard, compass courses, overland map-reading exercises and practice radio nets, not to mention signal-lamp and semaphore nets—and I should rather not mention them. Except for hourly 10-minute breaks, we never stopped. A little shrunken tea wallah from the village would be on hand for one of the breaks at least, morning and afternoon, to serve us from a small boiler heated by a charcoal grate he staggered along with. He could be heard coming from afar, for his scream was penetrating: "Anybody-waw TEEEEEEEEEE?!" It was better tea for a few annas than you could buy almost anywhere at home for two bits. I must have drunk a quart of tea a day and I was not much worse than the others. We drank tea till our teeth

53

began to turn black, though whether the tea was actually responsible was moot.

I was feeling a little more cheerful about things these days. We had acquired an additional battalion communications officer who was a radio specialist and were beginning to get our equipment. First Lieutenant William T. Bright flew from the United States to join us, bringing with him half the regiment's special radio sets. Bill Bright was a rather slightly built Texan with a mustache and a pleasantly foxy look and—what is an advantage in a soldier—an untemperamental nature. The division of labor between us worked out very well. He served as battalion communications officer in a staff capacity and as a source of needed technical radio information and I as the communications platoon leader in charge of the organization.

Two batches of officers were sent from the regiment to a British intelligence school at Agra, including Logan Weston. Under Brigadier Anderson, the school taught lessons learned by Wingate's Chindits. The course ended with a problem in survival. The students were turned loose in a great barren area to live off the land for three days. This was possible if you were good at stalking and shooting deer. If you were not, you could fall back on a five-pound tin of beef you carried—but not without disgracing yourself or, if you were one of us, compromising the issue of 1776.

We also had one of Wingate's officers—Colonel Scott—assigned to us as an adviser and Wingate himself visited us twice to see how we were getting along. I did not have a chance to see him, but Phil reported that, encouragingly enough, the legendary guerrilla warrior looked much more the scholarly than the rugged type. In the middle of December we had a week-long maneuver with Wingate's new force which, as the climax of the exercise, had the problem of infiltrating and capturing an airstrip we held. As the official record noted, "The maneuver was stopped when the units came in contact before reaching the field when it appeared that physical conflict might determine the side which won the maneuver." [1] This did not imply that there was any bad feeling between the forces. We were prepared to admire the fabled Gurkhas and did. The traditional proscription against their drawing their knives without letting blood and the consequent necessity for their pricking their fingers whenever they drew them to display the wicked, in-hooked blades to us appealed to us enormously; the more susceptible spirits among us promptly turned in their machetes in favor of Gurkha knives, which they carried throughout the campaign. We liked what we saw of the British too. They were doing the same sort of thing we were doing and doing it on far less pay, inferior rations, and no prospect of rotation home in under three years and eight months. This, and the knowledge that their homeland was being bombed, they bore stoically, reticently and cheerfully. They shamed us, too, by doing what they could to look smart during our joint maneuvers whereas most of us took the excuse to stop shaving and look like tramps. Phil came back with a report of a very neat raid on a kitchen he had seen a British platoon conduct, with the noncoms working the men into position by the use of imitation jackal cries. On one sector of the front the British opposing our battalion anticipated the calling off of the problem by trooping in to be taken prisoner for the sake of the food they could count on getting from our more bountiful mess.

We ourselves, being under British control, were on British rations. For the first few days at Deogarh we nearly starved. Later, when the system of supply had been straightened out and our rations increased to one and a half times the normal amount, we ate pretty well. Not to be overlooked was the fact that we received the British liquor ration of a fifth of whisky a month for officers and an ounce of nut-brown rum daily for all hands. It was not enough to make the desert bloom, but it showed that you had behind you those who accepted the fact that soldiers were men and would stand up for you and not, as in our country, politicians intimidated by frustrated, middle-aged females who would like to make the Army into a choir for mama's-boys.

With no off-post sources of either food or drink and no females at hand of a kind to tempt the appetites even of men who shot and ate vultures under the impression that they were turkeys (don't ask me how this could happen; all I know is that it did), our rations were on the way to being the obsession with us they were later to become. Guard was maintained day and night over the stores but was not 100 per cent effective. The insatiably hungry veterans of 3rd Battalion openly styled themselves Chow Raiders and wore the small can openers provided in 10-in-1 rations pinned to their lapels as battalion insignia.

The Intelligence and Reconnaissance Platoons had to train especially hard. They would be required to go out as much as 15 miles ahead of the parent unit—up to 24 hours' marching time—"snooping," as they called it. This meant locating the enemy and feeling him out (preferably without becoming engaged) and at the same time reconnoitering routes of march and supply-drop and bivouac areas for the column.

Logan Weston was picked by Major Beach, the battalion commander, to lead the 3rd Battalion I and R platoon. He was told to select the men he needed and train them for the job. "About 200 were interested," Logan wrote, "so from them we chose 55. These men were carefully selected and were thoroughly checked, past combat record and all." One of the criteria Weston set up was "that they had been in a hopeless combat situation during which time they realized their own helplessness and their need of God. These men, with very few exceptions, had trusted the Lord to deliver them in combat and they composed the best all-around platoon in the United States Army, bar none on any front. . . . But what I want to say about them is, that when they couldn't advance another step, then they went ahead on their knees (by prayer)."

In 1st Battalion Sam Wilson was given the position Logan Weston had in the 3rd. He recruited his organization as carefully as Logan did, but on a different basis. He filled out the cadre of practiced soldiers he started with by going to the guardhouse for recruits. His idea was that men who chafed most under the frustrations of training-camp life would do best in an I and R platoon. In our organization's guardhouse, which was already well tenanted, he obtained, as it were, the cream of the cream.

That Logan's and Sam's opposite approaches should have produced equally, and remarkably, successful results may be found disturbing by some. My theory was that to find men of daring you must look to those who hold this world in poor account, which includes both those who are outlaws of this world and in revolt against it and those whose thoughts and desires are fixed on the next, and that it does not much matter which you choose. Lloyd Osborne, on whom I tried this theory, did not think much of it. "The way you pick the men is secondary. What counts is the leadership they're given."

With the ardor of youth and a lively appreciation of what lay ahead, Sam would take his men all over the country at a pace little short of a run. Sometimes they would be gone two or three days at a time working out problems given them by Caifson Johnson on a treasure-hunt principle. One particularly grueling exercise nearly ended in mutiny. The platoon had taken a break at two o'clock in the morning, having been going hard since dawn, traveling fast under strict combat discipline. Sam heard one of the men mutter that he had had enough and was going to stay where he was for the rest of the night, no matter who said what. "Who's in it with me?" he asked. Several of the others indicated that they were of like mind.

It was a critical moment for a boy commander. The platoon was in a touchy mood to begin with, as Sam was well aware; his own spirits were at a low ebb. That morning one of the men had been lost—drowned—in a river crossing. The Betwa, at the spot they had chosen for the crossing, was narrow, although deep, and they had strung a line between banks. The victim, who could not swim and had a neurotic fear of the water, was midway in the stream when inexplicably someone sang out "It's breaking!" Thereupon the line did break, perhaps as a result of the victim's violent reaction. He went down like a stone.

57

Faced with insubordination and having only an instant to reflect, Sam decided on a hard line. He called the objectors weaklings and cowards and declared that if anyone was too tired to walk he was in no condition to stand up to what he was going to have to take from him, Sam, if he did not get to his feet and move out when the order was given. "According to the map," he finished, "there's a good bivouac area eight miles from here. When we get there we'll call the problem off for twenty-four hours and rest—sleep, wash and shoot some fresh meat." He paused. "On your feet," he said. "Let's go." Everyone got up together and the platoon moved on.

A great deal that concerned our organization was going on at a level high above our heads, but we saw only the results of it and not all of those. We acquired a new commanding officer, an American general immediately subordinate to Wingate, but he disappeared as mysteriously as he had come even before we knew we had him. It was not until later years that I learned why: General Stilwell considered him too fat.

By this time Stilwell had brought about the move of two divisions of the Chinese Army in India—the 22nd and the 38th —from the training camp at Ramgarh to the border between Assam and Burma to protect the advancing Ledo Road and prepare for the invasion of Burma, upon which the Allies had agreed. As usual, however, he was having difficulties with Chiang Kai-shek, who stalled on the decision to launch the offensive, which he wished to make conditional upon an amphibious assault upon southern Burma—for which the boats were lacking. "In other words," Stilwell wrote in his diary, "no fight. The little bastard never intended to." He added: "Says we mustn't risk being defeated in Burma. The effect on the Chinese people would be too serious. The little hypocrite. Even at expense of remaining cut off—still he won't risk defeat." [2] At the same time, while he would not agree to committing the divisions in Yunnan to the offensive in Burma, Chiang was willing for Stilwell to "go ahead and fight with the Ledo force [the two divisions from Ramgarh]. He is afraid that even concerted attack by all available forces has only one chance in a hundred and yet he'll sit back and let a small force take on the Japs alone." [2]

Then, on December 18, Chiang gave Stilwell full command of the Ledo force. Stilwell wrote to his wife to put the date down "as the day when, for the first time in history, a foreigner was given command of Chinese troops with full control over all officers and no strings attached. Can you believe it?" In his diary he said, "It took a long time, but apparently confidence has been established. A month or so ago I was to be fired and now he gives me a blank check"—an overoptimistic conclusion, as it was to turn out. "If the bastards will only fight, we can make a dent in the Japs. There is a chance for us to work down to Myitkyina, block off below Mogaung and actually make the junction even with Yoke [the Chinese divisions in Yunnan] sitting on its tukas. This may be wishful thinking in a big way, but it *could* be." [2]

Stilwell's object was to obtain Galahad for use in conjunction with the Chinese from Ramgarh in the campaign he was outlining in his diary. He was never reconciled to the assignment of Galahad to Wingate, who would have employed it in his planned descent upon the Japanese line of communication in central Burma. This operation, which was to involve five brigades, mostly flown in, would be by far the most ambitious of Wingate's undertakings in long-range penetration and would, he believed, force the Japanese to relinquish northern Burma. Stilwell, within a few days of receiving word of the planned dispatch of Galahad to India, had sent an eyes-alone message to General Marshall saying he trusted that the provision for Galahad to be under Wingate was not a final decision.[3] Marshall's reply was that the decision should be made by Admiral Mountbatten after hearing Stilwell's views.[3] Evidently Stilwell did not accept the implied restraint on his initiative, for in the middle of November General Marshall had to send an eyes-alone clarification (albeit an ambiguous one to a civilian eye), ending with a bit of a rap:

59

All American troops in China, Burma, India (including Galahad) are under your command. As Deputy Commander to Mountbatten you are to employ your forces, including Chinese troops attached by the Generalissimo, so as to insure an effective united effort by South-East Asia Command. Galahad was dispatched to India to take part in long-range penetration operations. If these operations are to be commanded by Wingate, the American group should operate in combat under his central direction. The individual and unit training as well as administration and supply must remain the responsibility of General Stilwell. However, their training must be closely co-ordinated with that of the British. . . . We must all eat some crow if we are to fight the same war together. The impact on the Japs is the pay-off.[4]

This was still not good enough for Stilwell. He persisted—and finally had his way. "He felt passionately," General Slim wrote, "that all American troops in the theater should be under his direct command, and had been angered when they [the Galahad battalions] were allotted to Wingate."[5] Admiral Mountbatten gave in to him on the issue.

General Wingate received the tidings that he was to lose Galahad from the colonel in charge of our training, at the airport in New Delhi. Colonel Hunter quotes him as having said, "You can tell General Stilwell that he can take his Americans and . . . [the language here being of even more than Old-Testament plain-spokenness]."

As a result, I suppose, of high-level changes of mind about how we were to be used, we went through several reorganizations. Perhaps because Americans as a nation have a gift for organizing, we tend to meet any new situation by reorganization, and a wonderful method it is for creating the illusion of progress at a mere cost of confusion, inefficiency and demoralization. The final reorganization left us with a regimental headquarters (though the designation "regiment" was always carefully avoided) and three battalion headquarters with the battalions themselves each divided down the middle into two so-called combat teams—a singularly poor choice of terms inasmuch as combat team, by long-established usage, means specifically a combination of infantry and artillery, and we had no artillery.

The reorganizations added to the impression we had of indecision about us at the top, as did the long period when we had no designation other than as a casual detachment. When finally we were given a name, the effect of it was worse still.

It was Lieutenant Scott, Chas. R., who brought the news of our christening to a bunch of us in the orderly room. "Well, it's out," he announced with a hungry grin. "What we are to be called. Have you all got pencil and paper—those of you who can write? Because it'll be a lot for you to remember. Here it is. Five Thousand, Three Hundred and Seventh Composite Unit Provisional. And the Provisional is in parentheses."

"Good God!"

"Where'd they ever get such a number? It sounds like a street address in Los Angeles."

"It's your fault! One goddam Signal Corps lieutenant in a battalion of infantry and it makes us composite!"

"Compositry is the queen of battles."

"Provisional! You know what that means? Any minute the War Department can think better of you."

"Yeah? Well, they can't think it too soon for me."

"It's a name to set the blood stirring. It's a name to inspire songs!"

Winnie Steinfield raised his hands and with the gentle manner and wavering voice of the Mock Turtle sang:

"The Five-Three-Oh-Seventh Comp. Unit, Provisional,
Sinned on a scale that was super-Divisional."

In view of the American tendency to regard change as in itself a good thing—the condition precedent to being up to date —you cannot expect our Army always to understand that an enduring continuity suggested by a name like the Queen's Own Royal West Kent Regiment (the heroes of Kohima) can do something for an organization that a mobile snack bar cannot—

61

not that we had a mobile snack bar either. In time we grew attached to our unhandy appellation, the hopeless inappropriateness of which came to seem in itself appropriate. The backhanded pride the organization developed as the record of its iniquities and accomplishments grew apace found expression in the syllables Five-Three-Oh-Seventh pronounced with indulgent exasperation. But that was with time. At the outset the name seemed depressingly of a piece with the one (as I recall) regimental formation we had, of which the most conspicuous feature was the lack of all insignia, guidons, flags, and as much as a single drum to march by.

Our feeling that we were in a vacuum was shared to some extent by the War Department itself. On January 13 a Memorandum for the Record was to be written in OPD which, referring to a request that had been made of China-Burma-India Theater Headquarters for information on the status of Galahad, stated: "In view of the overriding priority given to assembling and movement of Galahad by OPD and the personal interest of the Chief of Staff in this project, it is considered that the Theater should have kept the War Department better advised." This was to be followed by a telegram two days later to General Stilwell pointing to an apparent contradiction in his reports: "Your Ammdel AG 150 Jan. 8 stated plans contemplate continued operation in conjunction British Long-Range Penetration Group while your Copir 5 Jan. 7 [the day before] indicates complete release from Wingate centralized control and probable employment modified long-range penetration role to spearhead Ledo Chinese."

Nevertheless, without much help from above, the 5307th had begun to acquire a sense of being. One factor was the steadying influence of Colonel Hunter and, in 1st Battalion, of Lieutenant Colonel Osborne (as he had now become, having been promoted along with Hunter and the other battalion commanders). Each in accordance with his temperament, they gave an impression of being unworried, confident and knowing what they were about—the essentials of leadership. The other factor was the life at Deogarh, which was a hard one but withal a good one, the best the 5307th ever knew. Work does for you what nothing else can do when you feel it is producing results. You were grateful to the men in your platoon and proud of your fellow officers. And that made all the difference.

That is not to suggest that the 5307th had become the model of a disciplined unit. At Christmas part of 3rd Battalion took off over the hill as a body, flagged down an express train on the Great Indian Peninsula Railway and commandeered transportation to Bombay, where they laid the foundations of the 5307th's future reputation before they returned. At the same time a rash of firing in the camp at night had begun to make the place sound like a Western frontier town. The discharge of even a single unauthorized round in garrison is a scandalous thing in the Army, comparable only to popping sportively with writs of anathema in the Church.

At night on Christmas Eve the men really let loose, or, as Winnie Steinfield expressed it, "sought release through an externalization of inner tensions." The usual few shots rang out, only this time the example was picked up all over the camp. Soon it sounded as if all the small arms we possessed—and few units our size had ever had such fire power—were being discharged. In addition, tracer bullets from machine guns were crisscrossing on their way to the horizon like red-hot bees. "Oh, little stars of Bethlehem . . . ," Winnie sang in his doleful voice. Magnesium flares hung over the landscape, bathing it in their baleful illumination while colored signal lights zoomed into the firmament. It looked more like a scene of battle than any I have ever witnessed.

Officers sent out by battalion headquarters to apprehend the miscreants were later found—by officers sent out after *them*— dancing about like satyrs, firing revolvers into the sky. It was the only time I ever saw Lloyd Osborne angry or even ruffled, and he was enraged. (The night before he had caught a sergeant shooting off his carbine between the tents and, finding him drunk and disorderly, had flattened him.) A British major

63

whom we had invited to stay over for the night, after explaining apologetically that since nothing had been planned it would be a quiet occasion, surveyed the appalling scene with the sangfroid of his nation.

"I can't help wondering what it's like here," he observed, "when you're *not* having a quiet occasion."

On January 1, 1944, the 5307th came officially into existence under General Orders Number 1, as a regiment. Under General Orders Number 2 of the same date, Colonel Hunter took command of it. Under General Orders Number 4 of January 4, command of the unit passed to Brigadier General Merrill. (General Orders Number 3 had changed us from a Composite Regiment to a Composite Unit, since it would not be fitting for a mere regiment to have a general officer commanding it.)

Frank D. Merrill was then thirty-nine years old. He had been a classmate of Colonel Hunter's at West Point. Having enlisted in the Army as a private at eighteen, he had taken the competitive exams for the Point six times before the authorities were willing to overlook his astigmatism and accept him. Some years later he attended the Massachusetts Institute of Technology, graduating with a B.S. degree. In 1938 he went to Tokyo as assistant military attaché, remaining until the eve of the war. He made the most of his opportunities in Japan, learning the language, associating himself as closely as he could with the Japanese military, accompanying the Army on maneuvers, and even sending his two sons to a Japanese school. (Mrs. Merrill tells how Japanese visitors at their house were astonished to hear the younger child speaking their language like a native, while she refrained from pointing out that he might well do so since it was the only language he knew.) The attack on Pearl Harbor found Merrill on his way to Rangoon. He remained in Burma and joined Stilwell upon the latter's arrival in March. Two months later he accompanied Stilwell on the famous march over the Chin Hills into India. Then a major, Merrill in less than two years became a brigadier general as

64

Stilwell's assistant chief of staff for Plans and Operations, G-3, for the China-Burma-India Theater.

General Merrill's popularity with his new command seemed assured from the time of his arrival at Deogarh. His personality was appealing. He had a down-to-earth, smiling simplicity and a shrewd, politically wise geniality and charm. In that, Frank D. Merrill reminded one a little of another F.D. He resembled Franklin Roosevelt slightly in appearance too, though he had a full face, and more, perhaps, in speaking voice, for Merrill was a New Englander (from New Hampshire) if not a graduate of Groton and Harvard. But there was more to the impression Merrill made than personal likability. When he spoke—and he soon addressed us—he sounded as if he knew what was what and spoke with the authority of the theater, as was quickly clear that he did; this was a novelty for us. He evidently considered that we had been neglected, and the improvement he promised was not long in coming. This took the form chiefly of copious issues of equipment and abundant American rations. The 5307th felt like an ingenue who, after hanging about in various anterooms, has suddenly been discovered and given top billing.

"It's the wonder-working power," commented Winnie. It struck us that the attention we were getting could have been given all along, had the theater so desired.

There was, of course, a price. Soldiers are not fitted out and fattened to look pretty. As Colonel Hunter was later to write, "Although not completely equipped or, by any stretch of the imagination, fully organized and trained, it was decided in January that the unit could function and it was ordered to move to a forward staging area in Assam." Stilwell gave Merrill an order directing the 5307th to close in Ledo by February 7 and proceed at once to northern Burma to operate in conjunction with the two Chinese divisions then on the front.

At the time of Merrill's arrival we had only just begun to receive the animals that, apart from our own backs, were to provide our sole means of transport and perhaps our major subject

65

of thought and expression. "Under normal circumstances," an official report was later to point out, "a training program would have been initiated to improve the condition of the animals, train them to willingly accept and march under pack saddle and load, and fit and adjust their individual equipment. Because of the exigencies of the situation, such training could not be accomplished. There was no opportunity for conditioning marches. Consequently, pack saddles, pads and accessory equipment could not be adjusted until the march began down the Ledo Road. Many of the men who led pack animals past the IP [Initial Point, or starting line] led their particular animals for the first time that day. Many of the pack saddles were on the animals' backs for the first time and did not fit. Nearly every animal in the regiment developed a sore back as a result. The sores progressed from bad to worse because there had been no opportunity to train the men to take preventive measures. Neither did they know about 'chambering' a saddle pad to immobilize a sore back and permit it to heal."

We were to have 700 animals by the time the last of them arrived, which was not until the very start of the long march into Burma. Of these, 360 were mules, big, handsome, intimidating brutes from home. We were to have had as many more but the ship bringing them was torpedoed in the Arabian Sea and all were lost. The deficiency was made up with 340 horses, originally from Australia. They had been with the United States Army in New Caledonia and more recently with the Chinese Army in India, at Ramgarh, where their condition had radically deteriorated; they had, for instance, not been groomed in over six months. In contrast to the mules, hardly any were to survive the campaign.

The necessity of assimilating all these hundreds of horses and mules, coming as it did on top of the harassments of preparing the regiment for departure, gave the camp the atmosphere of a fantasy. Anyone taking it seriously would have given up then and there. It is doubtful if more than one in twenty of us had ever touched a mule or considered that his life lacked fulfillment on that account. Nevertheless, a leader had to be provided for every animal, and the 160 men of the two pack troops assigned to us did not stretch very far. One of the troops, which had been in the torpedoed ship, arrived only five days before 1st Battalion left for Assam.

Outside the warehouse tents emergency instruction in saddling and loading was being given to men who visibly did not know what had struck them. Here and there, with all the self-assurance of 14-year-olds escorting their partners for the first time across the floor of a dancing school, lines of soldiers were leading mules to water or to picket lines. Elsewhere, helpless, skill-less, exasperated infantrymen were trying to saddle or ride horses that required breaking in all over again after their retrogression at Ramgarh.

But the real fun came with the river crossings. For these exercises, an estuary-like expanse of the Betwa was chosen. To navigate the first mule across, after the bell-mare had been taken over, Colonel Osborne called upon his ex-book-reviewer. I can only guess what he expected, but the truth is that I was far more at home both with draft animals and with bodies of water than I was with communications. All the same, I had never had to deal with them in conjunction before.

Anyone who thinks a mule on land is balky should try launching one across a 100-yard-wide river. The most complicating factor, I found, was that I got over my depth just before the mule got over his, so that while he still had his hoofs on the bottom I was tiptoeing around him like a ballet dancer in slow motion, my toes barely touching. The saving grace was that with his legs under water he could not kick. Since I had no traction, I could not pull him back when he turned toward shore. All I could do was swim around after him and by pushing his head keep him turning until he was headed out again. It follows that we kept on describing circles.

"Let's move him out, Lieutenant," said Osborne placidly from his seat on the bank, which was crowded with nonparticipants.

"Yes, sir."

Possibly because there was no senior mule ashore wearing lieutenant colonel's leaves to stiffen his resolve, my antagonist proved to have less perseverance than I. However, even after I had succeeded in maneuvering him out over his depth he made a few last attempts to go back, and we described some more circles. The animal, with whom my relationship seemed to me both intimate and ill-defined, had a head nearly as big as my torso. Finally he accepted his fate and set his ears for the opposite shore. I slipped down his back and clung to his tail, as recommended by the cognoscenti. It was evident from his speed that if he once got away he would leave me behind no matter how I struggled to catch up. The sight may have been a droll one. Certainly four soldiers who were crossing in the other direction in a little pneumatic rubber raft appeared to find it so. It was interesting to watch the change in their expressions as my mule made a sharp turn and struck out for the frail craft with the unmistakable intention of climbing aboard. The voyagers bent frantically to their paddles, but to little avail. The mule had nearly closed the gap before I was able to work my way back up to his head and turn him. We did a few more circles before resuming our course. Coasting along, alone but for the straining mule in the pleasantly gurgling waters of the Betwa with the shore of the Princely State of Gwalior on the other side, I came to a conclusion about life that has proved worth remembering: there is no use trying to anticipate what it has in store for you.

Early in January Admiral Lord Louis Mountbatten visited Deogarh. In preparation we were given a typed scenario for our guidance. This called for spontaneous demonstrations of enthusiasm by the troops, but it was never used. An advance party, after making our acquaintance, had the script recalled and the occasion was allowed to run its natural course—which it did very advantageously. After being met at Lallitpur by an honor guard which we had formed—rather expecting the skies to fall —the Admiral drove a jeep around the camp with General Merrill and watched demonstrations of our weapons. He appeared to be favorably impressed—except, as it later transpired, by the bathtub he found available to him. It was only upon reporting to his staff his disquiet over this evidence of American softness in the field that he learned of the great pains the 5307th had been to in order to provide what it considered would be the minimum requirements of a British lord.

The visit by the Supreme Commander gave the unit a pleasant sense of consequence which was the more welcome in that General Stilwell, although exclaiming in a letter to his wife at this time, "If I could just have a couple of U.S. Divisions!" never got to Deogarh. As he explained in another letter to her, "I get numerous howls to come up to Chungking or come down to Delhi but so far have managed to fight them off and remain with the troops." He was at that time in Burma with the Chinese forces at the head of the Hukawng valley; he reported that "progress is slow; the jungle is everywhere and very nearly impenetrable." [2]

If Stilwell did not come to see us, we had at least, as a curiosity of the theater, been for some time attracting other high-ranking visitors from New Delhi. Their accommodation, in fact, became something of a problem, and Hunter was heard to remark that he had hardly ever seen so many generals gather around to watch a colonel work. With the time of our departure for the front imminent, a number of newspaper correspondents converged upon Deogarh to collect material against the time when the ban on publishing anything about us would be lifted. One was Dave Richardson of *Yank* magazine, a lanky redhead who was a bona fide sergeant in the Army yet entirely on his own, without superiors or subordinates—an ideal situation in the service, as it is in any sphere of life. Wearing our uniform but free of responsibilities, he could have been, as it seemed, alone among us in being guiltless of original sin. He was the only one to accompany us on our mission. The others included Charles Grumich of Associated Press, Frank Hewlett of United Press, and James Shepley of *Time* and *Life*. Shepley was riding in a jeep with Merrill on the way to a river-crossing exercise when he ventured the view that the name "5307th Composite Unit (Provisional)," while of course an honorable one, lacked something from a news writer's point of view. He said he proposed to call the outfit "Merrill's Marauders" in his dispatches.

"What do you think of it?" he asked.

"Unh."

And so it was as Merrill's Marauders that we left Deogarh for Burma.

III General Stilwell wrote in his diary, "The Long-Range Penetration Group [he apparently never mastered our official designation] is arriving at Ledo January 20 and expects to jump off February 15. My God what speed." [1] The exclamation was sarcastic. As it worked out, it was January 27 before 1st Battalion was even able to leave Deogarh and the end of the month before the last of the unit had done so.

Our departure was marred—I suppose the term would be—by a near homicide, and a multiple one at that. At 11:30 at night midway in our exodus, a British investigation unit brought in a report that three Indian dhobis had been wounded in the tent they occupied in the vicinity. In the morning a muster of all men was held in the presence of some Indian soldiers who had witnessed the shooting. Two privates from 3rd Battalion were identified. In the course of a formal investigation they confessed and were turned over to the provost marshal at Agra. The dhobis' offense was to have refused them rum.

That was not quite the full extent of the 5307th's valedictory. Following the departure of the main body from Deogarh, Lieutenant William Scott of 2nd Battalion, who was in charge of the rear-guard detail, was aroused as the train rolled across the flat plain of the Ganges by the sound of firing from behind his car. He looked out and to his horror beheld a row of rifle barrels thrust out of the windows of the next car. His men were shooting at the Indians and the various ruminants as if they were riding through the wild West of the 1870's. Given the high quality of marksmanship in the 5307th and the apparent absence of casualties, however, the assumption was warranted— for whatever comfort it afforded—that the intention was not to inflict corporal injury.

The trip from Deogarh to Margherita, which was situated a few miles short of Ledo, took ten days. It could have taken a hundred without my objecting. After the exertions of the past two months it was bliss to be able to lie about all day even on wooden benches, eight of us to a compartment, with nothing to do but talk, eat, buy tea from the vendors at the stations, and look out across the face of India as the train sauntered on its way or lay up on a siding to allow the slow-paced time of the Orient to catch up with it. (One section, dragging unconscionably, was discovered to have had a second train carrying 800 Indian laborers hitched on to it, putting 45 cars on the little locomotive.) There was even hot water to shave with if you were able to persuade the engineers to bleed the boiler and let you fill your helmet while the train was halted. I can close my eyes and—

"*Tea wallah! Tea wallah. . . .!*" Tweeeeeeeet Tweeeeeeet. . . . White cattle-egrets mirrored in still water. . . . "Aces back to back! Damn you, I don't know why I bother to draw when you're dealing." . . . *Click, click, clickety-click.* . . . "It was coming in from about two o'clock, so I gave it a little right windage, and the next round. . . ." Rag-clad crowds asleep on the station platform, like the victims of a violent natural disaster. . . . "Not a thing wrong with you that a pre-frontal-lobotomy wouldn't take care of. You'd feel like a new man." . . . Clusters of palms marking villages across the radiant green nap of the rice fields of the Ganges plain. . . . "But she says we can't on account of her roommate's asleep in the bedroom. Now, you're not going to believe this, but so help me, it's true. First, though, this roommate. Boy, was she stacked! You've heard of the well-

72

known brick. . . ." Griffin vultures doing obsequies on the carcass of a donkey, house crows on cornices, a small falcon on a telephone pole. . . . "O.K., I'll concede you the existence of God if you'll concede me that mankind is not necessarily the center of the universe or even particularly significant in God's over-all plan." . . . Gray water buffaloes, half hippopotamus, stolid, proprietary, with heads outthrust horizontally, pulling makeshift plows followed by human figures like attenuated, brown-skinned wading birds. . . . *Clickety-click, click, click.* . . . The human spawning grounds of Allahabad, Mirzapur . . . and Howrah, the outskirts of Calcutta, the proximity of United States Air Corps installations and the imprint of American culture. "*Sah'b bakhsheesh!* No-mamma-no-poppa-no-brother-no-Uncle-Sam-no-per-diem! *Bakhsheesh, sah'b!*"

We crossed the Ganges and rolled on to the Brahmaputra, the first and second holiest rivers in India, our orientation pamphlet explained, and the first and second dirtiest, we surmised for ourselves. After being ferried across to Pandu, we were put up at a transient camp, a sorry place. Ill-equipped to begin with to indulge the fastidious, its mess and its latrines were equally overburdened by the numbers of British and Chinese, and now American, troops awaiting transportation forward. "Pandu giveth and Pandu taketh away, but both very inadequately," Winnie Steinfield summed up. Across the road an American railway battalion had a camp. It was one of those which were taking over the Bengal and Assam Railway in order to speed up the movement of supplies to Ledo. (Before they had finished, these railroad experts from the United States were to give an impressive demonstration of the American Way. One of the steps they took, we heard, was to plot the increase in derailments to be expected from each additional increment of speed, correlate it with the amount of rolling stock available and the estimated duration of the war in Asia, and decide on that basis how fast to run the trains. The result was that in time every curve along the roadbed of the B. and A. was marked by cars lying on their backs down below, like dead giant voles with their paws in the air, while freight moved over the line at twice the rate ever attained before—and our side won the war.)

From Pandu we had a two-day, overnight voyage up the river in a paddle-wheeler that might have come from the Mississippi of eighty years ago. The mighty Brahmaputra, actually a greater river than the Ganges and one that has never been bridged, was shrunken at this season, and its interminable succession of sandbars, which must have made navigation a grueling task, gave it the aspect of a stream traversing a desert. It was like a nether world of the spirit, to which the imminence of what lay ahead lent added force.

Logan Weston, brooding over his platoon, reminded himself of John 19: 41, "Now in the place where he was crucified there was a garden," which meant to him that "Altogether too few of us who profess to love the Lord see the beauty of the garden in which our cross is erected. Our minds are so set and our eyes so focused on the place of suffering that we miss seeing the surrounding beauty. Many of us, unlike Paul, have not yet learned to rejoice in tribulation."

Sam Wilson stole out at night to the forepeak to look down at the stars reflected in the black water ahead of the ship. He had frightening spasms of self-doubt; the imagined sensations of being out in front of the unit with the enemy on all sides were becoming daily more real. As an antidote he turned to a passage he had read and reread in Ernest Hemingway's introduction to *Men at War*, grasping at the reassurance it offered— such as it was:

So when you have read it [said Hemingway of his anthology] you will know that there are no worse things to be gone through than men have gone through before. When you read the account of Saint Louis the IX's crusade you will see that no expeditionary force can ever have to go through anything as bad as those men endured. We have only to fight as well as the men who stayed and fought at Shiloh. It is not necessary that we should fight better. There can be no such thing as better. And nothing that can ever happen to you from the air can ever be worse than the shell-

74

ing men lived through on the Western front in 1916 and 1917. The worst generals it would be possible to develop by a process of reverse selection of brains carried on over a period of a thousand years could never make a worse mess than Passchendaele and Gallipoli. Yet we won that war and we must win this one.

From Gauhati, where we disembarked, we were carried forward again in the Bengal and Assam's atrocious, uncomfortable and filthy coaches. There were frequent lay-ups, and during one of these the men in a car down the train evidently spotted a couple of ducks beside the tracks and dived on them. The loud and bitter protests of the peasants who owned them brought us to the scene, but our search of the car, which had to be quick, revealed nothing—naturally. There were only a few smirks over the success achieved in the robbery of two of the inhabitants of that land, who were so impoverished they pounced upon the empty C-ration cans we tossed out the window. After the train moved off it was too late. We may have handed out some rupees by way of recompense. I am not sure. The incident passed without much to-do over it. Presumably it was the sort of thing that had to be expected. We were the soldiery.

At dawn on February 6 the train came to a final halt with a sigh of fatigue and we stumbled out. Everything was wet. After the desiccation of Central India, the dripping woods through which we marched were incredibly lush, like a botanical garden. We had our first dank smell of the jungle, our first lungful of the damp air that was to be the medium of our existence, as water is to a fish, from then on.

The staging area at Margherita was an assemblage of bashas —dirt-floored structures with bamboo poles for framework, woven split-bamboo siding, and palm-thatched roofs. We were in occupation only forty hours, and it was a time of mounting confusion relieved only by a talk given to the officers by a Baptist missionary on living off the jungle. Mr. Harold Young had grown up in northern Burma, and we looked on fascinated as children while with unhesitating authority he extricated specimens from a heap of vegetation he had with him and either munched them or extracted drinking water from them. Banana plants and bamboo were the chief vegetable sources of water. The former you squeezed and the latter you hacked into. Thanks to Mr. Young and the prevalence of bamboo in Burma, the bivouacs of the 5307th were more often than not to sound like a blacksmith's shop.

For the rest, we tried to get straightened out with our animals, which arrived in a train shortly behind ours, and assimilate the new supplies we were being issued. We were scheduled to set off on the evening of February 7 at eight o'clock, but at that time, amid scenes of turmoil such as various artists have considered representative of Hades, we were still having mules and pack saddles dealt out to us. Rear-base supply officers were running about with clipboards, platoons were being disentangled one from another, missing soldiers were being discovered (blinking in the beam of a flashlight) behind bushes fortifying themselves with a last, unauthorized meal, loads were being wrestled with by the light of campfires, freedom-loving pack animals were being rounded up in the woods. In fact, at precisely H hour the occupants of the basha housing 1st Battalion headquarters were clinging to the rafters while an overwrought saddle horse down below was kicking it to pieces.

Along about midnight the chaos of that last evening was magically resolved into a long and only dimly visible column in the road. Combat discipline was imposed. Silence came over the column like something tangible, and everything was changed. Down the line, passed back from man to man, came the words with which we were to grow so wearisomely familiar in the months ahead but which now struck with the force of a great Annunciation: "Put 'em on." And then, "The column's moving." In a moment the mule ahead of you, plucked out of his repose, lurched off with a start. You stepped off—and the march had begun.

By day the Margherita-Ledo area, which was the railhead for the supplies and equipment needed for the building of the road to China, looked like home. American transport and engineer teams were everywhere, trucks rumbled back and forth raising furies of dust, construction equipment was being unloaded and moved forward, installations of one kind or another were going up. Even at night there was traffic. In the headlights of the trucks that passed us we must have resembled a procession of forty-niners resurrected a century later in a boom town of the oil fields.

We had a 14-mile march that night. Coming on top of a two weeks' softening-up period of total idleness and combined with our inexperience with the mules, which we had never before been out with and hardly knew how to handle, it was a killer. Like many others, I was having my first walk in my newly is-sued shoes, and by the time dawn had broken on the other side of Ledo, so had my feet.

"This seems a lot of trouble to go to, just to get shot at," said Meredith when, about eight o'clock in the morning, we pulled into a grassy expanse in the woods that was to be our bivouac.

"This is the way I expected to feel on the last day of the campaign," I said. "If that's what it was, instead of the first, I could take it philosophically."

What with the animals and equipment to care for, the eating to be done, and the bright sky overhead, there was not much sleep that day. But the worst thing was my feet, which were raw. What saved me was the alternate footgear we had been issued. Pontiffs of podoculture among us warned that the feet would break down if the calf-high, rubber-soled canvas jungle boots were worn habitually, but after the heavy leather GIs they made you feel—in the established military parlance—as if you were walking barefoot over the bosoms of maidens. From then on, like about half the command, I wore nothing else.

In the evening we pulled ourselves together and took to the road again. We marched most of the night. We were, it ap-peared, moving "under cover of darkness" to escape detection by Japanese planes. Inasmuch as the Japanese had no planes at that time over the area in question but were able to recruit at will as many informers as they desired to report what went on in India by day or night, it obviously made no great sense to travel in a way liable to exhaust us before we ever reached the zone of combat, and the procedure was soon modified. It made life vastly easier for us and no one was disturbed when in due course we learned that the Japanese radio in Saigon had announced that we were known to be on the road and promised to bomb us off it. We still did some night marching, however, to avoid the truck convoys. Some thought had been given to sending our own unit forward by truck but the evident desirability of giving it further conditioning and a chance to learn to march with its animals swung the decision the other way.

The Ledo Road was well designed to separate the men from the supermen, as one toiling marcher put it. The construction of the road has been called the greatest engineering feat in the annals of the United States Army. From what we saw of it, we would not dispute the claim.

In February, 1942, the British had commenced work on a "Ledo Truck Route" that was to go to their northernmost outpost in Burma, Fort Hertz (Putao), and then south to Myitkyina (pronounced generally *mitch-in-ah*, more correctly *mi-yitch-in-ah* and in the 5307th, for mysterious reasons, *mish-un-aow*), the northern terminus of the Burmese road and rail nets. This project was soon abandoned. In November of that same year a plan was approved by Stilwell for the Americans to construct a road over a somewhat more southerly route to Myitkyina via Shingbwiyang, at the head of the Hukawng valley, with the object of ultimately establishing a connection with the Burma Road into China. The United States Engineers began work where the British had left off, and in the face of predictions that it was impossible. A wilderness of mountains rising from near sea level to two 4,000-foot passes had to be crossed, and the country was so little known to begin with that the distance from Ledo to Shingbwiyang—112 miles—was underestimated by 42 miles.

By February, 1943, a year before we appeared on the road, construction had reached Pangsau Pass on the border of Burma.

From April to September the work was held up by the rains, which in six months every year dump a hundred inches on the mountains the road had to traverse. In October Colonel Lewis A. Pick, an Army engineer from Virginia and an eminent specialist in flood control, took over command. From then on, work on the road (now known colloquially as Pick's Pike) proceeded day and night and without regard for weather or anything else. Cutting a shelf out of the precipitous, forest-covered slopes, preventing the banks from collapsing onto or out from under the road, and spanning the countless rushing torrents must have presented fantastic difficulties. But this is the sort of thing Americans are best at. Tillman Durdin in the New York Times reported that 13,500,000 cubic yards of earth were moved in the construction—enough to build a solid dirt wall 3 feet wide and 10 feet high from New York to San Francisco. On December 27, 1943, a month before we left Deogarh, the lead bulldozer broke out of the mountains onto the plain of Shingbwiyang. The last 54 miles of trace, comprising almost half the distance across the mountains, had been cut in 57 days. The bulldozer was followed by 53 trucks carrying Chinese troops to the developing battle a few miles to south.*

What we saw of the Ledo Road was a great, broad, raw gash through the forest dipping, rising, winding, cutting back, going on days without end, prevailingly uphill for the first half of the march, prevailingly down for the second but every mile of it steep. While the road was open for traffic to Shingbwiyang, much of it was still under construction or being improved. Crowds of local laborers with delicately proportioned figures and broad-brimmed hats tinkered at manual tasks, fastidiously spading the earth for a culvert or placing logs in an abutment

* Later, on the heels of the Allied advance, the road was extended down the Hukawng valley—in one flooded area over a two-mile-long causeway of logs—to Myitkyina, 260 miles from Ledo, which it reached in November. From there on to the Burma Road, 160 miles farther, the task was largely one of improving existing facilities. On January 28, 1945, only a few hours after the last Japanese had been cleared out of the way, the first convoy rolled across the border of China at Wanting, having traveled 620 miles from Ledo.

79

while burly GIs attacked the million-dollar-a-mile job, as they called it, with bulldozers, power shovels, earth-movers and front-end loaders in a spirit of getting it done before Joe's Grill ran out of hamburgers.

Cut through one of the world's obscurer corners, the Ledo Road brought some of the world's most diverse strands into juxtaposition. Trucks named Snake-Eyes and Sugar-Loving Mama, driven by Negroes from Alabama and 125th Street, shared the right-of-way with others driven by Cantonese and Yunnanese who, intoxicated at having latched onto the inexhaustible resources of the West, slammed their vehicles from one gear to another with a grinding scream that would set your teeth on edge and careened downhill at the risk—and often with the result—of plunging off a turn as if machinery were no more valuable than human life. Near the beginning of the road Melvyn Douglas, the Hollywood actor, was putting on a show at a base camp while a few miles farther along a quaint little tribesman of the head-hunting Nagas, who peopled the Patkai Hills in so far as they were peopled at all, was demonstrating the crossbow to us and accepting in return, with shy dignity, the world's one universal currency—American cigarettes.

From time to time we would pass a machine shop, a field hospital, an engineer encampment—often abandoned—or a Signal Corps station. One Engineer unit had motion-picture equipment and showed a film for us at the end of the day's march. At another spot some Army medics had rigged up a still, which Phil Weld's platoon discovered by hearing a sound of hissing near their bivouac. The proprietors, with what I suppose must be considered generosity, sold a fortunate few the last drinks they were to have for months. What made the deepest impression on us was a Negro Engineer regiment whose band stayed up most of the night playing "God Bless America" and "Dixie" for us as we passed.

I do not mean to suggest that there was a riot of activity. The chief impression the Ledo Road gave was of quiet—quiet merely emphasized by the clump of mules' hoofs and only too often by the sizzle of rain on leaves and puddles. Most of our encounters with our compatriots—all service troops—passed in silence too. They would watch from the roadside as we marched by and we would exchange looks without speaking. There was nothing to say. I fear the column as it moved somberly past them, heavy laden under the appurtenances of war, may have spoiled a bit the picture they had of themselves.

The 5307th was in good spirits. Apart from lunch, which consisted of a chocolate bar or the equivalent, we were eating well. At dawn and late afternoon a truck appeared with vats of hot food, and though breakfast was likely to be concocted of egg powder and ersatz sausage of soy-bean meal, there was often chicken for dinner and our mess kits were always piled up. Often, too, we were able to spend the night under cover, if on the ground, in the construction camps we passed on the way. (Once when we were promised unusually comfortable accommodations we found on arrival that a Chinese pack train had beaten us to it. There were many Chinese on the road, mostly in trucks.) But the marching, of course, was tough. One of the men was heard telling another, "After the war I'm going to get married and have ten children. And I'm going to line them up and tell them just what hiking over the Ledo Road was like. And if they don't cry, I'm going to beat the hell out of them." But there also was the satisfaction of discovering that we could take it. From remarks filtering down from the newspaper correspondents it was evident that the legend of Marauder toughness had been born. We did not feel tough—our complaints would have kept a corps of chaplains occupied—but it was gratifying to be thought so. Miles yielded to miles, the hills rose up before us and passed behind, and we kept on going. All around were the barbaric green ranges leading to the remotest fastnesses of Asia, and we, breathing the strange, new air that few like us had ever breathed before, were the farthest-flung column of our country's army.

The feeling of being an advance rivulet of a current of history was particularly strong when on the fifth day we toiled hour after hour to reach, after an eight-mile grade, the highest point of the road. It was the 4,300-foot Pangsau Pass, wind-swept, chilly, and open to an immensity of sky. On all sides there were vistas to impress the moment upon you. Behind, inching its way up the twisting incline, was the marching file of the battalion—the only time it was ever so fully in view—the mules under pyramids of mortars, ammo boxes and radios, the men spined with their weapons and hunchbacked with their packs. To our left, in the north, more nearly resembling a white-topped stratum of cloud than a range of mountains, was the snow-capped eastern escarpment of the Himalayas forming the border of China. Before us, to the southeast, lay the forested hills of Burma, into which the road dipped and, hidden by them, the farthest outposts of the newest of the many empires to have swept across the ancient continent in the course of time.

Two days before, some of us had crossed another kind of divide. One of the men in my platoon could not be located at mess call. He was a short, dark individual with an Eastern European name and slightly Mongoloid features and had always been something of a problem. I am not sure why this was except that he never quite fitted into the scheme of things and was always looking at you with puzzlement because you could not make anything of him. He might have been one of the Huns who invaded Europe fifteen hundred years ago inexplicably come to life again as an American draftee. As such, his difficulty in relating himself to anything would have been understandable. He had tried to learn radio repair from my able young New Yorker, T/5 Passanisi, but condensers, frequencies and grid leaks proved to be as much beyond his capacities as mine. On one of the marches out from Deolali, he had come up to me during a break and held out a handful of American bills which he had neglected to turn in for rupees as ordered: What was he to do? It was a time when I felt especially strongly that it had all happened a hundred or two hundred or a thousand years before. I had found no assignment for him in the platoon except to carry a Tommy gun. And this proved to be worse than nothing at all. When we found him the night he failed to appear for dinner, the evidence was only too plain that he had put the muzzle of his weapon in his mouth and pulled the trigger.

That was not the only fatality we suffered on the Ledo Road. A mess truck was on a steep downgrade when its brakes failed, and it plowed into a pile of logs at the bottom. Twenty men of 2nd Battalion were injured and one was killed.

There was a taint of death along the Ledo Road. The trace of the road had been the refugee trail out of northern Burma. Only two years before, hundreds, perhaps thousands, fleeing the Japanese advance had perished along the way of fever, hunger, exposure and exhaustion. One of the medical units we came upon had a collection of skulls that bore witness to the horror and we ourselves found whitened bones beside the streams in some of our bivouacs.

During the last few days of our march there was the sound of death too. It rumbled in the distance like a sinister kind of game played by giants. We were very brash at that time. "Let's hope it's just artillery and not thunder," we would say. It was.

The road grew ever narrower, twistier and more precipitous as we went on. For the last stretch of seven or eight miles we were going steeply up or down almost all the way. It was as nearly vertical as a road could well be, and then some. On the descent, under the weight of your pack, you came down so hard on your legs you felt you were going to be impaled on them. Climbing, you had almost to push down on your knee with your hand at each step. To encourage us, there was the roar of the Dakotas coming in for a landing in the valley. The noise grew continually louder, until finally we stumbled out of the mountains into Shingbwiyang. That was on February 16. Shingbwiyang was the site of an airstrip and other installations, including a field hospital, befitting a mushrooming supply base, it being the nearest thing to one we had on the far side of the Patkai Range.

Beyond Shingbwiyang the going was far easier. We were now at the head of the flat Hukawng valley, across which, with all

83

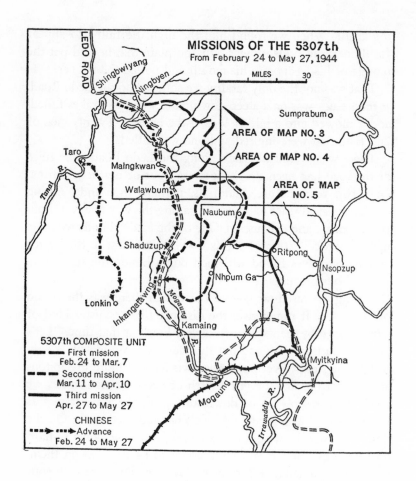

MISSIONS OF THE 5307th
From February 24 to May 27, 1944

0   MILES   30

AREA OF MAP NO. 3

AREA OF MAP NO. 4

AREA OF MAP NO. 5

LEDO ROAD

Shingbwiyang

Ningbyen

Sumprabum o

Taro

Maingkwan

Walawbum

Naubum o

Shaduzup

Ritpong

Nsopzup

Nhpum Ga

Lonkin o

Inkangatawng

Mogaung

Kamaing

Myitkyina

Tanai R.

Mogaung

Irrawaddy R.

5307th COMPOSITE UNIT
▬ ▬ First mission
        Feb. 24 to Mar. 7
▬ ▬ ▬ Second mission
        Mar. 11 to Apr. 10
▬▬▬ Third mission
        Apr. 27 to May 27
CHINESE
▬▬▶ ▬▬▶ Advance
        Feb. 24 to May 27

the convolutions of an intestinal tract, wound the many rivers that formed the headwaters of the Chindwin, one of the two main affluents of the Irrawaddy. Anyone coming up from southern Burma by motorcar could, in the dry season, go as far as Shingbwiyang—and no farther. The rusted hulks of vehicles abandoned by the refugees of two years before were still in

84

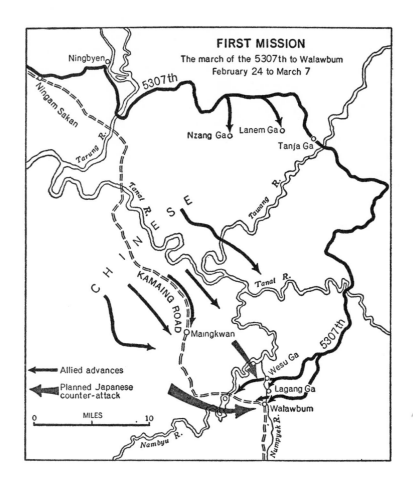

FIRST MISSION
The march of the 5307th to Walawbum
February 24 to March 7

Ningbyen

5307th

Ningam Sakan

Tarung R.

Nzang Ga   Lanem Ga
            Tanja Ga

C H I N E S E

Tanai R.

Tawang R.

KAMAING ROAD

Tanai R.

Maingkwan

5307th

Wesu Ga

Lagang Ga

Walawbum

Numpyek R.

Allied advances

Planned Japanese
counter-attack

0   MILES   10

Nambyu R.

evidence. From its terminus, starting at Shingbwiyang, the road
ran in a generally southerly direction down the Hukawng valley
through Maingkwan and Walawbum, across the ridge of the
Jambu Bum, which closed the valley on the south, on down
through Shaduzup, Inkangatawng and Kamaing (names which
so far meant nothing to us) to Mogaung and thence east to

85

Myitkyina and what would normally be called civilization. The Ledo Road was later to pass through the same area, though for the most part by an independent route. The existing road—the Kamaing Road, as it was called—provided the axis of Japanese communications through the Hukawng and Mogaung valleys, and it was down this road that the Japanese were being pressed by the Chinese, who had come over the mountains from India a couple of months ahead of us. So far—measuring in a straight line—the front had been pushed about 25 miles from Shingbwiyang.

About 15 miles below Shingbwiyang was Ningam Sakan, where General Stilwell had his headquarters. We were due to pass through it the day after we had come down out of the mountains, and in preparation for the occurrence we were ordered to shave that morning and to wear our helmets and otherwise to present as smart an appearance as we were capable of after ten days on the road. We felt a good deal of anticipation. Recognition is what everyone wants, I suppose, and having by now marched 140 miles with all our equipment we were having our first taste of pride as an outfit; it seemed safe to assume that the theater commander would show his gratification at our arrival. The occasion proved, unfortunately, to be one of those on which Stilwell missed the chance for an inexpensive gesture that could have repaid him in days to come. He did not show up for it.

At Ningam Sakan we left the road and turned east onto a broad trail that led through forest to the village of Ningbyen, beside one of the tributaries of the Chindwin, here known as the Tanai. This was to be the regimental assembly area, where we were to await the other two battalions, which had been following us down the road a day apart. The long march was beginning to tell on us. Walking in a formation, which necessitates accommodating your pace to that of others and often either marking time or racing as the column telescopes in and out in the mysterious fashion of marching bodies, is a very different matter from walking on your own.

Possibly because Ningbyen was the end of the line—for a few days—it seemed to recede before us. The ten miles that separated it from Ningam Sakan were interminable. One thing that delayed us was a series of abandoned entrenchments in which we became involved. The debris of war was still in evidence—shell containers, rusting helmets, cartridge casings—and in the distance the thud of artillery was louder than ever, together with a crunching sound we learned to recognize as the bursting of bombs dropped by our airplanes. There was little talking as the column moved on.

When the light began to fade we had still not reached our goal, but General Merrill and Colonel Hunter, who had come by jeep, were standing beside the trail next to a patch of elephant grass to speak a few encouraging words and tell us we were almost there. It was at that spot, on the strength of an unaffectedly friendly smile, that the conviction was born, at least in 1st Battalion, that Merrill, like Hunter, was interested in us and would look out for us if he could.

We reached our destination on the Tarung River in darkness and had to grope about on the wide, boulder-strewn banks to find places for our animals and ourselves to settle in. It is never fun to make camp when you cannot see, and in this case we were practically out of food—and of course were no longer in reach of mess trucks. When men and beasts were finally disposed of, there was the sound of a plane. It was a Japanese plane, evidently. The alert was given—and there went our cigarettes too.

In the morning we crossed to an island in the Tarung, wading the hip-high water, and set up in a more comfortable spot, though we were more famished than ever. Later that day we took our first supply drop from the air and were able to gorge on the best packaged rations the Army provided, the so-called 10-in-1, which were put up to provide a squad with three meals. Subsequently General Stilwell, wading across to the island, paid us his first visit. The officers were called together to be presented to him and to shake hands. I was not present for this

87

but heard later that he had made a good impression. He spoke simply and quietly, saying that there had recently been two very encouraging developments. The first was that the Chinese were at last showing an aggressive spirit, the second that we had arrived—a well-trained, hard-hitting American outfit to get things moving. This, he said, was what he and everyone had been waiting for. We were going to find it rough going but he was sure we would not let him down.

Following Stilwell's visit, the officers were brought together to receive an explanation of the way the war looked in northern Burma.

To defend the Hukawng valley and the route to the south the Japanese had, it appeared, about five battalions and attached troops, amounting to perhaps 7,000 men. On our side were four regiments of the Chinese 22nd and 38th Divisions and the Chinese 1st Provisional Tank Group under an American commander, Colonel Rothwell H. Brown. Numbers were greatly in our favor but because of the terrain did not give anything like a proportionate advantage. Movement through the heavy forest and kunai, or elephant, grass that was often as tall as a man or taller was narrowly channelized. In the whole valley only the Kamaing Road was capable of carrying wheeled transport, and it only in the dry season. A platoon in a concealed defensive position could hold up a battalion and exact a stiff toll before picking up, moving back and repeating the process. While between us and our supply bases were ranges upon ranges of mountains, with only one road through them, the mere existence of which seemed almost a miracle, the Japanese could look back upon road, river and rail lines of communication that improved progressively behind them. The Japanese force belonged to the 18th Division, General Tanaka commanding. The division had taken part in the conquest of Malaya as well as that of Burma and had captured Singapore. It was what might have been called a crack outfit.

Against these veterans, with the advantages of terrain, the

88

Chinese—though naturally we were not told this—had suffered heavily. Earlier in the month Stilwell had written that "it had become evident that the 38th Division could not be depended upon for any further serious effort. . . . The division commander [General Sun Li-jen, graduate of the Virginia Military Academy and future Chief of Staff of the Chinese Nationalist Army] was showing a strong inclination to delay operations interminably in the hope of avoiding more casualties." [1]

Reading in later years of the campaign in northern Burma, one is struck by the meagerness of the forces engaged. Battalions here counted for as much as divisions on other fronts, or as whole armies in Europe. It was all either side could do to make a military effort here at all. One has the impression of two Goliaths fully extended and barely able to reach each other on this remote sector, and constrained to grapple—albeit with undiminished ferocity—with their fingers alone.

Stilwell's strategy, which he had twice so far attempted to carry off, was to get a force around and behind the 18th Division, in what is called an envelopment, and destroy it, which would leave the Kamaing Road to the south open to his Chinese divisions.

On the Japanese side there had been a growth of confidence. When the first shots were exchanged in October and November 1943, the Japanese had been almost contemptuous of the Chinese. Then in December they were sobered by contact with the material resources that the 22nd and 38th Divisions commanded. But, as the fighting went on into February 1944, Tanaka several times saw a grave threat to his flank come to nothing because the Chinese moved so slowly. That the Chinese repeatedly moved as though to envelop, then let the opportunity slip because they did not exploit it, suggested to General Tanaka a way to defeat his powerful but lethargic opponents. Since Stilwell was spreading his forces wide in order to envelop, Tanaka consequently was operating on interior lines. He decided that "though threatened by enemy envelopment, we will exploit advantages of operations on interior lines, and, by utilizing every opportunity, defeat in detail the slow-moving Chinese forces without coordination on exterior lines." [2]

To read accounts today of the opposing strategies is a queer experience for one who lived through part of it on the terrain and whose view of it was as limited as it was vivid. The picture of a Japanese commander disposing numbered and structured entities like the 55th and 56th Regiments, just as our commanders did, wrestling with much the same kind of problems that confronted our own, and having only human faculties to bring to them, was not one that would have suggested itself to us. We conceived of the Japanese as a pestilence that infected the land. Even the notion of a comprehensible future history of movements on our own side would have been hard for us to entertain; for who other than God could have kept track of what tens of thousands of individuals were doing as they blundered into unforeseen situations and, if they were lucky, stumbled out not knowing, very often, what had happened? It was hard enough for us to follow the movements of the next platoon or keep track of what the battalion was up to in the depths of the sea of vegetation we inhabited.

One thing was clear enough at the start, however. We were a long-range penetration group and we were going to have to penetrate, specifically go around behind the enemy and burst upon him in the rear. We were to invigorate a campaign that was lagging. Phil Weld had brought back from an encounter with Arch Steele, a friend of his from *The Chicago Daily News,* an estimate that the success of Stilwell's whole operation depended upon us. We were to be the leading element in his third attempt to envelop the Japanese in the Hukawng.

"What's the story?" one of the sergeants asked when I returned from the session at which we were given the layout. He addressed me by my unadorned last name; word had circulated among the enlisted men that calling an officer by his title of rank in the possible hearing of the enemy would expose him to special danger and for some time, with a solicitude unusual

90

among them, they had been practicing a man-to-man style of address.

The platoon gathered around and I passed on what I had learned. It is possible that I did so with an air marking me as the supreme font and source of intelligence on World War II. I wound up by passing on the order that all nonessential equipment—blankets, mess kits and the like—was now to be turned in for removal to the rear to make room in our packs for the rations we should have to carry from now on, enough for four or five days at a time. I also advised everyone to shave and bathe, since it was not certain when the next chance would come.

On February 24 we rolled out of our ponchos in the black dark, wondering why we had ever been born. We were still allowed fires, though, and a can of C-ration stew with biscuits and a canteen cup of coffee put a somewhat different face upon things. We felt around for our equipment and our mules and were loaded up when dawn broke. A detail was to remain behind for a couple of nights to build campfires and mislead the Japanese, whose airplanes were assumed to be observing the area.

To get in behind the Japanese and cut the Kamaing Road, which was our objective, we were going to have to swing wide around their right flank. It was to take us eight days of marching, as it turned out, but to begin with it was not certain how far east we should have to swing in order to avoid the enemy. To find this out, General Merrill detached an intelligence and reconnaissance platoon from each of the battalions and sent them out ahead, with Sam Wilson's platoon from 1st Battalion in the lead. After some 18 miles, Logan Weston's platoon from 3rd Battalion was to turn off on a trail to the south to ascertain if they were yet beyond the Japanese flank. Lieutenant Grissom's platoon from 2nd Battalion was to do likewise a couple of hours farther on. Sam's platoon was to continue following the trail eastward for another few miles, when the trail itself turned to the south, toward the village of Tanja Ga. If he found that

Tanja Ga was not held by the Japanese (who were reported to have a platoon there) he was to push on to the Tawang River, a few miles beyond, and find a stretch where the regiment could ford it, should both Weston and Grissom find the way blocked. Altogether, Sam had a march of over 30 miles in store—all of it out ahead of everybody through an unknown alive with all the possibilities with which the imagination could endow it.

Sam and his men were off long before the rest of us, at 1:00 A.M. They moved as fast as the necessity for nerve-straining vigilance allowed, but this was not very fast. The trail had to be examined for footprints; the platoon had to stop continually to wait and listen. These expeditions were as much in the nature of stalking operations against a foe lying in wait, God knew where (or stalking the stalker), as they were marches. At dark at the end of the first day, after 17 hours on the trail, Sam called a halt for the night. The platoon pulled back into the woods and outposts were placed to keep watch on the trail in both directions. It was only the trail that could bring danger. You had to learn a reversed system of values. Trails, which you had always thought of as friendly, were here the enemies, while the nighttime forest, almost the symbol of childhood terror, now meant blessed safety. You had only to lie quietly in the darkness of the forest and you were back in the invulnerable refuge of childhood's bed. No one could reach you without betraying himself with every step as he floundered among the myriad noise traps of leaves and branches.

Until now the platoon had been traveling east, not toward the enemy but roughly parallel with the front. During the first day and the next morning the mission retained some of the exhilarating air of an adventure, a quality of not entirely counting in the sense that it counts when you risk being smashed up in an automobile collision, irrevocably, in the ordinary world of wet asphalt, neon lights, and speeding traffic. This was the Burmese forest, exotic and not quite credible, and this was an exercise according to the book. It still had a little the character of Figure 14, page 23, of the training manual or the desperate circumstances in which Jim Hawkins found himself aboard the pirate ship; it was not happening to you for keeps, you could look forward to putting the book down.

Then, about 1:30 the second afternoon, there was an instant of paralysis and simultaneously a conscious awareness of a shocking, unbelievable racket. A machine gun had cut loose in the silence. The platoon recoiled off the trail. The tattoo of the machine gun was followed by a fury of firing. The effect was of hearing from an adjoining room, while tiptoeing through a silent house, an outburst of maniac hysteria.

"It's behind us, Sammy!"

Sam nodded. It was not only behind but at some distance, not nearly as close as it had sounded at first. "All right, let's go," he said in a voice that sounded foreign to him. The men moved back onto the trail as the signal went down the line, and once more the platoon was in motion. But it was not the same, and no one had any hope it would ever be the same again.

There was fighting behind them, there were Japanese between them and the rest of the unit. They were cut off, isolated. To some it was as if an umbilical cord had been cut. They were alone. It was impossible to put the enormity of this knowledge out of mind. The scene before them was a mirror of it. The earth was no longer firm underfoot.

The firing had not lasted long. But a couple of hours later, with the same stunning suddenness as before, there was another outbreak. The horrible clamor went on, obscene, blasphemous, cut short at intervals by silences expectant and malevolent. The direction from which it came was slightly different this time.

In a low voice, consciously held steady, Sam said to his platoon sergeant, "They must both have bumped the Japs, Weston and Grissom both. First one, then the other." Next it would be his platoon's turn, Sam thought, looking down the trail ahead.

Sam's surmise as to what had happened was correct. Weston's platoon, turning south off the trail the other two platoons were following, had gone four or five miles and was approaching a village called Nzang Ga when his lead scout signaled to halt and stood listening. The trail was only a footpath, the jungle dense on both sides. Weston walked forward, past the three-man shock group and the second scout. The lead scout was Corporal Werner Katz, a naturalized citizen and veteran of the Spanish Civil War and Guadalcanal. He told Weston he had heard sounds ahead.

"It could be Chinese," Weston murmured. "Be careful. Don't shoot unless you're positive they're Japs."

He and the other scout covered Katz as the latter advanced, then stopped. Weston and the second scout then joined him and resumed firing positions. Katz went a few steps farther, to a bend in the trail.

"They're Chinese," he said in a louder, more relaxed voice. "They're waving us to come on."

He had seen, standing in the trail about 30 paces ahead, an Oriental-looking soldier beckoning to him and smiling. Katz started forward and had gone a step or two when the man up the trail brought his hand down smartly. On the instant two machine guns broke the silence and Katz hit the ground where he stood, firing as he fell. Behind him Weston and the other scout, diving for cover—the former behind a log—opened up too. Both would have been killed, nevertheless, had the Japanese traversed their guns instead of firing directly down the trail, at Katz, who lay in a slight depression just below the line of fire. Raising his head, Katz was grazed by a bullet along the nose—apparently from an Arisaka rifle. But he saw he had got one of the Japanese, who lay sprawled on the trail up front.

The fire from the Americans was accurate enough to throw the Japanese off and Katz was able to worm his way back. Then, two firing while one crawled, the three extricated themselves. Once disengaged, Weston ordered the platoon to fall back. His mission was only to discover if the enemy was in the neighborhood. "I think we could have knocked them off, though," he reported later.

The Japanese could be heard moving in the thick woods, trying to get around the platoon's flanks. But, having raised regimental headquarters on his radio, Weston received instructions to pull back all the way to the main trail, there to await the main body and cover its flanks, and he had no further contact with the enemy.

Katz was shaken—not unnaturally. The bullet that had grooved his face had needed only an inch's deflection to erase the prospect of forty years or more of eventful life, of complicated interactions with others inexhaustible in their consequences, that Katz had before him. Just that little bit, and the future would have closed over, without a trace, the skein of a life's effects stretching toward eternity.

A few miles away the outcome was otherwise. The hot stillness of noon hung upon the village of Lanem Ga when a patrol of Grissom's platoon, which had made its turn to the south after Weston's, headed in across the open ground. The village had been deserted by its inhabitants. But it was not empty. The second burst of machine-gun fire Sam Wilson's platoon had heard caught the lead scout, Private Robert W. Landis—a native, like Weston, of Youngstown, Ohio—and killed him instantly. The Japanese who held the village occupied the higher ground and had a clear field of fire. The patrol pulled back. It was not until the next day that, returning and finding the way clear, the platoon was able to recover the body of the first Marauder lost in action.

Among those in Sam's platoon, threading down the trail toward Tanja Ga, the longing to rejoin the regiment was like an undertow which had to be fought physically. They stopped more than ever to listen, their faces distorted as they sought to project their hearing through the diabolically uncommunicative screen of leaves. "This is it," a voice—his own voice—kept saying to Sam. He was aware of a continuing tremor of fear around his heart, but he was detached from it, not understanding why it should be there, for at this time he had the feeling— later to desert him utterly—of having an inherent immortality by virtue of being himself. His previous military experience kept unreeling before his eyes, in vivid fragments. He looked down the line of taut faces, each responding to his glance with instant inquiry. He had never quite realized how many the 47 men were who constituted his command; the file stretched all of 150 yards. It had never come to him with such force before, either, how precious each of their lives must be to them. What was courage when you were being brave with the lives of others? In retrospect, the instruction he had given at the infantry school at Benning on raiding parties seemed merely glib. What had it to do with this? The thought of miscalculations he might be making disclosed a whole menagerie of hideous possibilities. He blamed himself for not having done this or that differently in training.

There was nothing to indicate that his doubts were shared by those ahead of or behind him—thank God! The machinery was working. Though each resolutely ordered step was leading in what all of them doubtless felt was a fatal direction, away from the mother unit, jobs were being remembered. From his position directly behind the two scouts he could look back and see that the men were keeping watch in accordance with the platoon's standard procedure, one looking to front right, a second to front left, a third to treetops on right, a fourth to treetops on left. . . . He drew comfort, too, from the knowledge that his second in command, bringing up the rear (the platoon sergeant having to be ready to take over should the tail of the column be attacked) was a first-rate soldier. Edward G. Ammon, later to be commissioned in the field, was a burly, heavy-set, tobacco-chewing 210-pounder who had rejected the carbine his position called for (the heavier the responsibilities the lighter the weapon) in favor of a shoulder-breaking BAR which he handled like a popgun while carrying the additional, staggering burden of an extra bandolier of BAR ammunition slung cavalry-style across his chest. . . . The platoon marched almost soundlessly, though the thud of the mules' hoofs jarred in the stillness. Watching for signs that troops had passed along the trail, they sniffed also for the odor of a Japanese patrol mysteriously emitted, telltale to Sam's Pacific veterans.

With the other I and R platoons having both hit the enemy, everything now depended upon the route to Tanja Ga being found clear. It was difficult to believe it could be. Artillery, mortar, and even machine-gun fire could be plainly heard from less than five miles away, where the main battlefront lay. Ahead the view was always closed by a bend in the trail. Always there was a bend to be rounded. Each one had to be sweated out. From first to last that was probably the worst part of the campaign for those who had to endure it: *what was around the next bend?*

Uniforms were blotched with dark patches, wet with the sweat of heat and the sweat of fear. Bend unfolded after bend, stream followed stream—down one bank, up the other . . . hand raised . . . halt, stop, listen . . . on again . . . another bend, another halt. . . . Then came a village and worse tension as the separate, solitary scouts went out across the open ground, an almost unbearable sight, epitomizing the fate of man himself amid the emptiness and mystery that menace him. The platoon, covering them as best as it was able from the positions it had taken up in the shadows, waited for the horror of the machine gun's clatter that could cut them down. But nothing happened.

They pushed on.

Finally there was Tanja Ga itself, a collection of bashas in a wide clearing waiting as if under a spell, in a silence more ominous than any yet. The scouts, as they stole forward, their weapons slippery in their tight clutch, saw emplacements . . . and the suspense tightened. Sam watched with teeth set. But the emplacements, and the village itself, proved to be empty. The platoon immediately occupied the best prepared positions against the possibility of the enemy's return, for the abundance of bootprints leading in all directions indicated that Tanja Ga served as a patrol base. Leaving part of the platoon to hold the village, Sam reconnoitered the surroundings with the rest, as

97

far as the Tawang River, where he found an adequate crossing place.

Sam's relief and excitement were both intense. It was evident that they were now around the right flank of the Japanese and behind them, for Tanja Ga was well beyond the battleline. They had the information they had been sent to get, and good news for the commanding general. The SCR 284 was unloaded and set up and with the arrival of darkness and the hour for the regimental net to go into operation they at length made contact with Merrill's headquarters. Atmospheric conditions were bad, however—the perennial complaint—and it was quickly lost. It proved impossible to restore.

But Merrill had to be reached with the information that would mean so much to him. Sam decided to ride back, taking one man with him. He had a horse, a splendid black animal, that had caught his eye at Deogarh and that he had wheedled out of the sergeant in charge of the corral against the competition of some of his superiors. At 10:00 P.M., tired as he was from the exertion and strain of two days on the trail, he swung onto Pride-and-Joy and, with his companion on one of the platoon's other horses, set off into the night back along the way they had come. It was a 22-mile ride in darkness and on the whole more nerve-racking than the march out had been. There was no reason to suppose the Japanese had not closed in over the trail behind them; the firing the platoon had heard to the rear could well have meant that they had. The sound of the horses' hoofs kept the two men in constant apprehension. In the quiet forest the cantering seemed to shake the earth. But pushing a spirited mount in a dash by night through the enemy's territory was at least fitting to an heir of Virginia's traditions, and Sam felt not entirely out of his element.

As it turned out, it was not the Japanese he needed chiefly to worry about. His greatest scare, if not his closest call, came as they were crossing a stream. As his horse stretched to climb the farther bank, the saddle turned beneath him and he found himself on the ground with his left foot caught in the stirrup. He

98

was struggling desperately to free it, lest the horse bolt, when two big cats, as it sounded to him, bounded onto the trail 30 or 40 yards ahead; they could have been either leopards or tigers. They were spitting and snarling, as if they were fighting. The horse reared, and to Sam's mind the only question was now whether he would be trampled upon, dragged bouncing over the rocks up the stream bed, or attacked by savage carnivores, or all three. His companion was 75 yards or more back down the trail. Moved chiefly by the threat from the cats and recalling that wild animals can sometimes be frightened by the human voice, Sam shouted at them—the first words that came into his head. "You don't want to tackle me, you crazy cats!" His voice was strident and the note of hysteria in it was probably just what was required to unnerve a tiger. Certainly it made Sam's blood run cold to hear it. "I'm too damned tough for you!" he yelled. "Stringy and full of bones! You'd break all your teeth!" He managed to extricate himself and then his carbine from the saddle. He fired in the direction of the animals but over their heads, not wishing to risk wounding and maddening one of them, and that sent them scurrying off. Hurriedly he got the horse and saddle straightened out; the shots would have aroused any Japanese within half a mile.

They escaped safely the area of the encounter with the cats and dawn found them approaching one of the villages they had passed the day before, with Sam again well in the lead. Craning his neck to see what lay ahead, he lost his helmet—and perhaps saved his life. Dismounting to retrieve it, he decided to cross the clearing on foot. An early-morning fog greatly reduced visibility. Part way over he suddenly found himself confronting through the mist an American soldier who had stepped into view and was now aiming a .45 automatic at him. It turned out to be an OSS lieutenant attached to Grissom's platoon, into whose perimeter Sam had walked. However, there was no joyful, easy exchange of salutations by compatriots. "Get out of this village, please," was the amazing greeting he received

99

from the OSS man, whose white face and tense accents gave Sam an idea of the mood of the unit. The men he saw looked drawn and on edge, too, still showing the effects of their first action and the death of one of their platoon members. Having concealed their foxholes as they had, they obviously had no relish for the spectacle a fair-haired, hatless youth would provide dragging a horse through their position. He could imagine the turn it must have given them when he appeared unheralded and unaccountably out of the forest from which they had been waiting all night long with strained nerves for the Japanese to attack. He could also imagine what might have been in store for him if he had cantered up suddenly out of the fog without giving time for his uniform to be recognized.

After riding through Grissom's platoon, Sam felt an overpowering sense of relief and security. He was back behind the outposts, back behind the MLR, the main line of resistance. Freed from the weight of anxiety, he was ready to float away.

About four miles farther on, Logan Weston stepped out onto the trail in front of him. He raised his hand. "Hi, Sammy," he said, with a smile. This was where the side trail to Nzang Ga led off, which Weston's platoon was blocking. Weston's presence was always calming and reassuring and the spirit of the platoon was businesslike and unexcited. Being conducted through his position, Sam thought, was like being accompanied to the door by the pastor of the church at Jamestown.

Merrill was elated by the news Sam brought and outspoken in his praise for the conduct of the reconnaissance and Sam's energy in reporting its results. Hunter, with paternal pride, dropped a word about the way things were taught at Benning. Merrill at once spread out his map and after consulting it briefly directed that the three battalions move as fast as possible over the route Sam had reconnoitered.

"And now, Sam," he said briskly, "I mustn't hold you any longer. You'll be wanting to hurry back to your platoon."

Sam wondered whether in going over that trail again he

would partially forget his apprehension in his weariness or his weariness in his apprehension. He found that neither was much mitigated by the other. But the main thing was that—though three times seemed to be asking rather a lot of his luck—he made it.

IV Two days of marching brought the main body to Tanja Ga and on February 28, behind a line of outposts formed of Sam Wilson's I and R platoon, we forded the Tawang River by moonlight. From bank to bank the Tawang was almost a mile wide, but this was the season of low water, the river was shrunken, and we were able to cross without going in over our waists. Guidelines had been staked out to keep the column on course in the dark; we could not afford having mules fall in with their priceless loads. After marching another three days we reached the Tanai Hka, the Chindwin proper, another broad and beautiful river with clear water, a sandy, rocky bed, and forest on both sides. We were now directly behind and over 15 miles to the rear of the battle going on in the western part of the valley. Both at Tanja Ga and on the Tanai we received supply drops.

From the start supply drops were events in our lives, though we took them much more for granted now than we did later when we had learned how easy it was to miss them for one reason or another. The Dakotas roaring in from Dinjan, in Assam, provided almost our sole concrete link with the known world, the main evidence we had that it was still there. We would stand about gazing up at them like the votaries of a cult that afforded frequent but still impressive demonstrations of divine intervention. Uncle Sugar was back there, looking out for us! The callous tyrant of our recruit days was fussily solicitous of our needs now we were up front, though the amount he could send us in the face of the enormous difficulties was little enough.

Grain for the animals was free-dropped in half-filled sacks (full sacks would have exploded like melons on hitting the ground) and these were nearly as dangerous as bombs to heads below. The K rations, ammunition, and medical and signal supplies were floated down on red, white, blue and green rayon parachutes. There was a festival air about the drop field, but this was deceptive. Taking a drop was a strain on us. The battalions, which usually were strung out under cover, each a mile or two in length, had to assemble around an open area. We were like sea serpents which must leave their element to come up on land and expose themselves to danger in order to perform some vital function. The airplanes, returning repeatedly for the dropping run until the kickers finished discharging the cargo, advertised our presence, even though they flew as low as the terrain would allow. We could never tarry where those gay parachutes had flowered in the sky; we had to distribute the supplies fast and get out.

The advantage the Japanese had in having only to hide and wait and hold on in a country which favored just such a strategy would have forced us to pay an exorbitant price for any successes, despite the Allies' superiority in numbers and virtual command of the air, but for one asset we had: the local population was with us. Thinly settled as the hills of northern Burma were, that factor made a critical difference.

The Marauders took an immediate and lasting fancy to the Kachins. They seemed to be everything that the hostile, thieving, devious, cringing Indians—Wogs, to the 5307th—were not: friendly, open-faced, natural-mannered, smiling. An unspoiled people, one would have called them a generation ago, with fine, aristocratic features and unusual charm. In an exchange of glances with a Kachin you felt a rapport you might not achieve with your Indian bearer for years, if ever. It pleased

103

us to tell one another that there was something about them like Americans. Our passage through their villages had a social character, as if we were seeing well-bred friends after a short time apart, and it was this way even with the women, who, bare-breasted as they were, were unconstrained and unaffected—a joyful contrast to the peasant women of India, who fled, running like ostriches, at our approach, and to the sheeted women of the cities, with black slits in their cowls for them to see through, calling up images of the walking dead. Unless we were totally without food ourselves, even our worst reprobates would find a biscuit or a piece of chocolate for the little Kachin children who tagged along beside us to the edge of the village fields, not to beg but in simple excitement. At best the Kachins' material possessions were of the most meager, and now their simple economy was disrupted by foreign occupation and war and many of their villages were emptied, the paddy fields untilled. Neither their cheerfulness nor their dignity seemed impaired by poverty or hardship, however.

Mounds decorated with little flags or what resembled bundles of cornshucks on sticks were always in evidence in the villages. These were intended to propitiate, entice, or exorcise the nats, or forest spirits; I was never sure which the object was, and one must suppose that it does not matter. While our missionaries had been at them and had converted many, more or less, the Kachins were mostly animists, and this may have had something to do with their simple and appealing character. Certainly it must have provided another bond between them and the forest, in which they were so at home, and helped make them the invaluable allies we found them.

The British had organized Kachin levees, several hundred strong, and our own Office of Strategic Services also had been training Kachins by means of the agents it dropped or landed by airplane deep in Burma to live among the inhabitants, arm their patrols, and send out intelligence. We came to know the little Kachin patrols well and were enchanted. Waylaying the soldiery of the Japanese invader as they did in their artful ambushes, they made us think of a Robin Hood version of the Boy Scouts, clad (when in uniform at all) in green shirts and shorts. Some of the warriors could not have been above twelve years old, and while some had highly lethal burp guns slung around their necks, others carried ancient muzzle-loading fowling pieces. These latter, indeed, because ammunition could be improvised for them, were prized weapons, and OSS had been at pains to scavenge a number from home for distribution in northern Burma. Often we had a Kachin patrol with us and we never, if possible, moved without Kachin guides. The Kachins not only knew the country and the trails, but they also knew better than anyone but the Japanese where the Japanese were, and often they knew that better than the higher Japanese commands.

Why the Kachins should have sided with us is not as self-evident as we might like to suppose. It is true that they had suffered badly under the Japanese, who were constrained to live off the country, and that we meant relief from the Japanese. But we also brought the Chinese in train, and from long habituation the Kachins disliked and feared the Chinese at least as much as the Japanese. If, none the less they gave their help to us, it was presumably because they expected that once the Japanese had been cleared out they would be able to live their lives as before, free of both the Chinese and the Burmans, their other hereditary foes.

To enlist the co-operation of the Kachins was a concern of the British and an important job of one of the most important members of the 5307th, our British liaison officer, Captain Charles Evan Darlington. Phil Weld spoke of Evan as having the face of a Spanish grandee, and though I should never have thought of the comparison myself I see what Phil meant: there was the aquiline nose, the noble brow, the narrow, black mustache. For the rest, Evan was a sturdily built English type with the Englishman's special and deceptive capacity for pursuing the romantic and idealistic with a matter-of-course casualness and understatement, so that he seemed quite ordinary until you stopped to think about him. Although under thirty years of age, he had been a political officer for the area before the war, which had entailed his being all things to all Kachins: justice of the peace, counselor, adjudicator of contentions, doctor, and personification of the Empire. For five years his home had been in Maingkwan, which was the chief village of the Hukawng valley and now the immediate objective of the Chinese advance. When the Japanese invaded, he had walked out over the refugee trail to Ledo with his wife and two-week-old daughter. On arrival, their sole remaining possessions were the clothes they were wearing—shirt and shorts in his wife's case, shorts alone in his—and they were without a crumb to have carried them another day. Returning to Burma with the Allied advance, he had been devoting himself to preventing the worst depredations of the Chinese against his wards, the Jingpaw, as the Kachins called themselves. It was a task, one judged, requiring some diplomacy.

Evan had a brother happily married to a Kachin wife and he himself spoke Kachin fluently. There could be no doubt that he had been a trusted friend of the Kachins. In days to come, as we pushed south through one village after another, the inhabitants recognized and gave him a joyful reception. He was a harbinger of spring after a two-year-long winter and one who was unmistakably a favorite in himself. Knowing the country as he did, Evan was indispensable not only as a supplier of guides but as a guide himself.

At the Tanai, while awaiting the supply drop, General Merrill held a staff meeting at which he issued attack orders to the battalion commanders. These were based on instructions he had received from General Stilwell to move as fast as possible to Walawbum and there block the road.

It was learned after the war that until we reached the Tanai the Japanese Divisional Headquarters—thanks to communications difficulties—was unaware that its position was being flanked by American troops. Then, somehow, General Tanaka heard that we were already at Walawbum, well behind him.

"This was the chance Tanaka had awaited," says *Stilwell's Command Problems.* "Quickly analyzing his situation, he decided that the Chinese 22nd and 38th Divisions were moving so slowly that he could contain them with a small rear guard while the main strength of the 18th Division hurled itself on the Americans." To this rendezvous the unwitting 5307th was now preparing to speed under forced draft.

The site of the rendezvous, as determined by the intentions of the two sides, was to be along the Numpyek Hka, a stream that flowed directly north, its waters ultimately reaching the Tanai. Along the Numpyek lay the villages (reading from north to south) of Wesu Ga, Langang Ga, and Walawbum, a few miles apart. The southernmost, Walawbum, lay not only on the Numpyek but also on the Kamaing Road, which approached from the west and then, upon reaching the village, made a right-angled turn to the south. The 3rd Battalion, leading the regiment, was to go through Lagang Ga to Walawbum while the 2nd turned off before Lagang Ga and marched westward through Wesu Ga, across the Numpyek, to cut the road three miles the other side of Walawbum. The 1st Battalion was to have the not very glorious role of covering the access trails and serving as a regimental reserve.

Such was the pressure for haste that 3rd Battalion was ordered not to wait to receive its full share of the drop made to us on the Tanai. It had to take off after receiving little better than a day's ration. We had to leave sickening quantities of supplies behind on the huge sandbar in the river where we took the drop. The waste of war is difficult to get used to.

The previous day, before reaching the Tanai, Weston's platoon, which had been in the lead ever since the crossing of the Tawang, had run into a Japanese abatde, a trailblock of felled trees crisscrossing each other. Crawling around and through the branches, they expected to be shot at but were not. They had, at the same time, a distinct sensation of being under observation. After they had left the Tanai, still in the lead, the feeling they had of the near presence of Japanese grew stronger.

107

There were booby traps on the trail, which they managed to detect and dismantle without running afoul of any of them, and fresh Japanese bootprints. They were sure now that they were on the heels of a Japanese patrol. How closely on its heels they were became apparent when in time the bootprints began to have water still oozing into them. There was nothing to prevent their walking into a trap, but equally there was nothing to do but press on as they were. Moving through the jungle, if they had tried to bypass the enemy, would have been slow and costly in time, and from experience Weston knew that when a roadblock is to be thrown in it was important to get it done with the least possible delay once contact with the enemy was made.

Weston was an infantry scientist, and when, about half a mile from Lagang Ga, the inevitable happened and they caught a burst of fire from up the trail, the platoon's standard operating procedure went instantly into effect. The lead squad, plunging to cover, established a base of fire while the two following squads headed immediately off into the woods, one on either side of the trail, to work around the flanks of the Japanese gunners. Thirty yards or so beyond them, they began to ease in toward the trail to catch the rear elements of the patrol which they deduced from their acquaintance with the enemy would probably be emplacing themselves at about that spot to form the far end of a so-called S-shaped position. Discovering themselves outflanked as they heard the Americans closing in, the Japanese hurriedly pulled out.

Weston and his men also knew from experience that the Japanese patrol would probably set up another ambush when it had gained enough lead . . . and then another when it had again been dislodged. And so it went. After each contact one of Weston's flanking squads would take over as the point and lay down the base of fire the next time they were hit. In this way the squads were rotated. The Japanese patrol, kept off balance by the vigor with which Weston's platoon was pressing it and evidently nervous, was hasty in its firing and did no dam-

108

age. Weston judged that it was about equal in strength to his own bunch and that its mission was a delaying one.

Having been, in fact, slowed down, Weston's platoon was overtaken on the outskirts of Lagang Ga by the van of the battalion. It was decided that the two would separate here and move on Walawbum by different routes, one on the far side of the Numpyek, the other on the near. Accordingly, the main body turned off to the south and pushed on to the river against the same kind of opposition Weston had been meeting; it was to reach the river at a point directly across from Walawbum at nightfall. Weston's platoon continued on in the direction in which they had been moving, due east. They fought their way through the village of Lagang Ga, advancing by a succession of thrusts, and infiltrated across the Numpyek with the Japanese still firing on them, though from a greater distance. The low, heavily forested west bank of the river afforded scant defensive possibilities and they pushed on south along the river toward Walawbum. They were moving almost blindly. The shadowy silences yawned chasmlike around them. They had fought that afternoon for two and a half hours and they were still going in deeper. Twice they saw Japanese sentries, who disappeared ahead of them; one leapt up like a grouse not ten feet from Weston and had crashed off into the woods before anyone could raise a weapon. Darkness caught them struggling in a fog through a swamp and they bedded down where they were, in as secure a defensive array as the terrain would allow. Weston gave categorical orders: no fires, no noise, no movement. The sound of anything stirring was to be instantly grenaded. Helmets were to be used as latrines.

The 2nd and 1st Battalions, strung out in that order, were taking a more northerly route to the Numpyek. On the previous day, March 2, the scouts reconnoitering the route surprised two Japanese and killed them both, and these two, left where they had fallen on the trail, were the first of the enemy, dead or alive, that most of us had seen. An hour before they had been the victors of Singapore, the omnipresent, inhuman, uncannily

109

resourceful enemy, the protégés of Satanic and possibly invincible forces. And now it was all over with them. They were quite harmless. They lay flat on their backs, their limbs spread, at the end of a trail that led back to a Japanese farm or town and to school days that contained no hint of the footpath through the elephant grass of a valley in northern Burma. You tried to conceive of some wrongdoing they had once perpetrated that led logically to the sentence now executed upon them, a mortal error of which you were innocent, so that in a just universe no such sentence could be executed upon you. But you knew there was nothing in it.

The tension increased all the next day as we moved eastward to our certain collision. Nothing counted any more but the forest to which far-reaching chance had so arbitrarily brought you—so arbitrarily and so irrevocably. Up ahead the scouts, nearing Wesu Ga, were fired on from across a small field. The lead scout fell to the ground and the Japanese, believing him killed, rushed forward, whereupon he raised himself up with a Tommy gun and emptied a full magazine at them. Two were killed and five others fled.

Wesu Ga was evacuated ahead of us by the Japanese and 2nd Battalion moved on through. The next day it crossed the Numpyek, continued on two miles farther west, then turned south off the trail into the heavy forest. Hacking its way through, it reached the vicinity of the Kamaing Road at nightfall, close enough to hear the Japanese laughing and shouting in the distance. Closing in on the road at dawn with the expectation of having to fight to put in its block, it found that, although the Japanese had dug in to protect the road in that sector, they had pulled out during the night, doubtless drawn southward to meet what appeared to be the most immediate threat, at Walawbum. The battalion set to work feverishly to improve the Japanese foxholes against what it knew was coming.

The Americans had reached their objectives. The 3rd Battalion had cut the road the day before across the river at Walawbum, and now 2nd Battalion had cut it several miles farther west and nearer the front. They had arrived ahead of the two Japanese regiments which had been disengaged from action farther north to accomplish the 5307th's destruction, and which were now on their way.

There were plenty of Japanese in the vicinity as it was, however, and their reaction to the sudden appearance of the American force was hot and swift. When at dawn it had laid in upon the Japanese positions on the road in Walawbum with a barrage from its heaviest weapons, 3rd Battalion had stirred up a storm. The Japanese rained in mortar shells and attacked violently on the flanks, losing heavily as they ran into the booby traps and ambushes the combat team had set. Most of the 75 Japanese estimated to have been killed by the 5307th this first day fell in those fierce encounters. The combat team that had borne the brunt of them was now in its second day without food, but it was not food but ammunition for which it was sending urgent calls.

Americans and Japanese were running into each other on every side. There was no front to speak of in the kind of fighting that had developed. At dawn the first day a party of seven Japanese carrying an officer on a litter—four of them found later to have been already wounded—walked into Lagang Ga, where a 3rd Battalion command post was located, and were cut down by a machine gun. It was later whispered that one of the Marauders murdered the helpless litter patient by cutting his throat with a trench knife, but no one had the stomach to try to establish the facts. Out of the pockets of one of the Japanese lying in the grass, I noticed later, had spilled witnesses of two of the needs that work most powerfully upon men of every race: a cheap little gilded Buddha and a contraceptive device, pink in color. It is hard to say which is the more unnerving, the thought of your enemy's inhumanity when he is alive or the spectacle of his humanity when he lies dead. It was not long after the litter party met its end that the paddy field which the combat team at Lagang Ga was trying to clear for a drop field

111

and landing strip for the little liaison planes we depended upon to evacuate our casualties was assaulted by a Japanese patrol, one perhaps with vengeance in its heart. There was a ferocious scrimmage before the attackers, held off by wounded Marauder machine gunners, broke under the American mortar fire and left ten dead on the field.

In the kind of fighting that built up for three days to the climax of the battle of Walawbum, the 5307th's commanders were not much safer than anyone else. A Japanese machine gunner was chased from a hiding place not a hundred yards from General Merrill's command post at Wesu Ga just before he could let fly. Colonel Hunter, having gone forth with a small patrol to meet Colonel Rothwell Brown, commanding the Chinese 1st Provisional Tank Group, at a village a few miles to the north, ran instead into a body of Japanese at the rendezvous site. The Americans shot and killed two and dispersed the rest but shortly afterward had to take to the woods to escape a detachment of 50 Japanese moving southward. (The tanks which were to have supported us were unable to get through.) Lieutenant Colonel Beach, commanding 3rd Battalion, having had one narrow escape when a Japanese stepped out on the trail ahead of him only to have the top of his head shot off by Beach's orderly, had another narrower still when he undertook a personal reconnaissance of Walawbum. There had been no sign of the enemy in the village for three hours and Beach asked for volunteers to go over and investigate. He wrote later in a citation for his orderly, Joseph F. Sweeney, in a characteristic passage: "All officers and men volunteered at once. Due to the mission, I only chose one man which was Sweeney. I told Sweeney of the danger and he remarked, 'I will follow you through hell if necessary.' " The Japanese were still there, all right, but the ex-railway policeman and his orderly got within ten yards of them before being discovered. They had to take to their heels then. They just managed to make the bank of the river when the enemy opened up on them with two machine guns and a platoon of rifles. Under cover of machine-gun fire from their own side they succeeded—against the odds—in getting safely back across.

The Americans at Walawbum were under a singular misapprehension. They had a good idea that the enemy was bringing up reinforcements and forming for an offensive. The Japanese attacked several times on March 5, only to be thrown back from the riverbank by 3rd Battalion's automatic weapons, leaving more dead behind, and all that day the two sides dueled with their mortars in preparation for the showdown. To the south American fighter planes could be seen and heard strafing and dive-bombing the areas designated as probable enemy concentration areas by the 5307th's air liaison officers or by smoke shells from its mortars. But what the Americans thought was that in massing their strength the Japanese were engaged in a desperate effort to open the way for their forces fighting the Chinese in the north to escape with their heavy equipment. From Stilwell on down, as the official history points out, they were convinced they had trapped General Tanaka; it did not occur to any of them that it was for the purpose of destroying the 5307th that Tanaka was getting his forces in line.[1]

There was no doubt in the 5307th, however, that the Japanese were pressing harder all the time.

It was Weston's I and R platoon, isolated on the other side of the river, that first found itself in serious trouble. After the night in the swamp, the platoon had moved south toward Walawbum through the early-morning fog and had found a small clearing on high ground at a bend in the river from which it had a field of view upstream and down and could see into the village, about 600 yards distant.

Early the next morning the Japanese came after it. Attacking first from the south and losing five men almost at once, they commenced to feel out the platoon on its other sides. After beating back one assault after another for three hours, the Americans found that they had the enemy all around them except at their backs, which were to the river. Weston had formed his platoon in a kind of modern, small-scale version of the British

113

Square, a three-pointed star, with one squad to a point, and was using two Tommy gunners as a mobile reserve which he could shift to meet each new attack. Thanks to the coolness of his Nisei interpreter, Henry Gosho, who, close enough to overhear the voices on the other side, would translate the leaders' orders, he generally knew where to expect the attacks to hit. The two forces were almost on top of each other, but so dense was the vegetation that for the most part they were firing blindly.

Three Americans had been hit. The first, Pete Leitner of Lake Okeechobee, had been dragged back to cover in an extraordinary act of heroism by Weston, who had had to run the gamut of automatic weapons fire from only 20 yards away to do it. Leitner now was lying in a depression at the center of the star "under a low ceiling of lead coming from all directions," as Weston expressed it. One of the other wounded men, Sergeant Lionel Parquette, had been hit in the head and never regained consciousness. "He was a Catholic and the first of my men ever to die on the field of battle," Weston wrote. "It was a heavy cross for me. Another, Lappier, had an artery cut in his left arm. . . . Pete [Leitner] called for water and we moistened his lips. During lulls in the firing, we lay in a prone position beside him and led him to the well from which, if any man drink, his thirst shall be quenched (John 7:37). He soon dropped off into unconsciousness from which he never again revived, but as his eyes closed, a brilliant smile swept across his pain-streaked face." A characteristic picture emerges of Weston the minister comforting the dying as Weston the infantryman, methodically ordering the dispositions appropriate to the situation, steadies the living.

The Americans were running low on ammunition, and the Japanese, seeming to scent that the time for the kill was approaching, redoubled the fire of their grenade launchers. Getting word over his voice radio at this juncture that the main body of his combat team had moved in across the river from him, Weston bethought himself of its big 81-millimeter mortars. He quickly put in a call for their help. The noise was so terrific that his operator could hardly hear but he managed to make the request understood and transmit the co-ordinates of the spot where they thought the Japanese were concentrated. Across the river Lieutenant William Woomer—known from South Pacific days as "Woomer the Boomer"—had one mortar already in position.

The first round was wide and over, the next closer. Alfred Greer, Weston's platoon sergeant, who was giving directions, then asked for a smoke shell, took a bearing on it when it burst, and sent new figures over the radio . . . then amended them. The thud of the explosions was like the tread of a giant taking earth-shaking steps toward them. When the giant had almost reached them, he stepped squarely upon the enemy. There were screams and cries that Hank Gosho reported to be calls for medics. Then, in response to Greer's further directions, the blasting footfalls—there were now two giants at work—strode the whole arc of the perimeter to the south and back again to the north.

"Good!" the operator cried. "The last one blew two Japs clear up into the air forty yards out front!"

The fearsome march of the mortar bursts "temporarily delayed their attempt to clean us up," Weston wrote. "This gave us a chance to get our second wind so we braced for the *banzai* attack we knew was coming." When it came, it came well coordinated and from all directions at once. So small was the area the platoon held and so massed the assault that the attackers on opposite sides of the semicircle were running into each other's fire.

The position had clearly become impossible and the combat team commander ordered Weston to withdraw. The platoon steeled itself for what it could expect to be the worst so far. Under cover of the mortars and the fire of a line of skirmishers on the other bank, the Americans withdrew to the river, closely followed by the Japanese, who could look forward to catching them at a dreadful disadvantage as they sought to cross. Two of them stripped off their undershirts and staked them up to mark

115

the lane to be used for the crossing and to guide the fire from the opposite bank. Under the protection of this fire and what concealment was provided by the smoke shells Woomer's mortars had thrown in, they began to cross two or three at a time. One of the first over was Norman E. Janis, a Sioux chief from Deadwood, South Dakota. He had turned to watch Werner Katz and another bearer bringing Leitner across on a litter improvised of bamboo poles and fatigue jackets when in the nick of time he spotted a Nambu machine gun thrust out from the bushes on the opposite bank aimed at the litter party. He drew a bead . . . and the Japanese gunner fell across his weapon. Chief Janis was one of the crack shots of the regiment, and with his M1 he accounted for six more Japanese during the crossing. Two other Nambus emplaced on the river were knocked out with Browning automatics before they had fired ten rounds. Weston was in the last party to pull out. The crossing was completed without a single casualty.

It was against the block that 2nd Battalion had clamped on the Kamaing Road several miles to the west, at the point of the 5307th's deepest penetration, that the Japanese hurled their heaviest punches. After moving in at dawn, the Americans had just got their weapons set up when the Japanese force whose foxholes they had taken over appeared down the road, marching back. "I could feel the muscles trying to cross in cramps and the blood pounding in my face as I gingerly moved my position and peered down the road," Captain Fred Lyons recalled in an account he subsequently wrote. The thought he had was the thought everyone must have when his first action begins: "This is it!" It opened with the ear-splitting tattoo of one of his machine guns, which caught a file of seven Japanese in its burst. "Then," wrote Lyons, "the firing began in earnest. More Japs ran into view, so close you could see the bronze star shining dully on their bouncing little hats. The Tommyguns paused only for reloading as one after another the Japs ducked and melted away in the grass."

The attack was the first of six strong ones the Japanese made

A column of the 5307th marching down the Ledo Road, which in this forward section, near its descent into the Hukawng valley, had at that time only been roughed out. *U.S. Army Signal Corps*

Brig. Gen. Frank D. Merrill climbing down from a Kachin basha on the way to Walawbum, February, 1944. *U.S. Army Signal Corps*

Capt. Evan Darlington of the British Army with Kachin guides and part of a column of the 5307th on the way to Walawbum. *U.S. Army Signal Corps*

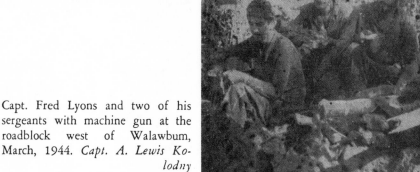

Capt. Fred Lyons and two of his sergeants with machine gun at the roadblock west of Walawbum, March, 1944. *Capt. A. Lewis Kolodny*

Using an M-209 converter, a code clerk enciphers a message to Base requesting a supply drop. *Charlton Ogburn, Jr.*

Trying to establish radio contact with Base. Sgt. George at the set, Lt. Bright (second from right) leaning forward behind him. *Charlton Ogburn, Jr.*

The supply-drop plane, a Dakota (C-47), appears through an opening in the bamboo overhead. *Charlton Ogburn, Jr.*

Watching supplies descend by parachute from the drop plane. *Charlton Ogburn, Jr.*

Steep hills, heavy packs, and everywhere the forest. The march to Shaduzup, March, 1944. *Charlton Ogburn, Jr.*

Part of 2nd Battalion crossing the Tanai River over a native bridge of bamboo on the way to Inkangatawng, March, 1944. *U.S. Army Signal Corps.*

Lt. Col. George A. McGree, Jr., just before losing consciousness while commanding 2nd Battalion in its last action, near Myitkyina, May 27, 1944. *Capt. A. Lewis Kolodny*

Firing a mortar during the siege of Nhpum Ga. *Capt. A. Lewis Kolodny*

A trophy of the fighting at Nhpum Ga. *Capt. A. Lewis Kolodny*

Medical Corpsmen of 1st Battalion cooking deer meat for the wounded near Hsamsingyang. *U.S. Army Signal Corps*

Col. Charles N. Hunter, in center, with Capt. Tom P. Senff on left and Lt. Col. William Lloyd Osborne on right at Naubum discussing the imminent march to Myitkyina. *Lt. Edward Sievers*

Officers of 1st Battalion. Lt. Col. William Lloyd Osborne, commanding, is in center of front row, behind map. Next to him on the left is Maj. Caifson Johnson. To the left of Maj. Johnson is Lt. William T. Bright, wearing cotton hat. Directly behind Lt. Bright is Lt. Samuel V. Wilson. Second from the left-hand end of the entire group is Lt. Philip S. Weld. To the right of Lt. Col. Osborne is Capt. Tom P. Senff and directly behind him is the author. Lt. William Lepore is in the front row at extreme right. Taken at Naubum before the march to Myitkyina, April, 1944. *Lt. Edward Sievers*

Bringing in a casualty of the fighting at Myitkyina.

Fording a river near Myitkyina.
U.S. Army Signal Corps

Crew firing a .30 caliber heavy machine gun near Myitkyina. *U.S. Army Signal Corps*

Winners and losers of a fight at Myitkyina.

Japanese prisoners from Myitkyina.

Lt. Gen. Joseph W. Stilwell awarding medals at Myitkyina. At extreme left is Gen. Wessels, commanding the Myitkyina Task Force. In the middle of the row is Capt. John J. McLaughlin, 1st Battalion Surgeon. Col. Charles N. Hunter, second from left, had to borrow a shirt at the last moment when it was realized that a medal cannot be pinned to a bare chest. *U.S. Army Signal Corps*

that day on 2nd Battalion. In between, they shelled it. This was the first artillery the 5307th had encountered, and it drove home a point that was to be driven home with all of us that day and the next. There is nothing quite like artillery when the enemy has some and you have not. Except when our planes were overhead keeping the gunners in their foxholes, the enemy's pieces had a free field with us. Having nothing with which to reach them, we had to sit and take it. However, 2nd Battalion gave the advancing infantry a hosing with all the small arms it had and killed over a hundred while itself suffering only six casualties, of which one was fatal. The doctors had their first experience of treating a serious injury under fire. A boy hit by a burst from a machine gun was brought to the aid station with his intestines perforated and hanging out. An operating table was improvised of a litter resting on medical carrying cases. While anesthesia was being given, the aid station began to catch machine-gun fire. The technicians and everyone else dove for cover, but Major Rogoff, the battalion surgeon, and Lew Kolodny had to stick it out, standing where they were. Lew was hit by a splinter while they worked with concentration against death, which seemed poised in different forms over both them and the patient. In the end all were spared. They washed out the patient's body cavity with plasma, sprinkled it with sulfa, closed up the perforations with purse-string sutures and got the boy safely sewed up.

In taking over a section of the road the battalion had also taken over a section of the main telephone line between the Japanese forward command post at Maingkwan and the rear echelon at Kamaing. Sergeant Roy A. Matsumoto, one of the Nisei interpreters, tapped into the line and while the block was held was able to monitor the traffic on the line. One message was from a Japanese sergeant who, after giving his position away by reporting the location of the 2nd Battalion in reference to it, stated that he had only three men with rifles to protect the ammunition dump under his charge and begged "help and advice" from his commanding officer. Merrill, relaying the information to Stilwell's headquarters, suggested that such help and advice as lay within his power be delivered by a dive bomber.

During the day—March 5—Matsumoto overheard reports betraying confusion and anxiety among the Japanese all through the area. Stilwell recorded some of them in his diary: ". . . casualties very large, we cannot protect river crossing . . . every man in the next few days must fight hard. Enemy is very strong and we must destroy him at all costs . . . cannot hold much longer if help does not come . . . no help available, fight to the end."

Late in the day a call was heard from Tanaka's headquarters ordering the 18th Division to withdraw. The attempt to destroy the 5307th, of which we never knew, was being abandoned. One reason for this was apparently that Colonel Brown's Chinese Tank Group, pushing down from the north, had preempted the trail from Maingkwan to Wesu Ga that the Japanese 56th Regiment was to have used in the attack on the 5307th. It had also, when its advance had been held up by a marshy stream, fired into the 18th Division's headquarters under the impression it was being opposed by a Japanese rifle company. The bulk of the 18th Division, in the east, was ordered to swing around the 2nd Battalion's roadblock by a secret trail and regain the Kamaing Road to the south. The 56th Regiment, in the north—as it developed—was to tackle the Americans on its own, apparently in an effort to throw them back and safeguard the retreat.

By the time Tanaka's order for the withdrawal came through and was intercepted, the 2nd Battalion had been fighting for 36 hours without food. It had used the last of its drinking water and was running low on ammunition. For all these reasons its commander decided to withdraw and rejoin the rest of the regiment along the Numpyek. The men were nervously as well as physically exhausted after their first ordeal of combat and the isolated and exposed position of the battalion had begun to create jitters. Reports were circulating among the troops that "thousands of Japs" were coming after them. There was an end-of-the-world feeling and a sense of desperate urgency while preparations were made to pull out. Nevertheless, and despite the confusion in the black darkness, the withdrawal was made in good order at midnight. Captain Evan Darlington and the scouts who led the return march, being apprehensive of booby traps, drove a mule ahead of them—providentially, since the animal was shortly blown up.

After a night in the kunai grass, 2nd Battalion arrived at Lagang Ga early in the afternoon of the 6th, just in time to share with 1st Battalion the worst artillery going-over the 5307th had so far had to take from the Japanese. They were getting us ready, presumably, for the assault the 56th Regiment was going to make.

The scene was one that I can see in my mind as vividly as ever. Our battalion headquarters was on the edge of the paddy field that had been cleared for the liaison planes and also on the edge of the pretty little Numpyek River. The fly-covered remains of the Japanese litter party that had blundered into the command post two days before was only thirty paces away in the weeds along the river bank. Phil Weld was husking a handful of rice from a basket someone had found and divided up, pounding it in his helmet with the butt of his trench knife preparatory to straining out the chaff with a mosquito headnet. We were waiting for a supply drop and, as always at such times, were starving. I was helping the veterinary officer treat a mule with a saddle sore deep enough for him to have got his fist into it. It was a pastoral scene, like an English painting of the eighteenth century, and it was fixed in my mind like a painting at the instant when, in fact, all motion was arrested by a sound that, while not loud, had an awful authority. To Phil it was like a "toboggan slide rustle of air overhead." What I first thought was that we were hearing the rocket swish of a signal flare. We looked at one another. Then, 75 yards behind us— BANG! The scene that was to prove etched on my consciousness exploded as men snatched up weapons and helmets and dove for cover and as mules and horses broke loose and took to the

119

woods. There were three more reports from a distance followed by the insinuating, compelling whinny—"*shu-shuing,* like evil buzzards flying overhead," Phil wrote—and then three quick crashes close by.

Everyone was digging frantically. A number of the men had discarded their entrenching shovels on the Ledo Road and had to scrape out holes with their helmets; they went at it like terriers. My disposition always to see the future in terms of its direst contingencies had for once stood me in good stead and I had held onto my shovel despite the weight it added to a pack. I could think of nothing but getting underground, but while I dug I was aware of Tom Senff lying face down nearby, too sick with dysentery to dig or perhaps even to care. The awareness was only somewhat less painful than my awareness of the shells coming in at intervals like ghostly express trains. When I had finished my trench I told him to get into it. He shook his head.

"Don't be a damn fool. Get in it. I'll dig another."

"Go to hell," he murmured, with a distant echo of affability.

I am ashamed to say I was relieved. When I saw in India the depths to which human beings could be reduced by circumstance I knew I could never think the same of mankind again. Now, pinned down in my slit trench by fear, as by a savage ape, I knew I could never think the same of myself again either.

Nothing, I believe, can prepare you for the experience of being fired on—all the books, all the motion pictures, any amount of imagination. The realization *these people mean to kill you* strikes as if no such possibility had entered your head before. They mean to kill you! The well-intentioned, good-deed-doing, vulnerable, sensitive, lovable you, the you who never thought of doing anybody any harm and had never desired other than for everybody in the world to be happy. They mean to kill you as if you were a Thanksgiving turkey or a mad dog. They mean to blow your entrails out. And they may well succeed. Why not? Insensate instruments of malice, they may well do it; and, looking like something in a butcher's shop, you will be covered over with this musty-smelling, alien earth, the golden edifice of your future, sunlit tower upon sunlit tower reaching skyward, leveled to this indifferent leafmold acrawl with ants. Your soul hammers against the unalterable walls of cause and effect: *Not here, not now*—the universe could not encompass such a monstrous and arbitrary cruelty!

The report comes that one of the first shells scored a direct hit on the 4th Platoon—Meredith Caldwell's platoon—killing one man and wounding another, and that the next salvo bracketed the 3rd Platoon, wounding three. You can picture the bloodstained foliage, the irrational position of the dead man, with the fixed, white-eyed gaze. Poor bastards! But better they than you. Yes, better by a damn sight. Better Tom Senff than you. Better almost anybody in the world. Oh, God, here comes another one, right for the pit of your stomach . . . *wheu-wheu-wheu-wheu-wheu*-BAM!

Tom Senff, who was then Battalion S-3, had pulled himself up and got hold of a voice radio. He put in a call to Meredith Caldwell to find out what his situation was. He said later he would never forget Meredith's reply. Meredith, it is necessary to explain, was expecting his first child and since the due date was in May, the month the rainy monsoon begins, he referred to the infant as Monsoon Minnie.

"Oh, God," said Meredith between artillery bursts, "please let Monsoon Minnie have a pappy come May!" He clicked off his set without any of the "over and out" routine he normally made an elaborate performance of.

Meredith, when we saw him, said the first shells, which came in just after his platoon reached its assigned position at the north end of the paddy field, went over his head and landed about a hundred yards behind him. "The next ones went right over and landed fifty yards behind me—right in the middle of the platoon. I thought: the next round is for you. So I got down just as flat as I could and tried to crawl up in the helmet. Sure enough, the next salvo landed just to my right. The closest one was just five feet from me. It sent up a geyser of mud but I wasn't even scratched. The next shells were fifty yards in front

121

of me. I saw I had some wounded, so I decided to run to the battalion aid station and get Winnie Steinfield. Winnie replied in his solemn, gentle, aquatic-mammal's manner: 'Now, Meredith, you know the Army regulations are that the wounded are supposed to be brought to the aid station, and I am not supposed to go running around northern Burma like a country doctor—but I'll go this one time.'

"So," said Meredith, "he grabbed up his little snake doctor's grip, and as the shells were flying we both assumed the National Guard Crouch and lit out back for the platoon. Unfortunately, Myers was dead. A damn fine soldier—from Mississippi. One of the company cooks came out of the grass looking like a hamburger, so he was Winnie's first customer."

Meredith was then ordered to bring part of his platoon down to the river to help guard battalion headquarters. After making his dispositions he lost no time in digging in. "I was in a hole with a Mexican runner," he told us later, "and every time we could hear the shells coming, he would start praying in Spanish. I told him not to be bashful and keep it up. I told him I was a Presbyterian and we just had one prayer and I had forgotten all of it but 'Forgive our debtors,' and I wasn't a damn bit concerned about them."

Near Meredith's position Sergeant Robertson, a veteran of Guadalcanal, and one of his men were digging a foxhole when, sitting down to catch their breath, they looked down . . . and directly between them saw a hand grenade. Two Japanese had slipped up behind them and taken a grenade off one of the Americans' own packs, only before heaving it they had unscrewed the fuse instead of pulling the pin. When it failed to go off, the Japanese threw one of their own. It landed behind a helmet and blew it all to pieces but did no other damage. Before they could throw another, Sergeant Robertson snatched up his '03 rifle and in an extraordinary feat of hipshooting with a bolt-operated weapon got both of them. Apparently they were the spotters for the Japanese artillery. They were armed with nothing but a radio and some grenades. "If they'd been in our army," said Meredith, "they'd have got the Congressional Medal of Honor."

Phil Weld wrote in his notebook:

L-5 pilots badly frightened, sweating, crowded in hole, asking, "Is the Infantry out in front?" A few minutes later they take off with wounded, the sound of their motors warming up brings another salvo smack on strip even as they lift into the air, a hazard any groundling would fear more than the perils of remaining under the shelling.

Colonel Osborne at command post singularly unruffled—not surprising in view of his heavy shelling at Bataan. Merrill and Hunter appear—Merrill very much the poised field commander calmly smoking pipe and debating whether to commit us. . . . Leave Owens at command post and return to move 1st squad to furnish a security light machinegun crew at riverside trail. More shelling. Little to do but dig—while I go up to lead element of 2nd Battalion to warn them Sammy's I. and R. platoon due to return about dusk and not to shoot them up.

Sam had been at the command post that afternoon to report that he had been close enough to one of the Japanese guns to hear the breech-block clang and the firing orders being called. He gave the air liaison officer the location as just under the "W" of "Walawbum" on an aerial photograph we had.

"It's a long way from the Top of the Mark, isn't it?" he said to me. We had had drinks together there during our last evening of freedom in San Francisco.

"Too damned far!"

Sam looked unnaturally bright eyed, like the rest of us, but otherwise no different for the narrow escape he had had the morning before. He had been leading a patrol a few miles to the north along a trail paralleling a stream when one of his men reported having seen through the vegetation what he took to be a horse's tail. Sam crept forward to the bank of the stream to investigate. He had come within fifteen feet of it when the bushes on the other side erupted with rifle fire. It is hard to see how it missed him. As he hit the ground, a grenade exploded

123

close beside him, ripping into his pack. At the same moment, his own patrol opened up, killing one of the Japanese riflemen instantly. Sam himself, raising up, saw one of the enemy swing onto the horse. He snatched his carbine up and shot and killed both the horse and its rider, who proved to be a major. They saw two Japanese flee, though blood on the foliage showed that at least one had not got away unscathed. We heard with delight that Sam had confirmed the picture we had of him by holding a critique on the spot to demonstrate how his Tommy gunners could have brought down the two who had escaped had they moved faster.

During one of the lulls in the firing we rounded up the animals as best we could. From then on they endured the firing stoically. It may have been the sudden excitement of their human masters that sent them off in the first place.

Late in the afternoon I had to take several of the mules and their handlers and help bring in our share of the supplies that had been dropped at Wesu Ga—the drop having been switched to Wesu Ga from Lagang Ga on account of the shelling. The drop field looked the way our drop fields always did, as if a tornado had struck a village and left nothing of the houses but their contents, but after Lagang Ga it presented an idyl of incredible serenity and charm. I could feel my soul opening up once more like a sea anemone unfolding. It blossomed with love for my fellow men, who were hauling and packing the cargoes.

To our stupefaction we came upon a tank at Wesu Ga. It squatted on the trail, indolently powerful, making harsh, rumbling noises in its depths while its Chinese crew lolled at leisure, looking careworn but entirely at home with the monster. The last vehicle of any kind we had seen was a two-week march to the rear, and I had not known there were tanks of any kind on our side in Burma.

Though I had never heard of him, this was one of Colonel Brown's machines, of course, and Colonel Brown himself was at Wesu Ga. So was General Merrill now, together with the commander of the leading battalion of the 113th Regiment of the Chinese 38th Division—General Sun Li-jen's division—which had been following us down the valley and was now beginning to arrive. A meeting of the three commanders was held. The latest intelligence was that the Japanese were falling back rapidly from Maingkwan, with the Chinese 22nd Division following up. It was decided that Merrill would pull the 5307th back that night and that it would be replaced by the Chinese 113th Regiment.

What was not known to the conference was that the bloodiest engagement at Walawbum was even then shaping up on the sector held by 3rd Battalion. Before the orders to the 5307th to withdraw could be given, the Japanese had thrown their main punch at Walawbum. The 1st and 2nd Battalions did not know much about it until it was over, for Lagang Ga caught only the artillery part of it.

Starting about 5:30 [says Phil's notebook], Nips fire concentrations about every seven minutes. Soon learn fallacy of believing you can't hear passage of shorts. Shells bracketing us on all sides and frequent slow-moving fragments clatter in leaves around us or hum slowly overhead like giant bees. Thankful nearly everyone in platoon has a shovel or pick. As dark falls, scrabble for dear life with helmet and pick, crouching cravenly at each report, praying fervently and feeling somehow debased for powerlessness to hit back.

About 7 PM Sgt. Owens comes in with order to pull out platoon by 7:30. All relieved at not spending the night here, but no fun packing horses while shells burst all around. Animals placid through it all. Move quickly single file across paddy field to command post tree, where flat on belly amid din of shells Caifson Johnson gives order to pull back to far side of Wesu Ga paddy field. Congestion of animals and intermingled columns and platoons.

After I had left Wesu Ga, leading my small detachment back to Lagang Ga with our loaded mules, I soon found we were

125

breasting a river of men and animals. Up front we could hear the shells exploding.

"Hey, you're goin' the wrong way."

"We're moving out!"

That was easy to see. The withdrawal had a note of something more than just haste about it. That did not make it any easier for us who were going in the other direction. Yet I had to keep on, both to report to Colonel Osborne and to collect the rest of my platoon. It took about all I could do to walk against that hurrying column of men, daylight fading, the artillery growing louder every minute. I told myself that, haunted for the rest of my life as I knew I would be my the memory of that afternoon's overmastering fear, I should need a counterpiece, and the fact that I had at least been able to walk back on my own feet into what I had been so scared of might serve.

The shells were crashing around the battalion command post —how close I could not tell—when we got back. We mustered what additional mules we could, loaded whatever equipment they could carry, and, leaving much behind, joined the exodus.

It was hard to be very happy about that evening's work. We could not help wondering if we had been routed. In retrospect, there seems to be more excuse for us. Not only was it the first time the battalion was under fire, but the fire was of a kind it could do nothing about. It is a cruel test of any unit's morale for it to have to remain in enforced inaction under a pounding without being able to throw even a rock back at its assailant. In addition, knowing little of what the other battalions had been engaged in, we had a sense that the 5307th had been a failure. We were as amazed as we were relieved to hear the next day that the operation in which we had played so peripheral a part was accounted a stunning success and that the exploits of the men in 3rd Battalion in the hours before we pulled out of Lagang Ga were such as to warrant their looking just as they did when we saw them next—keyed up, cocky, and exuberant, their pride effectively set off by the ravages of hunger and exhaustion in their faces, their pallor, and their feverish-looking eyes.

126

They had been in their third day on the riverbank across from Walawbum. They had already taken repeated assaults by the Japanese, who, spurred on by cries of *"Susume! susume!"* (Advance!) and *"Banzai!"* by their leaders, had come fanning out over the grassy clearing on the other side in successive waves. Each time they had suffered a bloody reverse. Their illustrious division had never before come up against another first-class outfit on even terms, and the experience must have left them sore and puzzled. On top of the physical hurt they had suffered, they were finding the roles reversed in another way: they were being made victims of a psychological offensive of the kind in which the Japanese themselves had always specialized. The instrument of the offensive was a nocturnal war cry that 3rd Battalion was to practice throughout the campaign. It was literally a two-syllabled obscenity, but as voiced it had the feral, doleful, spine-tingling wail of a wolf's howl. (That John George, with his special affinity with big game, should have originated it was not surprising.) Rising and falling from various fastnesses of the jungle at night—for it was sounded individually and, as it were, contrapuntally—it must have conjured up a picture of a legion of bloodthirsty ghouls.

On the third afternoon the battalion had a sense of something building up on the Japanese side bigger than anything yet. As John had reported, they had been hearing trucks bringing up reinforcements and also what sounded like artillery pieces being wheeled up. They had been catching heavy mortar fire, and as the afternoon wore on they began to be hit by flat-trajectory shelling—proof that the Japanese had in fact been moving in artillery. They replied as best they could with their mortars and for the rest kept to their foxholes as far as they were able, cleaning their weapons and getting their ammunition set. The position they held was on a bluff somewhat higher than the opposite bank, so that if they kept down the fire from the other side passed over them. The animals had a bad time, however. John said you could hear the bullets hitting them: *thud . . . thud*—an

127

awful sound. He himself got a bullet through his pack where it protruded into the plane of fire.

Around five o'clock the fire from the Japanese became more intense. Two 50-caliber machine guns with their stubborn, deliberate rate of fire, which could be imitated by clapping with the palms of the hands, raked the battalion's position from the sides of the field. Grenade-launchers added their wicked little projectiles to the swelling bombardment from the mortars and artillery; most dangerous of all were the tree-bursts of the 90-millimeter mortars. The declining sun was now behind the Japanese side of the Numpyek and full in the faces of the Marauders.

Then, out of the woods beyond the clearing, the attack broke. It was a bigger wave than any they had had, and there was more to come—far more. The clearing was full of running, crouching men, coming across under cover of everything the Japanese could fire. Again there were cries of advance! *Banzai!* Officers were waving their swords and in some cases leading the charge. A terrible excitement seemed to have seized hold of the Japanese, John said. On our side there was dead quiet: the bluff might have been unoccupied. Wave after wave of Japanese poured out of the forest, machine-gun crews among them, burdened under the weight of their weapons.

The Marauders waited motionless as an audience held by the climax of a stage drama. They gripped their rifle stocks, clutched mortar shells from which the safety pins had been drawn, held thumbs poised above the butterfly triggers of machine guns. They winced at the near bursts but did not move. Victor "Abie" Weingartner, a lieutenant from New York State, accounted one of the combat team's most daring patrol leaders, turned to his platoon sergeant. "Listen to them scream! We're supposed to be scared to death. It probably works on recruits." He was wearing the dirty mechanic's cap he had brought from the jungle battlefields of New Georgia, having—it was said— willingly paid a $100 fine for not being equipped with a helmet at the last showdown inspection.

128

The Marauders held their fire until the first wave was about forty yards away, nearly at the water's edge. Then they opened up. The sudden din of a combat team's three or four hundred weapons all laying in at once made the eardrums rattle like tissue paper. The first rank of the Japanese went down like stricken figures in a ballet. But those behind kept on coming. They must have figured that under their blistering mortar, artillery and machine-gun fire the Americans would be pinned in their foxholes. In fact, the sheet of fire was ripping the forest apart and barely clearing the Marauders' heads. Wrote Dave Richardson: "Bullets smashed two BAR magazines on the bank of the foxhole where T/5 Bernard Strasbaugh of Lewisburg, Kansas, was stretched. Another bullet nicked his helmet. Strasbaugh was in the center of the attack, firing as fast as he could shove magazines into his weapon. When he spotted five Japs in a group running toward a dropped machine gun, he stood up, riddled them with fire, and flopped down again. He hit the ground just soon enough to escape a burst of fire."

The persistence of the Japanese was horrifying. When a machine-gun crew fell dead with its weapon another would rush forward, grab up the heavy mechanism and carry it a few steps and then go down in its turn, only to be replaced by still another crew. The Browning automatic riflemen and machine gunners on the east bank, hardly slackening in the deadly business, worked a slaughter. Soon the edge of the river was choked with bodies. Still the Japanese came on. Two bullets punctured the water jacket of the machine gun operated by Corporal Joseph Diorio and Clayton E. Hall. Calling for canteens, they poured the contents of every available one into the jacket and managed to fire 4,000 rounds, though Hall's hands were scorched when the gun became red hot in the process. A kind of madness had now seized on the Americans too. Cupping their hands to their mouths, they were yelling, "Come and get some more of it, you yellow sons-of-bitches," and calling to one another, "Get those bastards! Get those bastards! Oh, Jesus, that did it!"

But ammunition was running low. Logan Weston said that toward the end machine-gun belts were being replenished from rifle clips and none of the riflemen was allowed to retain more than eight rounds. All grenades that could be spared were sent down the river to the battalion's other combat team, which had its hands full with Japanese who had crossed the river down below and come up through the woods.

Said Major John Jones's official diary: "The spirit of the men during the attack was awe-inspiring. They didn't notice the shells whizzing by or the mortars exploding in the perimeter. Some of them stood up and shook their fists, imploring the Japs to come on." As the light grew dim, the Marauders were jumping up and shouting obscenities across the river at the top of their lungs. There were answering shouts from the Japanese, but only sporadic fire. The enemy, too, was apparently exhausting its ammunition.

At 8:00 P.M. a pack train of five mules loaded with ammunition arrived at the combat team's perimeter, and with it came a feeling of vastly greater security. At the height of the battle Sergeant James C. Ballard had volunteered to go to Lagang Ga for new supplies; contact by radio had failed. He had made his way to the regimental command post, a mile and a half away, under continuous fire, and had repeated the hazardous journey on the way back with the mules after dark.

By the time Ballard had returned the attack had been broken. The artillery resumed and continued until 10:00 P.M., when it petered out. At midnight 3rd Battalion quietly pulled out and marched to Wesu Ga.

It had been an incredible showing. The Marauders had suffered seven wounded and not a single fatality. Chief Janis alone, lying beside a machine gun and picking off any Japanese who threatened to come within grenade-throwing range, accounted for eight of the enemy. Altogether at least 350 Japanese had been killed in the clearing and in the river bed—and they had gained nothing.

The equipment we had abandoned in our somewhat precipitate withdrawal tended to weigh on our spirits in 1st Battalion. Among the missing items was, unfortunately, a bag containing $250 in silver rupees that had been turned over to my platoon to carry. An anxious search of the loads the next morning failed to produce it. Signal lamps and signal flags all were there—but no rupees. I had to report the mishap to Colonel Osborne. It made him, I must say, very unhappy. Equally costly and far more useful baggage had been left behind in the confusion, but there was something about the loss of the literal currency that caused Osborne special grief. Perhaps it was the thought of its falling into the hands of the Chinese. Weeks later he was still referring to it sadly from time to time.*

It was T/5 Passanisi, my radio repairman and the youngest member of my platoon, who took our losses hardest. My having had the platoon pull out "under fire," as he said, before it could load all its equipment had aroused in him the lofty, inaccessible disapproval of youth. He evidently felt he owed it to honesty to make me privy to his adverse judgment. I can see him now, there at Wesu Ga, in the gray of a foggy dawn, his head back, his lips set in a pained half-smile, his eyes narrowed, feeling on my account a shame I was apparently beyond feeling myself.

"What the hell did you expect me to do?" I said. "Conjure mules up out of nowhere to load the stuff on?" I was a little put out despite my esteem for Passanisi, who was one of the most valuable members of the platoon.

"If we hadn't been in such a hurry we could have put more on the mules we had," he declared.

It was a theoretical possibility, but I was not prepared to concede that it was a practical one, given the difficulty of finding anything in the darkness, the possibility of a shell's landing in our midst while we fished about, and the fact that the battalion was streaming out. All the same I had been feeling bad over

---

* Shortly after I had written this I was having lunch with Lloyd Osborne in the Pentagon, and the talk turned to Walawbum. "You may not remember this," he said, "and you may not even have heard of it at the time, but we had a bag full of silver rupees. . . ."

the way things had gone and had been turning over in my mind the possibility of doing something about it. "Maybe you're just the one I'm looking for," I said. "Someone to take a mule back with me to Lagang Ga to see what can be picked up."

He agreed that he was. We had actually got as far as to be leading a mule out of the bivouac onto the trail when the order came that we were to move out at 6:30, which meant we had to load up immediately. I could only wonder what might have awaited us in Lagang Ga had we not been intercepted. Later we heard that the Chinese whom we soon passed on their way there found the area and the abandoned items of equipment just as we had left them and that the 5307th had lost face with them—until they went on and saw the riverbanks piled with Japanese dead.

Not long after we had left Wesu Ga, heading east in the direction from which we had come four days before, firing broke out at the head of the column. We came to a halt. Just then the Japanese artillery opened up on us from a distance. The design seemed plain. Pinning us down with fire from their trailblock, the Japanese would work the column over with the guns they still had around Walawbum; the bursts could be heard coming up the trail. I suppose we had all had a little too much for the time being. As we lay there, pushing up into our helmets, the air liaison officer next to me was sobbing hopelessly. His nerves had already gone before he joined us. He had flown too many bombing missions over Burma and Thailand— too many missions from which too few bombers had returned. "You don't feel like flying any more?" his commanding officer had inquired. "O.K., we'll see if you like walking any better." So he had been volunteered to us.

The firing up ahead ceased and down the column came the word, "Doctors to the front!"

It was not for any of us, it transpired, that the doctors were needed. After the head of our column had been fired on from across a stream and had returned the fire with Browning automatics and mortars, our Chinese interpreter, evidently uneasy,

132

had called out to the other side and found that our assailants were of his own nationality. They had been confused by our helmets—a novelty for them, since they wore British helmets as part of their British-issued uniforms—and had opened fire under the impression we were Japanese. Four of them, including a major, had been badly wounded by our return fire. The members of the platoon that had inflicted the casualties carried the victims to the paddy field to which we were headed, three miles east of Wesu Ga, where the little retaining walls were quickly leveled to permit the Piper Cubs to land and pick up our wounded. The four Chinese were the first to be flown out.

After leaving the Chinese trailblock and the Japanese shelling behind us, we began passing a seemingly unending stream of Chinese moving forward as we moved back. This was the 113th Regiment, coming to take over our positions. They impressed us then, as they continued to impress us, as being clean, cheerful and philosophical. Being beardless, more delicate of feature, and apparently never too hurried to tidy up, they made us by contrast look like cave men. The coolies interspersed in the column, ugly and grinning, each carrying at a little jogtrot a veritable kitchen divided into two loads slung on either end of a pole, added to the impression that they had brought their civilization with them while we had left ours behind.

As the columns moved past each other, we heard cheering in American voices from up ahead. It grew louder, coming down the line toward us, and when it reached us we could see the cause. In the Chinese column a battery of pack artillery was moving forward with the infantry. We too cheered while the Chinese beamed. The pieces were only 75-millimeter howitzers and hardly a match for the 105's and walloping 150's with which the Japanese had visited humiliation on us, but all the same they were guns and they could throw shells and they were on our side and they were a stirring sight.

The next day, moving still farther east to make way for the Chinese, we came to the little village of Shikau Ga and to one of the idyllic streams of that country where we were to have two

133

days' rest and to catch up on our eating before moving out again for the next mission.

General Tanaka once more eluded the trap Stilwell had set for him. "Communications difficulties that kept Stilwell in the dark as to the movements and locations of the several units, plus the extreme caution of the Chinese 22nd Division, seem major factors in Tanaka's successful withdrawal from the Walawbum area," says *Stilwell's Command Problems*. It adds, however, that "the 18th Division had yielded the greater part of the Hukawng valley to the Allies, and the Chinese Army in India could celebrate a well-earned victory." In fact, as General Merrill told a staff meeting of his officers, "Between us and the Chinese we have forced the Japs to withdraw farther in the last three days than they have in the last three months of fighting."

In five days, the American Forces in Action Series notes in its history of the unit, "the Americans had killed 800 of the enemy, had cooperated with the Chinese to force a major Japanese withdrawal, and had paved the way for further Allied progress. This was accomplished at a cost to the Marauders of eight men killed and 37 wounded. Up to this point, 19 patients had been evacuated with malaria, eight with other fevers (mostly dengue), 10 with psychoneurosis, and 33 with injuries. Miscellaneous sickness totaled 109." Of the 2,600 men, more or less, who set forth from Margherita, about 2,300 remained to carry on.

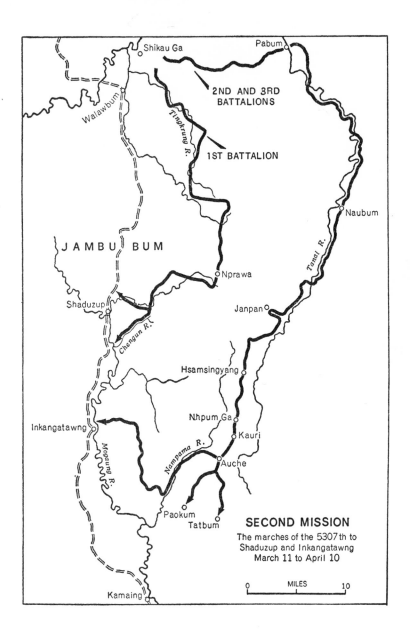

Shikau Ga
Pabum

Walawbum

Tingkrung R.

2ND AND 3RD
BATTALIONS

1ST BATTALION

Naubum

JAMBU BUM

Tanai R.

Nprawa

Shaduzup

Janpan

Chengun R.

Hsamsingyang

Nhpum Ga
Kauri

Inkangatawng

Nampama R.

Auche

Mogaung R.

Paokum
Tatbum

SECOND MISSION

The marches of the 5307th to
Shaduzup and Inkangatawng
March 11 to April 10

0   MILES   10

Kamaing

V We generally fared well in the neighborhood of the Chinese. We could barter cigarettes for rice and tea and often bum real coffee from the American liaison team attached to the Chinese unit. Boiled with a bouillon cube, the rice made a princely dish. Northerners, who believe rice is supposed to go into puddings, would cook it with a chopped-up fruit bar from the K ration and sugar from the liaison team and extol the result. If we were bivouacked beside a river and the situation permitted, grenades tossed into the water would bring a lot of fish, belly up, to the surface. Roasted in sections of bamboo, they were edible, if not tasty, and with the rice helped fill the stomach's void. That was always the problem. K rations would sustain life, but they provided no bulk. Even when our stomachs had shrunk, so that when ultimately we had a chance to eat a meal we could not, their incessant demands for something to work on were a torment.

For two days in Shikau Ga we ate and swam and lived mostly naked in the sun. Even the dour mules unbent and rolled in the sand. Like times of happiness in retrospect, the passing hours had an Indian-summer air, and you wanted to cling to them. At least that is how it was when we had heard what our next mission was to be.

Another, but deeper, envelopment was in order. Moving again around the eastern flank of the Japanese, we were to put

136

in a block on the Kamaing Road below the village of Shaduzup (pronounced with the accent on the second syllable). The spot selected was about 30 miles south of Walawbum by road and was to prove to be more than 50 miles by the route we had to take. The object was to undermine the Japanese defense of the Jambu Bum. This low range of hills, with its barbaric name, formed the southern end of the Hukawng valley. When you crossed it you entered the valley of the Mogaung, which led to the Irrawaddy—and the world. By Stilwell's direction and against the advice of Merrill and Hunter, the 5307th was to be divided for the operation. Colonel Osborne having been promised that his turn would come when he was assigned a reserve role at Walawbum, 1st Battalion was given the mission of striking south on its own at no great distance from the road, with the Chinese 113th Regiment following a day behind, while the other two battalions were to swing farther out and around before hitting the road in the same vicinity. On a map, the routes of the two bodies together form a figure suggesting the outline of the state of New Jersey, with 1st Battalion threading its way down the hilly, western border and the others completing the circumnavigation of the peanut-shaped area over a more circuitous but generally easier route.

The large-scale contour maps we carried made clear at a glance what the difficulty was going to be. There was only one trail skirting the Jambu Bum on the east, where 1st Battalion was supposed to go. With only one trail to watch, it was as certain as anything could be that the Japanese would have it well in hand.

Setting out first thing in the morning on March 12, we covered over 20 miles of the flat Hukawng valley in two days. The next 30-odd miles was to take us over two weeks.

Even before the end of the second day we ran into trouble. Shortly after noon Sam Wilson's platoon, well in the van, came to a spot where a body of Japanese, patrolling northward, had turned and gone back; there were the imprints of hobnailed soles and the cloven-hoof marks left by the canvas shoes with

137

separate big toes many of the Japanese wore. For two hours the platoon followed the steadily freshening southbound prints; it was the usual grim business of sweating out the bends. It came to a climax with a burst of Tommy-gun fire from up the trail, where the lead scout was out of sight. Then there was silence. The scout, John Sukup, when Sam had come up with him, reported that he had walked right on top of an Asiatic soldier when he had rounded a bend. The man had reached for his rifle and Sukup had turned his Tommy gun loose on him but he had got away. From ahead they could hear sounds of movement in the vegetation, and Sam, to guard against repeating the error of five days before, when we had shot up our allies, sent for one of the Chinese who had been attached to his platoon after that accident. He asked him to call out in the direction of the movement. A strange colloquy ensued, the Chinese shouting inquiries and a voice from the other side answering "*Wah . . . ? Wah?*" repeatedly and hesitantly. "*Wah . . . ? Wah?*" The uncertainty expressed by the voice was very human, but manifestly the man who was calling could not understand Chinese, and it was not a time to reflect upon the common destiny that makes all mankind one.

"Fire away," said Sam to his BAR man.

The deafening clatter of the Browning automatic produced a scream and an answering fusillade. In a short time Sam's platoon was under such heavy fire from the unseen enemy that, being under orders to avoid getting pinned down, he had to pull the platoon back into the forest and withdraw it northward. On the arrival of the main body, Caifson Johnson sent two rifle platoons on through to deal with the obstruction. They succeeded in driving the Japanese across a stream that lay in our path, permitting the battalion to cross. Lieutenant McElmurray, the rangy, red-haired, taciturn Oklahoman who led one of the platoons, had a man killed in the action, and in the first and last show of emotion we ever witnessed in him wiped his forearm across his eyes with a grimace of pain. "The first man I've lost," he said.

138

That was only the beginning of our trouble with that bunch of Japanese. Their stubbornness the next morning indicated that they had received reinforcements during the night, and we had to fight eight actions to advance a mile and a half. The Japanese would hold their position on the trail until our fire began to hurt, then fall back a couple of hundred yards, set up their machine guns and mortars and wait to blaze away at us when we ran into them again. It was the chronic problem; in the narrow corridor in which we moved, only a platoon or two could find room to fight. We would rotate our lead platoons but otherwise could not make our superior numbers tell.

What we did not know—did not have the remotest suspicion of—was that our adversaries were caught in a kind of nutcracker, or must have thought they were. At the other end of their column, as we found out several days later, they were having to fight much the same kind of action we were having to fight against them, for in their rear, firing on them from ambushes, was a patrol of Kachin Rangers led by an OSS lieutenant, James L. Tilly. The Japanese, pressed between the two forces, unquestionably took it for granted that they had been artfully trapped and would have been dumfounded to learn that in actuality the two actions were as unrelated as if they had been taking place in different theaters. At that time the United States Army and the Office of Strategic Services were fighting independent wars in Burma. Far from having received the copious information on Japanese dispositions that Tilly's organization had garnered, the 5307th had never even heard of Tilly's existence. The wonder was that the Tingkrung Hka did not witness a sanguinary collision between the Marauder battalion and the Kachin irregulars of OSS's 101 Detachment.

Colonel Osborne had a tough problem. If we kept on bucking our way down the trail, it might take us forever to get where we were going. The only alternative, however, was to leave the trail and head off across country. Uninviting as this was, it appeared to promise faster progress than the present course. Accordingly, he directed the forward elements to hold off the

Japanese while the rest of the battalion turned eastward into a dry stream bed, followed it as far as possible, then started cutting a path southward through the forest.

The holding action turned out to be a horrible affair that led to the relief of one of the battalion's high-ranking officers, and the award of a Silver Star to Lieutenant William Lepore. Lepore's rifle platoon was the forwardest element by some hundreds of yards, and in Sam Wilson's words was taking one hell of a shellacking while the battalion was preparing to disengage. Sam found Lepore's superior, the officer in command of the leading part of the column, in a state of near panic. He had an exaggerated idea of the strength of the Japanese and had been unnerved by the din of the fight and the dreadful sight of the wounded who were managing to get back, one clutching a hole in his chest, another voiceless from a gash a grenade had torn in his throat. He was actually preparing to abandon Lepore's platoon. "We'll have to leave 'em!" he was crying. A hot exchange nearly ending in a knockdown fight ensued between him and Sam, after which Sam took the situation in his own hands. With Lieutenant McDowell and a radio operator carrying an SCR 300 he made his way to Billy Lepore's beleaguered unit. While the weapons platoon behind them created a no man's land behind a screen of mortar fire, Lepore gradually got his platoon extricated and with the help of Sam, McDowell, and a few volunteers brought back the wounded and a few who were paralyzed with fear. Two men had been killed. One, a Sergeant Clark, had been shot between the temples. The other was a Chinese-American with his face blown off. Sam and Billy carried Clark by his legs and shoulders. Accompanied by the bearers of the other body and the rest of the platoon, they got safely across the broad draw separating them from the parent body despite the sniper fire they attracted and the shelling they got from a Japanese mortar until the weapons platoon, responding to an appeal on the SCR 300, silenced it.

The parent body under the officer with whom Sam had had the set-to was pulling out and losing no time about it. Sam and

140

Billy and the volunteers turned with a desperate haste to the task of burying the dead. The earth was hard—they were on a ridge—and the men had all they could do, digging frantically with the sweat getting in their eyes, to hack out grooves barely deep enough for the bodies while the two lieutenants cut some sections of bamboo and made crosses of them, binding the pieces together with vine. In the resistant ground, despite their best efforts, the crosses tilted forlornly. Only six inches of soil covered the two bodies. Sam stood on one side of the graves, fair-haired and still boyish looking though already wasted by the dysentery that dogged him through the campaign. Billy Lepore, stocky and swarthy with black hair, including a mat of it on his chest, stood on the other facing him. "The Lord giveth and the Lord taketh away," said Sam. "Blessed be the name of the Lord." Billy, a Catholic, crossed himself. "May the Lord have mercy on their souls." They stood looking at each other. Sam felt weary and empty—for the events of the afternoon had taken it out of him in more ways than one—and also on edge; for by now the little burial party was all alone on the ridge and the Japanese, for unaccountable reasons, had commenced to lay a thundering barrage on the hill just evacuated by Lepore's platoon. The two shook hands; Sam did not know why. Said Billy, "Let's get the hell out of here!"

That was the end of the action at the Tingkrung Hka.

The country we had to cross in bypassing the Japanese was a conglomeration of hills resembling the patternless jumble of waves in a tide rip and often so steep your feet would go out from under you while you were climbing. ("The steeper the hill the less distance you got to fall before you hit it. So what the hell are you complaining about?") Sometimes the slopes were too much for the mules; the packs would have to be unloaded and broken up and the pieces carried up or passed up from hand to hand. The platoons took in rotation the task of hacking a passage through the towering, tangled, resistant vegetation that buried hillsides, valleys and ridges together and reduced us in scale to crawling animalcules in its somnolent

141

depths. Within the platoons, officers shared with the men the labor of chopping. The young bamboo would slash out like saber blades when severed; the old, resisting like steel the blows of the dulled machetes, could hardly be cut at all. (The cuticle of bamboo has a high content of the material quartz consists of: silica.) Little of it would fall. You could cut a passage for hours, for days on end, and nothing would happen; the tops of the growth were too interwoven for any of it to break loose. So the bamboo had to be cut twice, at the ground and at a height above the peaks of the mules' loads. The head of the column sounded like a spike-driving crew on a railroad, but the jungle imprisoned the sound, as it did us, and within a small fraction of the column's length to the rear nothing could be heard. The men in the van struck savagely at the unyielding stems, as if the vegetation were an enemy that had to be done to death, until, soaked with sweat, their arms heavy, and gasping for breath, they would fall back to the end of the platoon and be replaced. It was like a column of slaves clearing a path for the pampered and despotic ruler of an ancient Asian empire.

We fought and toiled to reach Shaduzup as if it were salvation. But, Christ, how I hated its uncouth syllables! Shadu'zup! On to Shadu'zup! I pictured it as a cowled and sheeted figure like one of those ghoulish Moslem women. The days of that tortuous march were to remain forever living in my mind, though merged with other days of other marches that preceded or followed—not that it mattered; they were all alike anyway.

We were twelve hours a day on the trail, as a rule—whether there was a trail or not. When there was not, it was mostly a matter of standing and waiting while they slashed away up front. Pack, weapon, ammunition, knife, canteen, all grew heavier; the straps they were slung on cut into the flesh. You could sit down and lean back on your pack to rest your shoulders, but holding your head at a 45-degree angle was hard on your neck, and anyhow you might have to struggle to your feet again immediately. So usually you just stood, leaning slightly forward like an old farm horse in his harness to bring your

142

center of gravity over your feet. If a break were ordered it would pay you to take your pack off, but the mule-leaders had little respite. The mules lived only to get the spray of bamboo leaves that was just out of reach, and the palms of the leaders' hands were burned or their shoulders jerked half out of joint, depending upon whether they were holding the halter ropes loosely or firmly. One would hardly have thought it, but the continual yanking of the mules was a major trial to those who had to control them.

While we marched, men were continually falling out beside the trail, taking care to remain in plain sight lest they be shot in trying to rejoin the column. Dysentery was already the scourge of the organization; much of the command could have been carried in the morning report as walking dead.

On everyone's uniform there were dark, stiff patches. These were of dried blood, from leech bites. The country was infested with these repulsive little rubbery monsters, black worms with suction cups at both ends able to contract to pea-sized balls or elongate themselves to a couple of inches. They did give us the pleasure of going after them with the lighted ends of cigarettes. It required nice judgment to bring the heat close enough to persuade them to disengage without cooking them before they had a chance to. Unfortunately, Mother Nature—whose passion is for equalizing odds—had endowed the little pests with the capacity of clamping on and opening a lesion without your feeling anything, especially if you were asleep. Then after you had found one of them on you and got him off you were liable to have difficulty stanching the flow of blood, for their saliva contained an anticoagulant, a heparin-like agent, according to Doc Kolodny. Caifson Johnson oozed blood for days from some leech bites and one of the platoon leaders went around for an equal length of time with a ruby-red eyeball, the result of a leech's fastening onto it during the night. All of us were more or less bloody all the time, and the mules suffered worse than we; their fetlocks were generally dark red and slimy with blood.

143

In addition, eggs deposited in their lesions by a kind of fly hatched out into screw worms.

Compared with the combat platoons, the communications platoon had nothing to complain about. It was a fact, though, that after their work was over, at the end of the day's march, ours began. We generally had help in clearing enough of the forest to make room for our antenna, but the responsibility rested on us. The problem was a different one from opening a trail. It was not enough to hack out a tunnel; the roof of the forest had to come down. So we would cut farther and farther out and tug at the bamboo and vines, then cut some more and pull some more until a section of the canopy finally sagged to the ground. When we had cleared enough for our wire and had got it erected—and bamboo at least provided the world's best poles—we could turn to the job of producing enough current to heave our signal out through the woods and over the intervening miles to Merrill's headquarters, wherever they might be, and to our base at Dinjan, in Assam. This was done with a hand-cranked generator, which might be likened to an upended bicycle without wheels or handlebars; you sat on the seat and pedaled by hand. The drag on the crank was proportionate to the power output of the set you were working, and the AN/PRC-1 was designed to reach a long way. To keep it going was like forcing a bicycle uphill just before you have to get off and walk. It took everyone in the platoon working by turns to keep the glutton satisfied.

The mental strain of those evening sessions was worse than the physical, however. With dusk—and it was seldom that we were set up much before—an invisible curtain in the atmosphere shut down, which was difficult to penetrate. Sometimes we would try for hours to hear and be heard and not succeed. And without radio contact there would be no food, ammunition or medical supplies. In a way you were more lost than you would have been at sea on a raft. At sea at least you could be spotted from the air, but in the forest there was little chance of that. It was hard enough for a plane to find you when it had been told

144

where to look and a clearing had been marked for it with panels of white cloth. And as Lloyd Osborne pointed out to me in his undramatic but not unimpressive way one day when we had drawn blanks three nights in a row, it was a long walk back to Walawbum. Four days after a supply drop our rations were almost always exhausted.

Overhead the antenna wire would be etched against the darkening sky. Sergeant George would be seated before the set, little more than a curly-headed silhouette, with the silent figures of the relief men, standing or sitting, behind him. As evening wore on, the number of bystanders would be increased by visitors from nearby platoons drawn to the spot by the continuing *arraow, arraow, arraow* of the generator, the persistence of which had an unmistakable significance. Above it, the only sound would be the clicking of the key. It went over the same rhythmic pattern again and again. George's head and torso would move jerkily in time with the key as if he were trying to put physical force behind the electrical impulses. The crackle of the key was peremptory and didactic but supplicatory too. Then there would be a silence as George listened—an empty silence, presumably. Naturally. It was preposterous to imagine that by beating a little brass lever on a spring you could produce a reply out of that enormous and hollow night.

"They've probably gone to the movies."

The grotesque séance, in which you were required to believe, went on.

"Relief on the crank." A figure would resolve itself out of the darkness and with care the shift-over would be made with no slackening of push on the generator crank.

Finally—perhaps—there would come a tense, clipped whisper from George: "I've got them. The light, quick!"

A flashlight, dimmed with two thicknesses of carbon paper from a message pad under its lens, would throw a blue gleam on the instrument and, beside the key, the enciphered message giving our location and needs. George would start to send. We

145

would all hang on the clacking of that key. Contact could still be lost. If anything, the suspense was worse.

"Damn!" The receipt George had paused for was evidently not forthcoming.

"They want a repeat on the last ten groups," another operator, reading what George had scribbled on his pad, would whisper to me. George would try again.

The back-and-forth would go on. Then, taking you by surprise, George would whip the headphones off and in a spent but triumphant voice exclaim, "Roger on our transmission! All parts!" A cheer would go up, keyed to the quiet of the night— but a provisional cheer. Nothing was yet assured. Our message, owing to faulty reception, might prove undecipherable with no way for us to learn of it. We could never tell whether we had been understood until the scheduled hour of the drop arrived the next day.

When the hour came, you always heard the plane whether it was there or not. . . . Wasn't that it? No . . . no, it was gone. Yes, by God, there it was again! A plane for sure! A Dakota— couldn't be anything else.

There was no mistaking it, though the drone, after swelling on the ear, would fade again into inaudibility. In a moment it would come back stronger.

"There it is!"

Through the gap in the forest at the far end of the clearing you could see it beyond the next ridge. It was moving at right angles to us, quartering the area. It could not find us. We lost it again.

The air liaison officer was on the voice set trying to reach it. Soon he had evidently got it, for he was giving it directions. . . . When it reappeared it was almost on top of us, coming straight in toward our panels. It filled the valley with its roar as it swept overhead, a mottled green and brown giant dolphin on long, tapering fins, cherub and seraphim.

"I feel like a Jívaro," said Phil. "Was there ever such an awe-inspiring sight?"

146

"Never—for the communications platoon."

The first time we took a drop in the mountains, the planes had to fly home without unloading and return the next morning, for on the first trip they used up their reserves of fuel trying to locate us. We had been able to find only a tiny clearing to serve as a drop field. It was saddled across a razor-backed ridge and we had had our hands full cutting down trees two feet in diameter to enlarge it even a little. After the first appearance of the planes, an instinct had warned Colonel Osborne that we had better move our bivouac, and we pulled out just before it was mortared by a party of Japanese whom we subsequently chased off. The hills that pressed in upon the little drop field were not very inviting to anyone maneuvering an 8-ton egg-shelled, winged steel container burdened with four tons of cargo at 120 miles an hour, and there was the kind of altercation on the voice net between the air liaison officer and the pilot that we grew accustomed to.

"You're too high!"

"What do you want us to do? Hand it to you out the window?"

"You're all over the landscape with the cargo! For Christ sake, come on down. Those grain sacks plowed into the woods a hundred yards beyond the field."

"Well, Buster, it sure as hell won't do any good if we plow into the woods after them. And don't think we missed by much the last round."

"You're overshooting, you're overshooting. How do you expect to hit anything way up there? We'd like to get some of this drop. You can come down, I tell you. You got nothing under you for a hundred feet."

"Nothing but a hill at the end of the field and a downdraft. Suppose you just tell us where the chutes are landing and let us fly the crate."

It was not easy on anyone's nerves. At the end there were loads hanging from trees by their parachutes down the mountainside which we had to climb for and cut loose, not knowing

147

but what the Japanese were closing in. . . . On the other hand, before the campaign was over, two drop planes were to be lost with their crews.

Halfway to Shaduzup we met Lieutenant Tilly, who, if we had not heard of him, had heard of us and came out at dusk to meet us as we neared his retreat. Dropping in unexpectedly on the 5307th was not without its risks, and this Tilly seemed to appreciate. We heard him coming a long way off, as a faint voice from down the trail. "Hey, Yank, don't shoot!" he called. "We are friends. . . . Hey, Yank, don't shoot!" He kept repeating it until he came into view at the head of his little band of Kachins, marching into the muzzles of enough weapons to have lifted a Sherman tank off the ground. The appearance of an American officer, even one as informally costumed as Tilly, was unexpected, to say the least, but we had to believe what we saw. He introduced himself and was passed interestedly down the line. His innocent-looking young cutthroats under their Aussie hats with the broad brims turned up rakishly on the side appeared both businesslike and touching, especially when he brought them to attention before Colonel Osborne, himself doing an about-face and saluting with parade-ground formality.

Clad in a nondescript khaki shirt and a pair of curious, wraparound, blue, calf-length trousers, and with his own little Kachin army, fifty strong, Tilly seemed to have worked out a very satisfactory personal adjustment to the trying business of being at war. We stayed overnight at his hideout in the village of Jaiwa Ga, set among the familiar paddy fields on a ridge. With the surroundings posted by Kachins, we could afford to relax a little. After the strained and meager routine of our normal existence, the interlude at Jaiwa Ga was like a drop back into life—even into literature, into romance. There were perhaps a dozen of us who spent the evening together in the chief basha of the village: Osborne, Weld, Wilson, a few other Marauders and I, Evan Darlington, Tilly, and four or five Kachins, the dignitaries of the district. The Kachins smoked their crude, relatively innocuous opium, the Americans smoked their cigarettes,

148

the wavering light from the fire on the earthen hearth played upon the split-bamboo lattice of the walls and the thatch of the ceiling, both brown from the smoke of many such fires, and the subdued talk in two languages rose and fell, pitched in a ceremonial key as the principals exchanged tales of ambush and trailblock, deception and surprise, slaughter and escape. I sat leaning against a supporting pole in a half-dream, not sure how much of the impression I had came from the scene itself, how much from reading Joseph Conrad. Sam, who never missed the least part of the flavor of an experience, was in his element; he had earned a place in that scene and he filled it modestly and becomingly. Phil was moved to decide, as he told us later, that if he came through the present campaign he was going to join OSS and do the kind of job ahead of the Allied advance that Tilly had been doing. Exercising the power of life-or-death decision over some forty of his fellow countrymen, which as a platoon leader he could not avoid, went hard with Phil; rather than go on pretending to the kind of omniscience that was called for, he was prepared to run greater risks himself.

At dawn Tilly watched us saddle up with a wry expression. "Here goes the front," he commented sadly. "I won't be behind the Jap lines any more."

Says the official diary of the 5307th:

"20 March 1944—The First Battalion marched over difficult trails to Nprawa Ga where our lead platoon hit a Jap machine gun blocking the trail. We had one man killed and two wounded before the gun and crew were wiped out by mortar fire on their block."

On the way to Shaduzup I still had an inexpensive Signal Corps camera that had been issued to me. Fungus was already starting to grow between the elements of the lens and the deterioration of the emulsion was causing the film to jam, but the pictures it took, by the very reason of their poor quality and imperfections, have more the flavor of reality for me today than those taken with superior equipment by professionals as occasion made possible. A typical one shows part of the headquar-

149

ters section during a break in the march. Colonel Osborne, physically inert but thoughtful, is on the right in the cotton fatigue hat he persisted in wearing in place of a helmet. Ten feet up the trail Evan Darlington is talking to a barely recognizable Tom Senff, while in the center my colleague, Bill Bright, the battalion communications officer, is looking at the camera with the glum weariness we all felt but which he betrayed less than most of us. Bill had a favorite song, of which he knew, or was willing to vouchsafe us, only a few lines:

> I'm going to buy a paper doll that I can call my own,
> A doll that other fellows cannot steal.

When I whistle it today I have an urge I feel I cannot resist to find someone to listen to me while I try to say what it was like in Burma. The outlandishly inappropriate, wistful, sentimental ditty unleashes the whole flood of association.

There is the earthy, faintly acrid odor of the jungle floor, the heavy air, the sweet, chlorinated taste of the treated water you seldom could get enough of; you were thirsty again almost the moment you had drained your canteen. There is the flavor of the K-ration biscuits (the softer of the two sorts), flat and musty like the ground when you dug in it. There is the sound of voices habitually subdued, addressed unendingly to the one subject of unfailing interest: "Pack of Cavaliers for two lumps of sugar, anyone?" "Pork-and-egg-yolk for a cheese component?" "Coffee for a fruit bar?" "What am I offered for a D bar?" (The chocolate bars officially styled "D rations" were all that those with acute dysentery could eat, so with one of these for barter you could often get a whole K-ration unit.) There are the poor jokes. ("When I close my eyes I can see a steak hanging over the edge of the plate, french fries, apple pie à la mode." "You're lucky. When I close mine, I see a mule's behind. Also when I don't." "You remember that hefty blonde nurse at the British infirmary at Deogarh? Now I look back on her, she wasn't so bad. If I had her here now, I'd undress her— you know, slowly and lovingly, garment by garment. Then I'd

150

eat her." "Let the Chinese worry about saving face. Let's save ass and get the hell out of here.") There are the animal preoccupations of bedding down in the dark on a steep, wooded slope—the feeling about for a space long enough and level enough to lie down on (the communications platoon was generally late in turning in), the hard edge of a helmet's brim in the nape of the neck (a helmet makes a much better pillow than none at all), the utter despondency, if we have been marching down a dry ridge all afternoon, of having to endure an evening, a night, and at least part of a morning without water or coffee and consequently without food either, for a dry throat will pass no part of a K ration.

There was worse, too—much worse—and nothing brings that back like a certain four-note bird call that was one of the few sounds in the never-ending forest. When I imitate it I can almost believe for an instant that all that has happened since I heard it is a dream I had one night on the way to Shaduzup—or on the way to Weilangyawng, or to Hsamsingyang, or to Naubum, or to Ritpong. . . .

The first warning would be the low-spoken injunction that came down from the head of the column, passed from man to man: "Fresh Jap tracks. . . . Take a five-yard interval. . . . No talking." Weapons would be unslung. Time to get a round in the chamber; the rasp and click of bolts could be heard ahead of you and behind.

Your heart would leap as off in the forest a band of monkeys would set up an unrestrained din of whooping, humorless laughter. It had what Phil called an hysterical, end-of-the-world sound, and breaking out of the silence it was incredible and unnerving. Then it would abruptly cease, and that was perhaps even more unnerving.

"Column's halting."

That would mean the scouts were being sent out. The only sound then would be the soft stomping of the mules, and the clink of a harness ring—and the questioning, plaintive call of

151

that bird in a treetop. "Whee-oo, WHEE-OO," it went, at 10-second intervals. It had much the same quality as Bill Bright's Paper Doll song, and it was always to be heard when the column was feeling out a Japanese trailblock. "Whee-oo WHEE-OO."

In the breathless stillness the first rattle of firing was monstrously loud. It had the effect of a horrible moral shock, an unspeakable blasphemy. It was as if the pleasant trappings of the earth, the blue sky, the shimmering leaves of the bamboo, the trickly little stream, were all whisked away and you saw a death's-head leering into your face.

After the first burst the silence would close in again like the well-oiled door of a cage. Then explosions would follow one upon another as the Japanese brought their grenade-launchers to bear.

From the head of the column the order would be passed back, "Weapons platoon forward!" Then a minute later, coming up from the rear, "Clear the trail."

You got the mules into the dense growth alongside to let the mortar crews move through. Their heavily laden mules were the biggest of all, without doubt the biggest that ever came out of Missouri. From up front would come bursts of automatic-rifle and machine-gun fire and then the detonation of mortars, hollow sounds as if they were being fired inside a hogshead. From the middle of the column you could never be sure whose mortar bursts you were hearing unless the shells began to hit around you.

"Medics forward!"

The wounded who could still stand were mounted on horses. Litter cases were sent to the rear to be picked up by the Chinese following behind, who would provide bearers to carry them until we came on a paddy field we could convert into a landing strip, whenever that might be. A detail remained behind to bury the riflemen killed in the first burst and to erect another bamboo cross.

152

"Column's moving!"

You picked your way around a couple of dead Japanese lying like dolls on the trail and pushed on.

With fear subsiding, our other enemy took over: hunger. We were perpetually famished. Not only were K rations lacking in bulk, but every fourth or fifth day we ran out of them. We had two conditions—one in which we felt unfed, the other in which we *were* unfed. Elsewhere in the Army the talk might be of women. With us it was of food. Few of us could have classified as intellectuals, but no equal number of theological scholars, applying themselves to the central mysteries of their creed, could have elaborated more minutely analytical commentaries or have formed more abstrusely differentiated schools of thought than we did on the topic of food. Some idea of our absorption in food might be conveyed by an exegesis on the subject Phil Weld jotted in his notebook when he had a chance. Because of his large frame, Phil probably suffered even more than most of us from hunger. As indicated in his deposition, he would go so far as to pick up and eat the maltose and dextrose tablets that others would throw away unless actually starving. These brown and white squares resembled the tiles bathroom floors are made of and tasted much as such tiles must taste. I cherish a picture of an emaciated Phil later in the campaign, clad in jungle boots and the remains of a pair of GI drawers, panhandling for rice among the Chinese troops with the bright, kindly social manner of a Beacon Street hostess putting an odd sort of guest at ease.

Wrote Phil in his treatise, after noting that he had made himself highly irritating to battalion headquarters by protesting so vigorously the effect of malnutrition on the spirits of his platoon ("Pleas for at least a cupful of rice per man in the food drops summarily rejected") and recording his suspicion that there was a plot on the part of theater to starve us in order to take our minds off the danger from the Japanese ("But now know that such subtlety in a military command is highly unlikely"):

153

We learned to know a box of K as intimately as a monk his rosary and sacramental gadgets. Could extract everything from it but wax in carton, and this was our best wet-weather fuel. Never tried making candles but no doubt could if light allowed.

Breakfast—First the water to be boiled. Blackened canteen cup filled to brim, though packet directions said two-thirds of cup only for amount of powdered coffee provided; for a while an aid to ready boiling and to keeping bamboo ashes out of cup was the Ogburn lid executed by Deolali tinsmith.* Meantime, egg can opened either with key provided with can, which was left attached to the extended strip of coiled metal to serve as a handle, or with 10-in-1 can-opener (the insignia of Third Battalion), which preserved the can for later use as jam-pot. Soon as eggs browning, they put to side. [It is necessary to bear in mind that the components of the K ration, here dwelt so lovingly upon, were doll-sized.] With trench-knife inserted into cup handle, water was held over hottest coals to boil. Then one lump of sugar and coffee powder stirred in. Entire process a delectable ritual, all-absorbing. Eggs eaten with two of the soft biscuits from ration and some coffee. Next, half of fruit bar broken up into egg can with dash of water added, knife thrust through up-prized lid, and held over flame till water absorbed. Behold! nice jam, enough for third soft biscuit and two of hards. Linger over remaining weak black coffee and one had momentary illusion of being well-fed, but restraint still required to wrap other half of fruit bar and two biscuits and gum and extra three lumps of sugar inside cellophane packet for mid-AM snack. Hoarded sugar valuable currency. Six lumps would sometimes get fruit bar or D bar or cheese.

Through AM the salvage from breakfast allayed gnawing of hunger, as did gum—unless from Walla Walla Company of Nashville, Tenn., which always crumbled at first chew into candle-wax. But by 11 AM hard to forbear breaking into lunch unit for dextrose tablets, which if sucked in twos could, despite unpleasant taste, bring solace for 50-minute stretch.

Lunch—Depending on our strength of will, Owens and I would eat whole unit each or divide one and eat half. If half, it meant we had a pre-sleep snack to prevent dreaming of food all

---

* By "for a while" he meant he lost his. I still have mine.

154

night. Process of division intricate and closely watched even though complete trust between us. Too hungry to ignore fear of inequality. Cheese untinned and bisected after due consultation as to exactitude of division, then crackers—two each of softs, one and a half each of hards, with the odd one divided exactly on perpendicular stroke of "B" in NABISCO. Then, provided water nearby or reserve in QM bladder on pack [the bladder was an inflatable rubber pillow issued for use as a float in river crossings but often filled with water to supplement the canteen by those able to carry the additional weight], lemonade. Each always had plenty of lemon powder, since this least used item in ration. Alert scavengers near end of column could collect six or eight packets in a day. If good surplus, three or four in a cup. Fond notion it gave us vitamin C, deficiency of which said to abet hunger—something about Georgia Crackers eating clay because diet lacking vitamin C, and since we hungry enough to eat clay, perhaps also lacking in vitamin C.

This left no reserve, so afternoon dragged worst unless lucky enough to salvage half-empty dextrose boxes along trail. As time went on and many lost appetite from dysentery, these pickings good and my dextrose content way up—until one dozen eaten in one day, followed by revulsion at mere thought of these tablets.

Sometimes weak-willed enough to nibble at supper's D-bar, but this profligacy frowned upon.

Supper—Preparations same as breakfast with exception chocolate bar and bouillon instead of fruit bar and coffee and too often with corned pork loaf—vile concoction with a perfume flavor from apple flakes. (Can visualize the bedizened dietician who thought up that one—type to put whipped cream and pineapple on lettuce.) Some made cocoa from D-bar. For a while Sam's trick of shutting eyes and chewing together with soft biscuit gave illusion of eating a chocolate cake.

After an hour's interval we again hungry. Followed a period of old-maids' gossip of our eating habits at home: the best meals we'd ever had, ideal menu for first repast on getting out, etc. Voluptuous lingering over details like Latins discussing mistresses. Then second lunch (if we'd saved it), following noon procedure exactly. At last sleep, but after midnight constant waking up to gnawing in belly.

155

In a manner appropriate to a collection of wolves, supply and distribution system worked. In situation where every individual's food reserves as widely known as actors' incomes in Hollywood, chiseler would have small chance of concealing loot.

Rigid regime in preparation and consumption of rations, akin to measurement and dispensation of baby's formula, broken only when prospect of delayed drop reduced us to two-thirds or one-third of ration per day or when action imminent and air of abandon prevailed; most agreed with Caldwell: "I ain't gona die with any packful of rations, that's for sure."

It was during the last phase of the trip to Shaduzup that we had our greatest communications difficulties and Colonel Osborne dropped his remark about the long walk back to Walawbum. We had been making about two miles a day cutting through the forest when one morning we heard the mutter of a light airplane. It came from first one quarter, then another, and though we could see nothing beyond the trees around us we could be pretty sure it was looking for us; the Northern Combat Area Command was doubtless wondering where we were. Fortunately the column passed a small clearing wh'le the plane was beagling after us and I hied myself out to the center of it. The sound of the motor was the homeyist I had heard since I had sold my Model A Ford in Louisiana on the way to the West Coast. Soon I saw it gliding over the treetops and I waved the piece of white parachute cloth I carried as a handkerchief. When I had decided it was never going to spot me, it banked sharply, turned straight toward me and came by low overhead. After making its pass, which evidently was for the purpose of satisfying itself that the castaway below was what it was looking for, it came back and dropped a white sleeve with a weight on the end. After one more trip to make sure I had retrieved the missile, it wagged its wings and went off. I bore the trophy to Colonel Osborne with the efficient demeanor of a spaniel laying before its master a very dead fish—which was what the message inclosed in the sleeve proved to be. It inquired acidly when we were going to conclude our scenic tour of northern Burma and get to Shaduzup. Osborne decided to halt at midday for however long it might take us to get in to Dinjan. He personally composed a reply to the message and I personally ran it through Greater Garble (a libel upon our faithful M-209 converter by the radio operators, whose transmissions were far more likely to be to blame for unintelligible messages than the little cipher machine). It pointed out that we had fought thirteen actions since jumping off, and in the language was a restrained implication that if the addressees did not like the way we were fighting the war they could come fight it themselves. It also asked for a drop. That time we did get through to base. Northern Combat Area Command did not comment, but the next message we received from General Merrill was a generous one asking if it was a private war we were fighting or if others could join in.

For the last leg of the march to Shaduzup we had taken to the woods again because reconnaissance had showed the trails all to be blocked; if our expedition, which could easily end in disaster, were to have any chance of success we had to get in undetected, difficult though this appeared to be. Osborne had decided in consultation with Darlington that our best chance would be to descend from the hills down the gorge of a twisting stream called the Chengun and make our play where the Chengun flowed into the Mogaung River, a few miles below Shaduzup; at that point, as at Walawbum, river and road were adjacent. To improve our prospects of achieving surprise, as the hallowed phrase is, Osborne sent McElmurray and his platoon on a feint to the northwest, at a right angle to our route of march, to mislead the enemy into expecting an attack north of Shaduzup, where, according to Tilly's information, there were 300 Japanese with another 500 or 600 along the Jambu Bum, seven miles or so to the north.

McElmurray caught up with us again the next day after having pushed up the trail to within a mile and a half of the road. Partly, at least, because of his height, the carbine he was toying with made me think of a jackstraw. He made his report to

Colonel Osborne in a flat tone of voice and with an economy of words. Shortly before reaching a village about three fifths of the way to the road he had run into a couple of Japanese who, judging by the equipment they were found to have, were engaged in a mapping survey. The platoon killed one and the other got away—fortunately for the purposes of the deception. Shortly afterward the Japanese had started lobbing mortar shells into the village. Evidently they had got the idea.

As we moved on southwest down the ridgebacks, Evan Darlington was first to spot the Kamaing Road. He had climbed up into a tree and out on a limb. Parting the foliage, he had looked out across the wooded valley. "By God, I think I see it," he called down. Phil Weld, whose platoon was leading that day, set down his pack and carbine and climbed up beside him. Evan pointed to what resembled a fold in the forested range across the valley leading to a scratch of raw dirt and the two consulted over a contour map and took a compass bearing. It was just right for the road. The Kachin guides, smelling a pitched battle ahead, with shellfire, had quietly disappeared during the night. We could not say we blamed them.

For the past hour the going had been relatively easy, for elephants had beaten a wide, irregular track along the crest of the ridge, but this advantage was lost as the ground began to fall away. No two elephants of those which had traveled the ridge seemed to have descended by the same route; a skein of scarcely distinguishable trails unraveled down the slope in the direction in which the map showed the Chengun to lie. Phil had frequently to halt the platoon and double back to see if he could find a less precipitous way down than the one they were taking. Every hundred yards or so, in Phil's words, the leading men with machetes were brought up by a windfall of bamboo through which a cat would have found difficulty passing. Here only two men could work, one hacking at the tensed shafts of the low, bent stalks while the other shoved the butts to the sides and tucked them back. Once this pair had made a way large enough for a man, other two-man teams could follow, expanding the opening above and to the sides until a big enough tunnel had been opened.

After an hour they stumbled down a deep declivity into a rock-lined ravine through which a torrent of white water plunged into a deep, black pool. It was the Chengun. Patches of blue sky could be seen high above, but the density of the shade made the day seem sunless. One of those outbursts of uncomprehending, insane laughter from a troop of monkeys gave the moment a theatrical quality. Phil and Evan drank greedily and gratefully, filled their canteens, then, scooping the cool water up in their hands, splashed their faces, heads and necks, washing off three days' accumulation of sweat-salt and dirt. When the rest of the platoon had assembled and had a chance to drink and clean up, Phil set them to the task of digging out a zigzag cut for the animals down the face of the bank.

The rest of us soon began to arrive. The gurgling Chengun was an uplifting sight—and also a forbidding one. Except for a persistent rain the night before, water had been scarce for us. There had been nights when one could think of little but the enduring happiness a sufficiency of water would bring. I had not shaved for a week. Drinking the Chengun was one thing, however, threading its course another. The footing it offered looked chancy in the extreme. Most of what the battalion carried, it was true, would not be much affected by being ducked, but among the exceptions happened to be the equipment my platoon carried. You can fight a battle in a downpour but you cannot go about dowsing radios and cipher machines and expect to be able to exchange tidings happily with the outside world thereafter. I had been awake much of the night before accommodating myself to a cold trickle of rain that had found its way under my poncho, we had had nothing hot to eat or drink, including coffee, for thirty-six hours because any fires at all might betray our presence, and we were in one of our rations stretch-outs. These deprivations would not have been so bad had we been able to look forward to something better. But you could not do that without looking forward also to what was going to happen on the Kamaing Road. Until we had had our collision with the Japanese there would be no fires and no supply drop. So you did not look forward.

VI There were flat stretches in the Chengun easy of passage along sandy beaches or over a sandy bottom in shallow water, but alternating with these were pools formed by giant boulders across the stream bed where we were held up for as long as it took to build a causeway of stones across the bottom for the animals or to excavate a bypass trail along the slope of the ravine.

Phil, whose platoon was still in the lead, described how it was at one such pool after his four squads had taken turns heaving rocks into it:

When at last it was done, they called for Charlie Shytle and the chestnut mare—the animal that had pioneered all the most difficult passages to this point.

By exerting all his instinct for horse-handling, the Missouri boy maneuvered the mare down the bank to the edge of the deep pool at its foot. There she paused, flanks trembling, nostrils distended, blowing nervously and dabbing at the surface with her lips. Shytle, stripped to his shoes, stood at her forequarter holding lead-rope and halter.

"Let's go now, girl," he said in his flat, farm-country quaver. "Just keep your feet and we'll make it all right." And the pair stepped off into chest-deep water. The mare lunged, nearly lost her footing, regained it and surged forward to the accompaniment of a steady flow of blandishment, cajolery and imprecation from Shytle. At last they attained the sandy shallow of the far side.

161

"You need about a foot more stone and dirt along the bottom," Shytle called back to the working crew. "Then the rest of them can make it." Turning to the shivering mare, he slapped her shoulder and said, "Ho, you girl. You're good. You and me could lead 'em to Rangoon."

The growing weakness of the animals compounded the problem of getting them downstream—and getting them there quietly. One mule, finding itself slipping, dove from a 10-foot bluff into the water. It was pulled out with blood pouring from its nostrils as from faucets. Another, in the weapons platoon, fell over in deep water and drowned before it could be freed from the load that pinned it to the bottom; in shallow water a mule's head could be held above the surface. At every obstruction I anxiously watched the communications mules. Some of the slopes were so mean they could not be led up them— there was no room for the leader—and had to be urged up from the bottom and recaptured at the crest. Top-heavy under their swaying loads, unloving and unloved, they scrambled on up. God knows why.

In the late afternoon we came to a spot where a Japanese patrol had recently encamped, leaving the still-warm ashes of a fire, an improvised bamboo shelter, and some empty fish cans. They had ascended to what they evidently considered the highest point upstream from which any danger could conceivably arise, and as a result of their expedition the Japanese in the area would be enjoying an unwarranted sense of security with respect to their eastern flank. It was a stroke of great good fortune for us.

The order was given to "bivouac in place" and word was passed down the line that the food we still had left would have to last at least another forty-eight hours. For most of us this amounted at best to a six-ounce can of meat or cheese and a scrap of chocolate or fruit bar—apart, of course, from some of those bathroom tiles.

Soon after dawn the column was under way again. The river bed began to level out and the backwaters were shallower, but the halts were as frequent as ever; the most cautious reconnaissance of the stream ahead was now required. Sam Wilson was again up front and had once more put John Sukup, one of his best scouts, in the lead. At each bend Sam would hold up his hand to halt the platoon, strung out at wide intervals behind him. The scouts would creep ahead and for a full minute or two scrutinize the banks of the stretch of river that had opened out before them. Sukup, who had a reddish-brown mustache, was somewhat hard of hearing and perhaps for that reason was a particularly acute observer. After receiving the scouts' all-clear, Sam would double-check, ears and eyes strained, before signaling the platoon to move forward. The foliage hung motionless, the water tinkled and gurgled; there was no other sound or movement. More and more it appeared inconceivable that 800 men and over 200 horses and mules, fairly choking the defile of the Chengun, stumbling, splashing, perhaps even hee-hawing (for, as the War Department had soberly informed CG, USAF, CBI, in a special telegram, the mules had not been "devocalized") could move undetected upon an established Japanese position.

In time Sukup noticed that the vista of water and trees was lighter and airier than it had been. Edging forward around a curve in the river, he found himself looking out upon the expanse of a much broader, muddy river, perhaps fifty yards across, dazzling in the sunlight: the Mogaung. He heard the bray of a mule—not behind him, but across the water—and the *ponk . . . ponk* of an ax. In a minute or two Sam was beside him. Voices in an alien tongue could be heard, the bang of a pot, laughter.

The I and R platoon, which had left its transport behind to gain greater mobility, was well in advance of the rest of the battalion. Sending a runner back to report to the battalion commander, Sam divided the major part of the platoon and set up outposts upstream and downstream from the mouth of the Chengun.

On arriving at the scene, Colonel Osborne stood and gazed

163

speculatively across the broad, tawny river. The sound of the Japanese throwing grenades into the water for fish could be heard.

"I wonder what's on the other side," he murmured.

There was a pause. "Why don't I go see?" Sam asked.

The colonel looked at him thoughtfully. "Yes," he said finally. "Why don't you?"

Sam repaired to the northernmost of the two outposts. "I've got to go across," he announced in a low voice. "Who wants to go with me?" There was no response. It was the first time that had happened. Sam had, he knew, touched on a sore issue. A week before he had faced a small crisis in the platoon. Having offered to take an extra turn at the head of the column—a duty which experience showed had to be rotated among the platoons instead of being left exclusively to the I and R platoon because no one set of men could stand the strain continuously—Sam had been too sick to make good on the offer, as far as he himself was concerned, and had been back in the column vomiting while the platoon carried on by itself. Its concern over its leader's propensity for volunteering its services had been brought to a head. In a council with the platoon Sam had agreed that any volunteering he did in the future would be for himself alone and that he would not ask anyone to go along with him, except other volunteers.

In the silence that followed his announcement, the voices of the Japanese were audible.

"O.K.," said Sam, "I'll go alone. You can cover me going across and coming back."

One of the noncoms—Perlee W. Tintary—picked up his carbine and got to his feet. "Oh, hell, I'll go with you, Sam," he said.

The two men made their way to the river's edge and lowered themselves into the water. For a few yards in midstream they had to swim, holding their carbines out of the water with one hand. Hearing an insistent hissing whistle from behind them they turned and saw Sergeant Branscomb pumping up and down with his raised fist in the signal that spells "on the double" throughout the armed services. The expression on his face gave it added urgency. They pressed forward as fast as they could, crawled up the opposite shore and tumbled into the jungle. They reached cover just in time to escape detection by two Japanese walking down the river's edge. They could almost have touched the pair as they passed.

After a few moments' wait they wormed their way through the dense growth for several hundred yards until they abruptly found themselves about to blunder into a Japanese bivouac. They glimpsed some bashas apparently full of supplies—evidence of a significant encampment—and located the position of the road. It was all the information required of them. They worked their way back to the river. Sam took a deep breath to combat the pounding of his heart as he contemplated its immoderate vastness and estimated the time they would once more be at the mercy of chance. The return proved to be nearly a repetition of the first crossing. Nearing the other shore they saw their platoon mates were looking at them bug-eyed. Again Branscomb was signaling frantically. This time they made the shore about thirty seconds before a Japanese patrol passed on the opposite side.

Colonel Osborne was as little given to dramatizing his approval as his anxieties, but his solicitude as Sam reported to him, shivering with cold and fright, was sufficiently expressive. "That's all for you for this operation, Sam," he said.

Osborne had made up his mind quickly. After the animals had been unloaded he ordered them sent half a mile back upstream where they could not be heard. The battalion went into position on the high ground just back from the river to prepare for the attack. Radio silence was to be preserved, but we got our equipment, which had arrived safely, set up.

From observation posts they had set up in front of the main body, Phil Weld's men could creep forward to the edge of the embankment over the Mogaung and peer out through the undergrowth to a stretch of the other shore adjacent to the Japanese encampment. Like Iroquois warriors in the forest shadows gazing silently with burning eyes upon an outpost of the white invaders, they watched, fingering their weapons, while groups of Japanese soldiers in khaki trousers with wrap leggings, some with white shirts, sauntered to the river's edge to talk or scour their cooking utensils. The stars on their caps could easily be seen. The Nisei who had been sent up at Phil's request to translate their conversation reported that it seemed to concern nothing more vital than the evening meal.

After dark Osborne called his officers together and gave them their attack orders. With one of the battalion's two combat teams standing by for trouble, the other was to cross the Mogaung at three in the morning. Weld's platoon was to lead, followed by McElmurray's and then Meredith Caldwell's. At the first light of dawn the platoons were to move independently from the riverbank to the road, cutting the Japanese supply line and digging in against the inevitable violent counterattacks. "Keep your men from firing as long as you can," said Osborne. "Whatever they do, they mustn't start shooting while it's still dark. If they get in a jam, it's to be knives or bayonets."

At midnight Major Caifson Johnson, commanding the combat team picked for the attack, waded out into the river and crossed its deepest part, guiding on a smudgy lantern held by a Japanese sentry downstream, and satisfied himself that the river was fordable at the spot he had chosen for the crossing. Johnson, looking like a professorial kind of bear (or ursine kind of professor, perhaps) because of the massive pack he carried and his grizzly-style, reddish beard, was an outstanding figure of the Shaduzup operation. Although suffering acutely from amebic dysentery, he had been up with the lead elements throughout the approach march except for two occasions when he had fainted from weakness and illness. Nothing would persuade him to lighten his stupendous pack, though, even the time he fell into a hollow and lay there on his back, his limbs waving in the air, like a beetle, unable to get to his feet without help. Johnnie was to be one of the first across the river in the

166

dark of the next morning, following Phil Weld and his runner

Phil, who would be the first man of all, had a restless night
It is one thing to face the ultimate possibilities as one of a
crowd in the excitement of intense activity, quite another to
anticipate it lying alone in the dark with five hours to go—beyond question nearly all that remained of life for some of those
nearby . . . so why not for oneself? Could a kind and just Lord,
he asked himself, let that happen to Anne and the children?
He breathed the prayer he had spoken more than once during
the past month and, with luck, would speak more than once in
the weeks ahead: Oh, Lord, please get me home before too
long and in such shape that I won't give them too much of a
shock. . . . What, he propounded to himself, if he went to
Johnnie and said he would not go through with it? What difference would the damned roadblock make anyway? Burma
meant not a bloody thing in Allied strategy. It only mattered
to some general's reputation. . . . More than almost anything
else within reason a cigarette would have helped, but lighting
one would have been against orders even if he had not smoked
his last the day before. . . . He tried to anticipate the morrow,
then decided there was no use attempting to figure it beyond
moving out from the riverbank in single file. For the rest, it
would be the old "depending on the situation and terrain." He
could tell himself that this was the real thing, but it seemed
more like all those training problems. Jump off. Go through
the prescribed motions of soldiers attacking. The problem is
now nontactical. Assemble here for a critique. The attack was
a success because it followed the old principle of surprise. But
there was too much bunching up. The junior officers did not
appear to have control. If there are no more questions, form
company front and move out. He would have liked to have one
of the glib instructors there now. Still, if you could only do
what the book said, everything ought to work out. If. What
was it Sammy had told him were the two most important things?
As he recalled them, they were: Don't deploy till the last possible moment. And when you do, commit the smallest possible

167

number of men. He would remember that. Tomorrow would take care of tomorrow. . . . To his wife, whose anxious face he could see vividly, he said, "Don't worry. We'll just take it easy and it'll turn out all right." And he dropped into a fitful sleep.

About one o'clock Phil and the others in his platoon were awakened by the sound of truck motors across the river. In the stillness they sounded no more than fifty yards off but he knew that the road was at least a quarter of a mile distant. Further sleep was impossible. They talked brokenly and somewhat aimlessly, running over the details of the attack order and trying to think of things that had not been covered in discussion the evening before. Phil and his runner, Owens, divided their last K-ration component, a can of cheese.

As the time to move out approached, Phil led his platoon to the mouth of the Chengun to await the signal. There he found Sam leaning against the bank. While he crouched on one knee on the sandbar, he and Sam chatted in whispers. In a few minutes word came from Caifson Johnson that it was time. Phil straightened up, checked his gear, and stepped off into the water. Sam, shivering in his still-wet fatigues, stood up. "Good luck," he said to the figure disappearing in the darkness. Out of the night came "So long, Sammy."

Phil instantly regretted the reply, which struck his New Englander's sense of the proprieties as a melodramatic exit line. Why couldn't he have just said, "See you later"? He was to remain abashed by the memory through all that followed.

He could have been alone in the river, except for Owens, a couple of paces behind him. The current pressed his trousers against his legs. The water was cold as it rose higher. It had reached their waists by midstream. From there the dividing line between forest and sky on the far side was barely visible. As they went on, the water grew deeper. Phil decided that if it came above the breast pockets of his jacket he would have to backtrack and find another route since some of the men were eight inches shorter than he. Then, as the bank became discernible, the water began to recede. Within two yards of the bank he stopped and whispered to his runner, "Tell Johnnie it's okay. The water came short of my armpits. I'll wait here."

Sooner than he had expected he saw a line of dark objects above the surface of the water. Major Johnson stood beside him, the rest of the force strung out in single file behind him. "O.K., Phil. Move on upstream. Good luck."

With McElmurray's platoon forming the keystone of the block, Phil's was to be on the extreme right flank, so he had a good way yet to go. He had led his squad off perpendicularly to the route of the rest of the column when suddenly a light appeared downstream. Everyone froze where he stood. The thought that the movement had been discovered struck Phil and he braced himself for a torrent of machine-gun fire. The lantern advanced swayingly, then steadied as its bearer set it down by the water's edge. The rays illumined a shadowy figure which lowered a bucket and filled it from the river. Then the lantern moved off again. The collective unbreathed sigh of relief that went up from the column could almost be felt.

Dawn was still some time off when Phil led his platoon out of the water onto the bank. They were sitting there shivering with the water draining out of their clothes when Phil saw the figure of a man approaching from downstream. The shape stopped five yards away and was joined by another. He could hear whispering. Quietly he unsheathed his trench knife and crouched ready to spring. He meant to slap a headlock on the nearer Jap and sink the knife between his shoulders.

Then the shape whispered "Lillian" in an unmistakable Midwestern accent. It was the lieutenant in command of the adjacent platoon, which had climbed out of the river farther back and moved up by land.

"Russell," Phil whispered, feeling deflated and foolish.

The two discussed the best means of reaching their objectives. Since the Mogaung made an S bend between them and the road, they had the prospect of crossing it twice more. Soon the trees began to take clearer shape against the sky and Weld noticed that the hands and faces of the men around him were standing out white against the wet, dark-green fatigues. He judged the time was to be considered dawn. "Hey, Al!" he called in a whisper to Sergeant Overby, a veteran of Guadalcanal and New Georgia who was one of his squad leaders. "We're moving!" They headed out in single file. After pushing through some 50 yards of thick forest they came upon an open glade where bamboo shelters and the embers of fires marked a bivouac—deserted, surprisingly. Just then, from perhaps 200 yards downstream, came a rifle shot, loud, solitary, and fateful. It was followed by the deadly rip of a Thompson submachine gun at full automatic.

Meredith Caldwell had begun the battle of Shaduzup.

Meredith, when he had crossed the river, had been told by Johnson to wait on the bank till 4:30, then shove off for the road. Johnnie had been standing in the water directing the platoons to their positions. Inasmuch as he was to be on the extreme southern flank, at the opposite end from Weld, Meredith had to go some distance downstream. The bank where his platoon was to go ashore proved to be too steep to see over and he passed down through the platoon a call for two volunteers with fixed bayonets to climb up it. The word came back that there were no volunteers and that the lieutenant would have to pick two by name. Reckoning that he had been put on the spot, he prepared to go up himself. But he decided that if a Japanese head appeared over the bank he was going to blow it off with the Tommy gun he was carrying, orders or no orders.

The bank proved to be deserted, however. Meredith formed the platoon on the top of it in a skirmish line, fifty strong, backs to the river, ready to get up when the hour came and move in the direction he surmised and hoped the road would be in. At 4:28 he stood up and said, "On your feet—and pass it on." When they were all up he looked down the line and thought how strikingly it resembled a movie of World War I. He had enough presence of mind to feel out of place having to consult a big pocket watch of his father's instead of a wrist watch—like a railway conductor. "Let's go," he said.

170

At the same moment Major Johnson gave the order over the voice radios, the SCR 300's and 536's: "Move out." The 400 men who had crossed the river soundlessly headed into the forest, almost as quiet as ever, weapons at the ready.

Caldwell's platoon had advanced about 150 yards straight ahead when a young private from upstate New York whispered to him, "Look, Lieutenant, there's a road!" It was the Kamaing Road, and they were the first to reach it. "He and I walked out onto it together," Meredith told us. "I got just south of him so I could say to myself, 'Meredith, you are the furtherest man down the Ledo Road.' About that time I saw a Japanese sentry way up the road coming toward us. The private with me was one of the finest shots in the Army; I'd given him a telescopic sight to use in sniping. He threw his rifle up effortlessly and without seeming to take aim killed the Jap instantly with one round—at about eighty yards. At the same time another Jap appeared on the road and we heard a truck coming, so we jumped back into the bushes. Just as the truck—an imitation of a 1935 Ford—drew up alongside someone fired. I leveled in with the Tommy gun, aiming a little above the headlights, which were still on. A submachine gun ain't worth a damn at fifty yards, but at five it's deadly. The Japs in the truck we didn't kill outright we finished off with bayonets when they piled out."

In the bivouac area there were little fires agleam in the half-light. Some of the Japanese were tending these, some were pulling on their clothes, some were at the latrine when the firing sounded in the south. Before they had had a chance to react, the line of Marauders broke out of the woods and fell upon them. There was pandemonium and carnage as the Marauders swept through the camp. There were Japanese running from every quarter, like rabbits before a cordon of gunners. They pitched forward, sprawling or rolling with their momentum under the massed fire of rifles, Tommy guns and Browning automatics. In a few moments the bivouac area was cleared and the attack was pushing onto the road.

Weld's platoon made it safely over the second stretch of the

171

river they had to cross but the third looked formidable. There was first a dry, rock-strewn secondary channel, followed by a brush-grown knoll, followed by the river itself, followed by a 20-foot embankment, followed by the road, down which they saw two chattering Japanese riflemen running in the direction of the battle. If the Japanese chose to defend the road at this point, the crossing would be impossible, but Phil decided he must make the attempt to get his platoon there, as ordered. He and Overby made a dash for it and gained the knoll. After crawling to the other side of it, they had a view of the opposite bluff.

"Holy crow, look at the bastards!" said Overby. The Japanese were there all right. Overby gave a chortle of excitement. He was actually enjoying it, Phil thought. He was one of those rare ones who liked fighting, as if it were a game. "Ten, twelve. Two with a machine gun."

"Then," Phil reported, "things began to happen fast. The unmistakable, high-pitched crackling of Jap rifle fire broke out from the corner where the road disappeared behind the trees. Puffs of sand appeared 15 yards to our left rear. The rapid, hysterical bursts of a Nambu light machine gun tore short rips into the tarpaulin of silence that had covered us until this moment. Then from the bank behind us came a cascade of answering fire from our men. The din resembled the pattern of sound on a rifle range during a rapid-fire exercise—a scattered beginning of single shots, a crescendo of simultaneous triple bursts, tailing off into silence punctured again by irregular single shots.

"Behind us we heard a man's agonized cry.

" 'I'm hit. I'm hit,' the voice called. 'I'm hit. Oh, please don't leave me. Oh.' A series of short broken moans followed.

"It was a private named Page. Overby and I recognized his voice.

" 'Shut up, Page,' I called sharply as if I were reprimanding a recruit. 'Shut up and crawl for cover. We won't leave you.'

"We wriggled forward to get a better view of the bluff across the river. Looking downstream at this angle we could see the lighter patches of Japanese uniforms through the leaves. Overby raised his rifle, the old bolt-action '03 that, as a squad leader, he carried. He had removed the grenade-launcher. He raised the sight leaf with a steady hand, settled the stock to his shoulder and twisted his elbow into the sand as methodically as if he were on the drill ground dry-firing.

"The rifle report slammed. Twice more, between rasps of the bolt sliding forward and back, it slammed with ear-deafening shocks. The smell of scorched oil and hot steel mingled with the powder fumes. A helmeted head appeared and quickly disappeared as Overby sent two more shots across the gap. But the lumps of what could only be two bodies lay still."

Weld crawled back to the other side of the knoll, slid down into the dry river bed to where Page lay and dragged him down a little slope to a deeper part of the depression, farther below the plane of fire. A blood-soaked bandage from his aid packet was bound clumsily around Page's leg. "Now get this through your bean," said Phil. "By tomorrow you'll have a trained nurse feeding you orange juice."

"Yes, sir. Do you think so, sir?" Page was the smallest man in the platoon, meek and uncomplaining. To the customary "How's it going?" he generally answered, "Not so bad, but I'd sooner be back in Milford milking cows."

"Dammit, I couldn't be surer."

There were five of them who had to get back across the stream bed, Phil reflected: in addition to himself, Page, whom he would have to carry, Overby, and two others who had mistakenly followed them across. He called out to Overby. "Al, you can run fastest. I want you to go first and test the fire. It's that other machine gun that's the problem. When you get there, tell Norris and Wolfheil to get a mortar on it."

Overby ran erect, like a halfback, his knees high, back and neck straight, carrying his rifle weavingly before him as if it were a football. The second machine gun had opened up. In flicks of three the bullets were tearing into the ground no more than a yard behind him. They followed him up the bank and were striking no more than six inches behind him as he topped the crest and dove sprawling into the scrub. Phil let out his breath. But it was obvious the other two could never make it here. He sent them farther upstream.

They got across pretty much as Overby had, leading the puffs of dirt thrown up by the machine gun by a matter of inches. That left Phil to get across—with the disabled man.

"We'll start crawling now, Page," said Phil over his shoulder. "Just keep calm and hold onto my legs." He inched along, using his elbows as crutches, dragging the wounded man. It took all his strength. Every five yards he had to pause for breath. At last they reached the point from which the second two men had crossed. Atop the rim of the bank he could distinguish the face of his sergeant, Tinsley Norris, who was peering across at him. The *pung-plap* of a mortar shell leaving the tube rose above the continuing rifle fire. After the eternity that follows the discharge of a mortar came the roar of the explosion. Smoke pillared up from the far bank.

"That's them getting on the machine gun," Norris called.

"O.K.," said Phil. "In about two minutes we'll make a break for it. I want everyone to open up with everything we got. Soon as you start, I'll get moving."

He had Page crawl up on his back and across his shoulders while he lay there and slipped an arm under Page's knee, getting into position for a fireman's carry. Slowly he drew his own legs under him. Then the furious din of thirty weapons punctuated by mortar thumps broke out above him. Now was the time.

Slowly he struggled to his feet. He took a deep breath and started in heavy-legged strides across the opening. Fifteen, sixteen, he counted to himself. Gradually he increased his speed. He knew he was now a plain target, for bullets were cracking over his head and the dirt spat up before him. Faster, faster, he kept saying to himself: a moving target is twice as hard to hit. But his breath was coming short and his legs felt flabby. His toe hit a rock and he sprawled headlong, Page pitching over his

174

shoulder. By great good fortune, they had been thrown into a slight depression, below the plane of fire.

"Jesus, I'm sorry, Page," said Phil. "Clumsy ass, I am. I've hurt you worse than the Japs did."

"No, sir, I'm all right. Don't you think you'd better try it alone, sir? I'll just get you hurt. I can make it by myself."

The absurdity, in the circumstances, of these civilities struck Phil even as they exchanged them. "The hell you can," he said. "One more heave and we'll be there."

He got the wounded man across his shoulders again, gathered his strength, and lunged to his feet. Fifteen yards remained between him and the foot of the bank. The sprint he attempted was mostly a stagger as his knees weakened. Going up the cut in the bank, he could only walk, ponderously, clumsily. Hands reached out and pulled them over the crest and into the shelter of the forest.

"Where are you hit, Lieutenant?"

They could not believe he had not been scratched. The platoon guide laid a solicitous hand on his shoulder. "You've got no right to be alive, the way that lead was flying."

He checked the position of his men, who were disposed in pairs along the bank, on their bellies with their weapons in firing positions. Their faces, he thought, were like the sights of the home town after a long absence. It was only when he announced his decision to pull the platoon back to the command post for reassignment that they found the heart to tell him there was more bad news.

"What the hell's happened now?"

"We've got three more wounded out there."

One had been hit while trying to follow Phil and Overby to the knoll and the other two while trying to rescue the first.

As Phil crawled to the bank to see for himself, the original wounded man had just succeeded in heaving himself up over the edge, and now, minus helmet, pack and rifle, he staggered forward and fell. "Olsen and Susnjer are out there," he quavered. "They came to help me. They got hit bad. We got to help them."

The two, Phil found, were lying like grain sacks dropped from a plane at the foot of the bank. First one, then the other would moan. Milton Susnjer, a rolling-mill worker from western Pennsylvania whose crotch was a mess of blood called out weakly, "Olie's dying. Somebody help Olie. Oh, God, how I hurt!" Olsen had got it in the head and one leg.

The Japanese were firing now only in answer to the firing of his own platoon, when one of them spotted a target. But they were still there. While Phil fought a momentary wave of despair, Overby and Ernest Banks, a cowpuncher from Texas with curly brown hair, a habitual volunteer for dirty work, appeared from the rear. "Al and me thought you might use some help," the Texan said. "We got to get them before they bleed to death. You and me could run down there, each grab an arm and drag them up the bank, first one, then the other—before the Japs could ever get in on us, if we're fast." It was what Phil had had in mind, without wanting to ask anyone to run the gamut with him.

Overby, who had been scanning the far bank of the river, lowered himself to one knee. "I think I see one of them snipers, anyhow," he said. He raised his rifle, placed his cheek against the stock and squirmed into a better adjustment. The blast rocked him back a little. On the far bluff a dark shape in a tree dropped a few feet and hung there from a branch—a man's body. Phil threw the squad leader an admiring glance.

Divesting themselves of their rifle belts and rolling up their sleeves and trousers, Phil and Banks shook hands, braced themselves and shot down the slope side by side. They had dragged Olsen to safety before the Japanese had comprehended what was going on. It was not until they had made their second dash and had Susnjer nearly up the bank that they came under fire, and then the fire was wide of the mark. Susnjer had been shot through both thighs—a bloody but not critical wound. Olsen's wounds were relatively bloodless—but serious.

The Japanese on the road had collected themselves fairly rapidly and had gone over to the offensive—as indeed they had no choice but to do; it was their lifeline, not ours, that was at stake. Within two hours of our jumping off, all our positions along the road were under small-arms fire while on the east bank of the river the reserve combat team and battalion headquarters were being shelled by artillery. There was enough to do to keep our minds off it, however, as much as minds can be kept off artillery. We had to dig not only foxholes for ourselves but deep pits for the radios and operators. Everything now depended upon our getting through to base. It was not so much that we were out of food as that we could expect to run out of ammunition before nightfall. Colonel Osborne had stated in the message he had given us to transmit that if we could not get a supply drop by that afternoon it would be necessary to abandon the block and withdraw. He had also included a warning that the drop planes should have fighter cover and a request for fighter-bombers to deal with the artillery.

We ground the juice into the AN/PRC-1 as never before. The battalion's one irreplaceable possession, and looking as if it knew it, it straddled the bottom of its trench, inscrutable, temperamental, its favor beyond entreaty or purchase. It appeared to be humoring us, though. The clipped twerps in which it spoke had a reassuring vigor and authority.

The artillery was growing in violence, seeming to be feeling for the battalion command post.

"Shut up," said Bright anxiously. "I can't read."

In the morning reception was generally at its best, and that morning was no exception. I had never been so glad to hear a message receipted for.

Down on the road everyone had his hands full.

Caldwell's platoon had tried to get the truck they had shot up off the road, anticipating that when our planes appeared they would strafe the bejesus out of it and incidentally the platoon too. "But we couldn't budge it," Caldwell said. "We got a lot of supplies off of it, though—underwear, canned goods, and cooked purple rice, of all things. One of the Nisei said it was dyed that color for some holiday. It didn't bother us. We had ourselves a feed while we waited to see which way the hornets were going to hit us from after the brick we'd heaved. Colonel Osborne sent me a section of light machine guns and I had the sergeant in charge place them in a slight curve pointing south straight down the road. It wasn't long before we saw a movement at the end of the road. It was Japanese, and they kept coming. What looked like a whole company of reinforcements was headed toward us, marching in columns of twos—the target machine gunners dream of, of course. We held our breaths and held our fire too, to give the buyers of War Bonds their money's worth. Still they came on, apparently completely unsuspecting. Then the machine guns opened on them. The sergeant swears he counted sixty-odd bodies after the dust had settled."

Major Johnson's face lighted up when Phil came into his command post. "Boy, am I glad to see you! I've never been so glad to see anyone!" Having feared that he would be thought to have bungled his mission, Phil was relieved. He asked how the other platoons were doing.

"Damn well," Johnnie said. "McElmurray has a beautiful position. While the Japs were fighting you upstream, he had time to get well dug in. We're tied in all the way down now. The Japs have brought up some heavy mortars. They've tried one counterattack over on the left, but Coburn's machine guns mowed them down. God, it was a pretty sight. I happened to be up there."

Phil was sent forward to put his platoon in next to McElmurray's. He found the hawk-nosed Oklahoman in happy spirits, thoroughly at home in the world. A bullet had left a scorched mark down his shoulder where his lieutenant's bar would normally have been.

"By God," said Mac, "when they open up with that heavy over there you better keep your head down. The road is only ten yards off and the Japs are smack on the far side of it. Can't

178

be fifteen yards between lines. But it's too thick to see a thing.
... You were having quite a time over yonder. We could see
them Japs pulling dead ones off the road plain as anything.
How are you, anyway?"

"Pretty rugged. Lost my pack."

"Well, if you need a blanket, help yourself. Right over there
the Japs had a storeshed full of blankets and rifles and all sorts
of crap. We've been eating raw eggs all morning."

The Japanese heavy machine gun opened up then with a
chug-chug and a clanking of parts. It sounded as much like an
ancient flivver as a weapon. The two officers leapt into a hole.
For several minutes the din of firing on both sides of the road
made speech impossible. Twigs and leaves lopped off by the
bullets two feet overhead fluttered to the ground.

"Say, look at that damn Manuel, will you," said Mac.

Herman Manuel was a swarthy, squat Navajo from Arizona.
Crouched in a nearby hole, he was dropping shells into his mortar, his copper-colored face never changing expression. He
would hold the shell poised at the mouth of the tube. When a
shell from a Japanese mortar burst behind him he would drop
in his round, and the report, coming so close on the crump of
the other, could not be heard more than a few feet away. In
that way he did not reveal his position to the enemy.

"He figured that one out by himself," said McElmurray ad-
miringly.

McElmurray and Charles Scott, the fire marshal from Ohio,
were together that morning when a Japanese attack gave Scotty
one of the moments he had come for. The two spotted a Japanese officer. While Mac was getting his carbine to his shoulder,
Scotty felled him with a shot. In the next half hour, twelve Japanese were killed trying to retrieve the body.

Our Air Force showed up later in the day. It brought us the
vital supply drop and a respite from the shelling, which had
been growing worse. The enemy gunners laid low while the
doughty little Mustangs were overhead. The strafing made a

179

burbling sound, the dive-bombing a crunching like a giant crushing drums underfoot.

That evening the Chinese 113th Regiment began to arrive. The commanding officer, obviously eager to prove his unit and his people, insisted on taking over from us along the road without delay. We were nothing loath and the switch was made. By then the Japanese had no hope of prying loose the hold we had fastened on the road and, although we did not yet know it, they had broken contact with the Chinese pushing down the road south of the Jambu Bum and were falling back. But they were not through with us. Far from it.

Beginning with dusk, our enemies had nothing more to fear from the air. They knew where we were—on the high ground across the river from them—they knew we were helpless against artillery, they were murderous at our having caught them at such a disadvantage and inflicted such hurt, and they decided to stay up all night getting the most out of the artillery ammunition they had accumulated. We did not know how many pieces they had. The two they had opened up with in the morning were reported to have been augmented by an additional battery. We should also have found it hard to say which of the two types of pieces they had was the worse. There were the howitzers, 70 millimeters and perhaps 150's too, that we had met at Walawbum. Their shells arched in on you and could be heard coming a long way with a sound like that of a bird with whistling wings. (In fact there was a bird, a kind of hornbill, that made a sound so similar when it took off ahead of the column in the forest that we froze when we heard it, waiting for the detonation.) If you were exposed you had time to dive for cover, but you also had time for a protracted and sickening apprehension. The others gave you no time at all. The flat-trajectory fire of a 77-millimeter gun was like a whiplash. It came with a shriek. There was no suspense, only an instant of cowering contraction: boom-*whaaow*-BANG! and it was all over except the zip and whine of the shell fragments and the rain of dirt and bits of tree.

180

In the darkness, alone in your foxhole with nothing to take your mind off your plight or give your imagination anything else to work on, it does no good to remind yourself how overwhelmingly the odds are in your favor. It is of no significance that death is an end you have not always found unbearable to contemplate. It is not extinction itself but the circumstances that turn you coward. The death that haunts the battlefield is not the quiet oblivion that waits beside the sickbed; it is a vile monster crazed with evil that lurks in ambush to terrify you when it lunges, that shrills in the air and means to rip your vitals out with iron claws. That, even, you could probably take if it were you alone who had to take it. But it is not you alone; you are less vulnerable in yourself than you are in a wife or parent who stands to be struck down, without warning, with a bare slip of paper. A few years after World War I, when I was ten, I witnessed the burial, with military honors, of a soldier who had been killed in France. A rumor circulated that the exhumation of the remains preparatory to reinterment—itself an unspeakable thing—had disclosed that the incomplete human fragments had been pieced out with parts from a mule. The rumor must be supposed baseless, but the horror I felt then—though I had never known the dead man—remained the measure of what I imagined the anguish must be of those who received news of the death in war of one to whom they were close.

Fear has an identifiable taste. At least it has for me. It is a taste of brass. Every time a shell exploded it was as if my tongue had been touched by the two poles of a dry cell. And, Christ, they were coming close! One erupted a few feet away from me, turning a small tree into a column of sparks. All it needed was the minutest depression of the gun's barrel, a grain less of powder in the charge, to drop the next one right in on me.

They say there are no nonbelievers in foxholes. That is not true. But even nonbelievers may be reduced to the point of voicing a call of distress and a plea for help just in the hope, just on the chance, that there may somewhere be an understanding and a compassion that could be moved by it. Prayer, we are assured, brings comfort and courage, the peace that passeth understanding, to the believer, and it must be so. To the doubter, cringing in his hole in the ground, struggling grimly for every inch like a swimmer being drawn backward toward the cataract, it is evidence of how near he is to the end of his resources, how close to the brink he is coming.

One source of hope seemed to me to warrant one's faith. I noticed continually during the campaign that when things were really terrible it meant that they were on the eve of looking up. Of course, analysis might well have revealed that the principle amounted only to a trick of relativity—the worse things are the less it takes to make them look better—but I found it a help and at the moment did not have to worry over the fact that the converse of my principle was equally true. Another thing that helped was smoking. Extra packs of cigarettes had been dropped with our rations and there was no need to skimp. In addition to the slightly narcotic effect of the smoke—sufficient to separate you from reality perhaps a tenth of a degree—there was the comfort, not entirely negligible, of the warm glow of the coal in the darkness.

Once during the night I went down the slope to show the way to the medical aid station to some men with a casualty of the shelling. We were careful to display the blue gleam of a blackout flashlight and make appropriate sounds as we went, for it did not do to wander casually around our positions in the dark; a number of water buffaloes met their ends by doing so. A shelter had been quarried out of the sandbank, beside the Chengun, and in this the doctors worked on the wounded as best they could by candlelight behind a screen of ponchos. The wounded not being worked on lay in a network of trenches covered with blankets. Olson, from Phil Weld's platoon, was one of them. Phil had learned that while Olson was in Guadalcanal a man in the foxhole next to his had been bayoneted one night and Olson, being deaf in his left ear and not having heard him, blamed himself for the man's having died of his wound—which

182

was perhaps why he felt he had to rescue the man wounded in the stream bed that afternoon. Later, when trying to reassure him, Phil could hardly make himself understood. "Sorry I caused you all so much trouble," Olson said barely audibly. He was dying.

Colonel Osborne also had his command post on the lower slope—which meant only that that was where he was sitting. He was awake.

"How goes it, Oggy?" he asked.

"We seem to be doing all right, sir, up where I am."

The only one in the vicinity who I know slept that night was Tom Senff. He was one of those rare individuals whom almost nothing bothered. Once, though, he startled me by popping bolt upright with a smothered cry. "What was that?" He was only a few paces from me.

"I didn't hear anything special," I said.

"That *whooosh!*"

"Oh. I guess that was me blowing up my rubber pillow."

"Oh, for God's sake. I thought it was a shell coming right in on us," he said, lying down again.

"Well, I hope it scared the hell out of you," I said. "Your bloody regular breathing is the last straw."

For a time the shelling was particularly fierce. The Japanese gun crews must have been slamming them in like demons. When the racket slackened off, a voice of exasperation was heard in the darkness, controlled but distinct. "Where the hell are the other five thousand, three hundred and six composite units?"

There were sniggers audible from scattered points.

We did not come through that night unscathed. The worst incident was in Sam Wilson's platoon, which, occupying a forward slope, took a savage pounding from the flat-trajectory fire; the shells were throwing up dirt all around. After a particularly heavy cannonade that showered his foxhole with debris, Sam became aware of moaning a short distance away and of a voice calling "Sammy, Sammy, come quick! Old Allen is dead and

Young Allen's been hurt real bad!" Two scenes flashed into his mind at once. One was of Old Allen, as he was called (the two Allens were unrelated), telling him the day they had the bad time on the Tingkrung Hka that he would have to transfer out of the platoon, that he couldn't take it any longer. ("Oh, come on, Allen," Sam had said. "Don't leave us. You'll feel all right in a day or two.") The other was of Young Allen only the evening before imploring him, arguing with irrational vehemence, not to leave the platoon where it was. That night the two Allens occupied a double foxhole together. It was about 25 feet from Sam's. In response to the cries he heard after the shell burst, Sam snaked his way over to it. Lowering himself cautiously into it, he stepped on one of their feet. "Oh, I'm sorry!" he said. Only there was nothing connected with the foot. There had been a direct hit on Old Allen and it had blown him to pieces. Young Allen was somehow alive, and Anderson, the T/5 medical aid man who had cried out for Sam's help, was working on him and trying to comfort him. Allen called for "Sandy"—his name for Sam—then for Clarence Branscomb, the platoon guide. Sergeant Branscomb was later to be decorated for staying with the wounded man under the continuing barrage after Sam, exercising an option he had (reluctantly because he was protecting the right flank), got the platoon moved to the safety of the reverse side of the slope. Allen, as he failed, began to call for his mother. "A few moments after he died," said Sam, "it was day, the sunlight bright, the sky blue, the foliage across the river fresh and green."

It was about that time that there came a sound none of us who heard it will ever forget, for it was the most thrilling sound we had ever heard. Men who were groping in their packs for their rations, men who were checking on their platoons, men who were tuning up the radio, men who were peering at maps and making calculations stopped what they were doing and faces drained by sleeplessness, by fear, by exhaustion, took light and were twisted into lines of savage joy. *Boom-boom-boom-boom!* it came, from behind us, like four strokes of a trip-

hammer, followed by a singing as of a flight of arrows overhead. The Chinese pack artillery had arrived and was zeroing in with its four weapons! *Our* side was being heard from!
Boom-boom-boom-boom!
Take that, you goddam sons-of-bitches!
You bastards! You lousy bastards!
The brave little howitzers!

The effect on the Japanese was, indeed, sobering. The shelling that was coming our way eased off. And that was, for us, the end of the battle of Shaduzup.

The order came to pack up, and with far more energy than it would have been thought we possessed we fetched our mules from the picket lines and got them saddled up.

"What a night! I'm telling you, I spent a lot of it praying." It was one of the more profane stalwarts of the platoon who was speaking.

"Well, your prayers were answered," I said.

"Not by a damn sight they weren't! What I was praying for was a shell fragment in the fleshy part of the leg."

There cannot have been many in the organization who did not do so, at one time or another. It became a standard joke with us.

The mules picked their way down the disheveled slope and we headed upstream against a tide of Chinese coming down. The two columns jammed the lower reach of the Chengun, which resounded to the exchanges of *"ding how"*; Sino-American relations had never stood higher.

By then it was estimated that the number of Japanese killed in the fighting numbered 300, as against an incredibly low figure on the American side of 8 killed and 35 wounded. First Battalion had set an example of aggressiveness and skill of the kind Stilwell had hoped for. "Thank God," said the American liaison officer with the Chinese 113th, "you moved right in on the road. I'd been afraid you might just stay up on the heights and 'interdict traffic' with mortar fire." North of the block the battalion had put in on the road Japanese defenses were reported completely crumbled. While most of those manning the defenses were to escape down a bypass trail west of the block, the Chinese from the Jambu Bum were able the next day to sweep south down the road through Shaduzup and meet those who had relieved us.

That night we camped about a mile up the Chengun, next to a Seagrave medical unit, which had come down with the Chinese 113th. (Colonel Gordon S. Seagrave, the "Burma surgeon," had kept Stilwell's Chinese armies provided with hospital facilities and care ever since 1942.) The artillery exchanges in the valley on the other side of the ridge were now in another war as far as we were concerned and we gave ourselves up to what Phil called the pure, 100-proof delight of being alive. Over our small fires we delayed the moment of turning in, savoring the prospect of a night's sleep, the relief from fear, a warm meal. There is a peace of soul that comes from sharing an intense emotion with those around you, and what was in our hearts was in every case the same. We had come through it!

Phil, to whom more than to any of us the past forty hours must have seemed an eternity, wrapped himself in his Japanese blanket, gave thanks to God, and to the image of his wife, which was as real to him as it had been two nights before, said, "I told you we'd make it!"

Because our next move would be to rejoin the rest of the regiment over in the east, we had to reascend the Chengun, with all its arduous and treacherous passages. Going up must have been scarcely less hard than coming down; three of our horses collapsed from exhaustion and had to be shot. But all the way back to the trail from which we had turned off a week before into the forest there was little room in our minds for any feeling but relief. I should have been worrying about our long-range radio, which had gone out of commission, or at least have felt contrite when Colonel Osborne, concerned over being out of touch with the command, took a horse and rode to Shaduzup down the trail we had found blocked by the Japanese the week before. But that day, while we were lying up alongside the trail waiting for Osborne to return, my happiness was greater than ever. I had real coffee to brew in my canteen cup—the fruit of barter with the American liaison team, or perhaps of their charity. I had a shelter; Bill Bright and I had snapped our ponchos together to give us a canopy 10 feet by 6 in the form of a lean-to deserving its name of Poncho Villa. There we took our ease, receiving emissaries from the platoon, and bestirring ourselves only to fetch more dried bamboo for the fire. True, we were camped on a ridge with no stream nearby, but since it was raining copiously we were well supplied with drinking water by the runoff of the villa, which we collected in a helmet. We were even dry, more or less, thanks to the fire. And to top it all, it was believed—we believed, that is to say—that our fighting was finished for the season. The Allied advance, it was said, had already carried as far as had been planned for the current dry season—which was true; Stilwell had expected only to reach the Jambu Bum before the Hukawng became a quagmire. It was further said that, subject to our proving to be successful, the theater expected to re-form and expand the 5307th into a division for next season's campaign—which also was true. Finally, as everyone knew, it would not be long before all activity would willy-nilly be brought to an end by the Rains—as distinguished from the present inclemency, which was rain with a small "r."

That was the day I learned what happiness is. Happiness is what comes after unhappiness.

"Here's to William the Conqueror," said Bill, raising his canteen cup, "from William the Living!"

We even sang a little:

> *No-oh cares have I to grie-eeve me,*
> *No pretty little girl to decei-eeve me,*
> *I'm happy as a king, belie-eeve me . . .*

Then Colonel Osborne returned with the news. The Japanese had invaded India with three divisions. While the offensive had been foreseen by the British, it had never been expected to have

187

such power and momentum. The main Japanese force had surrounded a British corps in Imphal and one division had cut through to Kohima, where only a small British garrison stood between it and the Brahmaputra valley, which was the sole avenue of communication with Assam, from whence all the supplies for the 5307th and all those for China were flown. About the same time that Osborne got back—our long-range set having meanwhile been repaired—we received a message from Merrill's headquarters saying that our other two battalions had run into a Japanese offensive aimed at out-Marauding the Marauders and flanking the Chinese advance. Our assistance was needed as fast as we could bring it.

By the scale of these developments, the other news that Osborne brought, that General Wingate, after moving five brigades deep into central Burma—four by air and the fifth by foot from Ledo through almost impossible country—had been killed in a plane crash (at a singularly inopportune time, as it happened) seemed only incidental; he was hardly known to us as a man. It did nothing to restore to us, however, the sense of participating in an enterprise proof against ill-chance.

VII Three weeks earlier, and half an hour after we had pulled out of Shikau Ga on the trail to Shaduzup, the other two battalions also set forth, but they had been marching southward for several days by their more easterly route before they learned where exactly their attack on the Kamaing Road was to be made. There was, in fact, a two-day layover while orders from General Stilwell were awaited, which made it possible to bring in Painless Parker (Lieutenant James Parker, the dental officer) in a Piper Cub to fill cavities. The site picked for the attack was Inkangatawng, a village eight miles south of 1st Battalion's objective and similarly located at a place where the road was only a few hundred yards distant from the Mogaung River.

There was little about the 80-odd miles' march to Inkangatawng to suggest that the clouds were gathering around the 5307th—except literal clouds; the increasing frequency of downpours attested to that. No Japanese at all were encountered until almost the last moment. That said a good deal in support of Merrill and Hunter's preference—overruled by Stilwell— for a wide swing-around on the part of the three battalions together as contrasted with the close-in envelopment that 1st Battalion found so hard to execute. The march was completed in 11 days, the 2nd and 3rd Battalions reaching the road four days ahead of 1st Battalion. Reading about it, you have the impression of a *National Geographic* travelogue, although those who had to keep up the pace under the weight of their packs, sick or not, while the soles of their feet wore away from the abrasive action of the sand filtering into their shoes from continual river crossings may have had a different one.

For half the distance to Inkangatawng the route lay along the Tanai River, which here had cut a deep cleft through the jumbled hills. Midway in this stretch, at the town of Naubum, the Marauders acquired an auxiliary force of 300 Kachin guerrilla fighters. This force had been organized by another of the OSS officers, Captain Curl, a red-bearded Texan, and it specialized in ambushes, information-gathering, and rescuing downed Allied flyers. A week later and many miles to the south the Marauders were to be enlightened with an example of their unlikely methods in one of these departments when the Kachins led in a Lieutenant MacFarland from an American fighter-bomber group. MacFarland had landed a liaison plane in a field in the neighborhood to pick up another aviator, Lieutenant Jenkins, who had parachuted out of a disabled fighter plane. Jenkins was nowhere to be found. MacFarland set to work preparing the field for a take-off but on starting back toward his plane found that a party of Japanese had closed in on it. He crawled away, and after four days of wandering in the jungle without food stumbled upon a party of Kachins. He fled, with the Kachins in pursuit, but saw he would soon be overtaken. He halted and was approached by one of the Kachins bearing a placard upon which he was dumfounded to read: "Lt. Jenkins and Lt. MacFarland follow this man." Jenkins had been picked up by a patrol of our 3rd Battalion the day before. Curl's Kachin force kept the area patrolled and ambushed for miles around Naubum.

With Captain Curl at Naubum was an Irish Catholic missionary who had been living among the Kachins for over seven years. Father James Stuart was one of those vital individuals whose force of personality makes them stand out in almost any company. He had a genial face but one full of character, with

190

a prominent, pointed nose and a chin also prominent and pointed and with a dark cast even when he had recently shaved.

Father Stuart had remained behind in northern Burma after the general exodus in 1942 to look after his Kachins. The Kachins badly needed looking after, for the Chinese had cleaned them out utterly during their retreat. Major Jones in his diary of the 5307th tells of Father Stuart's first encounter with the Japanese: Alone with an assemblage of Kachin refugees at Sumprabum, which is almost as far north as you can retreat in Burma, he decided his best course would be to walk down the trail to meet the advancing Japanese. "About four miles south of Sumprabum, he ran upon an officer sitting on a horse in the middle of the trail. . . . Father Stuart said, 'Chinese?' The officer on the horse spat out of the side of his mouth and barked 'No! Japanese!' Then the Jap officer looked squarely at Father Stuart and said harshly, 'English?' Father Stuart, without batting an eye, spat out of the side of his mouth and snapped, 'No! Irish.' The Jap major smiled wryly." Father Stuart was left undisturbed with his refugees. If it was because of Ireland's neutrality that the Japanese left Father Stuart at liberty, they made a mistake. He gave OSS a great deal of help in the organization of the Kachins in the area.

Father Stuart became more or less attached to our regimental headquarters. While clad in ordinary khakis, he sported an Aussie hat with pheasant plumes stuck out of it and made a striking as well as popular addition to the force, the picturesqueness of which was further enhanced at this stage by the acquisition of some elephants. These had been taken by Captain Curl's force from the Japanese, who had originally taken them from the Kachins. The elephants were exceedingly useful in helping to clear a drop field fast, as well, of course, as in the routine business of hauling equipment. They and the mules had, however, to be kept segregated, for each evidently entertained the wholly understandable conviction that no such creature as the other could exist and when brought together they stampeded.

After leaving the Tanai and climbing almost vertically into

191

the hills, the column entered Janpan, which was the first Kachin town any of us had seen in which the inhabitants were leading more or less normal lives. All the conventions associated with such encounters were honored. On the American side, a clinic was set up and treatment dispensed to the ailing, while the indigenes for their part put on a festival and dance. Gongs were struck, a buffalo was gutted and spitted, and long lines of men and women in barbaric costume shuffled rhythmically and allegorically to the music of a kind of recorder, accompanied by the inevitable elderly dignitary in incongruous finery —in this case a blue Chinese mandarin robe. General Merrill was presented with a freshly slaughtered goat and rice wine and in turn, adhering faithfully to the script, dispensed imitation jewelry lugged over many a wearisome mile for just such a purpose. American, Jingpaw . . . good friend!

The main force pressed on through Janpan without delay. It wound along the crest of the ridge while the clouds lay in the valleys below. It marched on southward over steep mountain trails through forest and occasional villages of a few bashas and exotic names none expected ever to remember and by the week's end was ever going to forget: Hsamsingyang, Nhpum Ga, Kauri, Auche. From Stilwell came a message to Merrill: "Japs withdrawing down road. Jambu Bum fell today. Come fast now, Stonewall." At Auche the column turned off the main trail to descend the Nampama River. The object was the same as that which led 1st Battalion down the Chengun—to escape detection. In this case the column did not have to wade the river. It only had to cross it fifty times in the space of eight miles. Leaving the Nampama where it debouched into the valley of the Mogaung, the column made a U turn and headed toward Inkangatawng, 18 or 20 miles back up the valley. It was now in a vulnerable position. To the left of its route of march —that is, to the south and west—was a level plain across which the Japanese could move in force and with rapidity, even using motor transport at this time of year. Half of 3rd Battalion was required to block trails on the exposed side. Nevertheless, the charmed character of the expedition continued nearly to the end. Patrols scouting ahead of the column almost reached Inkangatawng before running into any enemy.

One contact was of course enough to stir up all the Japanese in the area. However, 2nd Battalion under Colonel McGee was able to ford the Mogaung and in the face of growing resistance to reach a point 300 yards from the Kamaing Road and dig in. This, as it turned out, was as far as the attack was to carry. Patrols sent out to envelop Inkangatawng, a quarter of a mile to the south, found it too heavily fortified for them to handle.

Apart from that ominous circumstance, the appearances were that this was to be a typical 5307th operation. There was the swift approach march taking the enemy by surprise, the hasty digging in, the repulse of ferocious counterattacks at heavy cost to the enemy, the hanging on under pounding by the enemy's guns, the respites between midmorning and midafternoon while fighter planes from India coursed the battlefield taking a heavy toll by strafing and dive-bombing.

Clinging to a roadblock in the face of a furious reaction was always nerve-racking and in this case was especially so in that the Marauders had little field of fire. Their perimeter fronted a jungle of kunai grass, taller than a man. That first morning it was only the lifting of the enemy's mortar barrage and the sound of shouting and of men rushing through the grass that warned them of what was to come—and then the attack was on them. All around the Japanese came running into view. At twenty paces the Marauders' line opened up. The effect was searing. The front ranks of Japanese went down and those behind were piled on top of them. . . .

During the day sixteen attacks of that kind were repelled. Only two of the charging enemy ever reached the perimeter. One was a lieutenant who kept on coming, crying *"Banzai!"* and waving his sword even when he had been almost cut in two by the 45-caliber slugs of a Tommy gun. He fell with his head on the edge of the Tommy gunner's foxhole, his sword severed. The other was a rifleman who got far enough to make

193

a lunge at a Marauder foxhole with his bayonet. The Marauder, unable to bring his own weapon up in time, seized the bayonet at the base and, holding on tight, scrambled out of his hole. The two struggled over the weapon until with a sudden lurch the Japanese let go and made a break for his own lines. A BAR man who had been trying to find an opening dropped him within a few paces.

While attacks like that were expected, the situation unfortunately had two novel features. For one, the general advance down the valley that the two battalions were supposed to be spearheading had failed to materialize. First Battalion had yet to reach its objective on the Kamaing Road and the Chinese in the north were making little progress; it seems to have been one of those times when Chiang Kai-shek was putting the brakes on his generals in Burma behind Stilwell's back. There was no spear behind the spearhead. For another thing, as a captured map revealed, two Japanese battalions were coming up from the south to protect General Tanaka's right flank and, being able to move and bring up artillery by truck, could well cut off the American force.

The bad news reached Colonel McGee at a time when his battalion was running low on ammunition and could tell from the sound of motors that trucks were already bringing up reinforcements for the Japanese who were nearly surrounding him. Having so far managed to confine his own losses to 2 killed and 12 wounded compared with known Japanese dead of over 200, McGee ordered his battalion back across the Mogaung. It was the beginning of what was to become a desperate retreat.

Further information on what the Japanese were up to was coming in. Stilwell's headquarters had learned that a Japanese reinforced battalion was preparing to move north along the Tanai River to outflank the Chinese above Shaduzup just as the 5307th's 1st Battalion was preparing to outflank the Japanese below it. General Merrill's orders were to block the Japanese advance, giving no ground beyond Nhpum Ga. As *The U.S. Army in World War II* was to point out, "This use of the

5307th in a static defensive role was a radical change in the concept of its employment."

The change certainly signified a trimming back of Stilwell's hopes, but the two battalions had a long way to go before they could even take up a defense. At all costs they had to beat the advancing Japanese to the trail running north from Auche to Nhpum Ga. By seven o'clock in the morning 2nd Battalion and half of 3rd, which had bivouacked overnight beside the Mogaung across from Inkangatawng, were on the march. All that day—the 25th of March—the now rapidly tiring column plodded southward through deep mud in a downpour so heavy that holes had to be cut in the litters on which the wounded were being carried to prevent their filling with water. In the afternoon it reached a village from which the most seriously wounded were able to be evacuated, but in the end the weather grew so bad that the liaison planes had all they could do to get off the ground without any load.

By that time an historic action—as every member of the 5307th was to regard it—had been under way for several hours on the trails leading northward from the Japanese base at Kamaing. There were two of these trails. They diverged just above Kamaing, one going through the village of Poakum and the other through the village of Tatbum, and converged again about two miles before entering Auche, the village from which the Marauders had left the main trail down from the north to descend the Nampama River and which they were now striving to regain. Lieutenant Logan E. Weston's I and R platoon had been detached to block the trail from Poakum and a rifle platoon under Lieutenant Warren R. Smith to block the trail from Tatbum. These two platoons, with a combined strength of 90 men, had to face 850 Japanese advancing in two bodies, one on each trail, and delay them for two days—long enough for the rest of the two battalions, pushing forward with all the energy they could summon, to clear through the trail junction below Auche. The technique they employed was that of successive ambushes.

Some part of the picture may be glimpsed in the two officers' terse report:

1410 hours, 25 March: Estimate 30 Nips hit Lt. Weston's ambush on the Poakum trail. Twelve Nips killed and one knee mortar [grenade-launcher] knocked out. Five of our animals wounded by mortar fire. . . .

1020 hours, 26 March: A reinforced platoon of Japs hit Poakum trail ambush and were completely surprised. Known dead —28. One knee mortar knocked out, one mule loaded with pack artillery killed. A dog with lead scouts of Japs pointed to one of our [machine gun] positions. . . .

1025 hours, 26 March: Approximately 100 Japs were completely surprised at the Tatbum ambush. Known killed—18. One knee mortar knocked out. . . .[1]

By the morning of the 27th the two platoons had held the Japanese up long enough for the main body to have passed the trail juncture. It was then, however, that Lieutenant Smith, holding a position only 100 yards below the juncture, had his worst time. With one of his blocks attacked by a patrol of perhaps double its strength, he fought a two-hour battle. Then, after getting all but five of his men withdrawn, he found that a 50-yard open stretch they had to cross had come under enemy fire. Smith, with great courage, maneuvered around to the side and by spraying the Japanese with his Tommy gun held them down while his men got away. He finally worked his own way back to the platoon by dashing from one position to another, firing from each and keeping the enemy confused.

The two platoons now joined forces, but by midafternoon the Japanese were not only ready to move frontally in force against the enormously outnumbered Americans but were about to get a company in behind them. Accordingly, the two platoons started pulling back up the trail to Auche. They retreated in successive bounds, one holding while the other withdrew through it and set up a position in the rear. These tactics bought the main force indispensable time. By the evening of the 27th the 2nd Battalion had set up a perimeter at Auche and the 3rd was strung out on the trail to Nhpum Ga. Weston and Smith's platoons had not only held up a battalion of Japanese for two days and killed over sixty of them but they had done so—almost incredibly—without suffering a single casualty themselves.

The day that followed was in some ways the worst in the 5307th's history. What made it so particularly was that the 5307th—all three battalions, just about to a man—was beginning to wear out.

The physical exhaustion resulting from seven weeks of marching through mountains, mud and water, from insufficient food, and from disease probably made us more susceptible to the nervous strain of being always in the enemy's territory— which was by far the worst part of it. Not to know from one instant to the next, week after week, when the silence would explode around you created a suspense difficult to describe. It ironed out all individual differences, and everyone in that heterogeneous organization looked alike. All faces—uniform in their emaciation to begin with—wore habitually the same expression of furtive intentness, sharp with the effort to exercise a sixth sense. Every time a twig crunched under foot it jarred your nerves because of the way it echoed inside your helmet; the echo made it sound as if it came from off to the side, from where an ambush would be. Maybe some kinds of danger are stimulating and ennobling, but if so, this was not one of them. You felt it as sordid, debasing, a steady contamination. It was corrosive, like an acid eating at the heart and nerves. Every minute was an enemy to be outlived; the hours were days and the weeks lifetimes. Worst of all, perhaps, was the way you came to see yourself, as a prey of apprehension, much as if you were pursued by guilt, and this further sapped your resistance to that which you feared.

In the five days before its arrival back in Auche, 2nd Battalion had marched 70 miles and made over 100 river crossings. During one of those days it had fought off continual attacks at point-blank range. It was soaking wet on its departure from Auche and it was still wet on its return. It was separated by at least five days' marching time from the safety of Chinese-held territory in the north, while the enemy, fresh and—for all that was known to the contrary—able to replenish its strength at will, was pouring northward at its heels.

Aware as it was of the numbers and proximity of the enemy, 2nd Battalion was surprised when the night it spent at Auche passed quietly. By 6:30 in the morning, when the battalion started moving out, there had still been no contact with the Japanese and the spirits that had been flagging the day before began to revive.

The battalion headquarters group was just leaving the village when the Japanese artillery started zeroing in. The first rounds were wide, but the fire moved in closer with every burst and was soon squarely on the target. A Marauder in the middle of the column received a direct hit and was blown to bits.

The outlook was bad. The trail from Auche to Nhpum Ga was four and a half miles long and followed the crest of a steep ridge; there was no way to move other than on the exposed trail, and though no Japanese were seen, the accuracy of the fire as the shelling searched up and down the column indicated that observers were controlling it. The trail was all up hill or down; in places it was nearly as steep as the declivity on both sides of it. Also it was slippery. Whenever it rained—and it had been raining hard—the soil of those hills turned into mud of the exact consistency of butter. While the shells whistled in and the jarring, nerve-shattering explosions cracked at front and rear and the wounded cried, men and mules slipped and fell and the morale of the marchers began to go. Panic, the obsessive, uncontrollable urge to get the hell out that extinguishes every other consideration, threatened to wreak more havoc than the shelling itself.

"Move faster!" The call was passed up the line to men who were already exerting their last strength to force a shambling trot. "Faster!" Some men threw away their equipment. The shells whinnied overhead and blasted the trail, there were more screams and moans from the injured, and over it all, bringing home to the fleeing column its complete powerlessness, as palpable as the steamy air for which the lungs labored, was the imagined, vast, demoniac exultation of the enemy. Yet the majority held fast. Men stopped and improvised litters for the maimed and struggled forward under the almost impossible loads. Medical corpsmen, answering calls for help, gritted their teeth and threaded their way back down the half-running column to bind up wounds and mount the casualties on horses. Muleteers whose animals slipped and fell and slithered down the accursed inclines dropped to their knees beside them and wiping the sweat from their eyes undid the buckles, got the packs off, fought the mules to a standstill, heaved the saddles back on, and laboriously reloaded.

By 10:30 that morning the bulk of the battalion had made it to Nhpum Ga. Some whose nerves had snapped were screaming at every shellburst. A big, burly Tommy gunner stumbled into the aid station Major Rogoff had set up by the largest of the four or five bashas in the village, shaking violently, tears streaming down his face. "Major, I'm not afraid, damn it!" he cried. "I tell you, I'm not afraid. I just can't help shaking." Men staggered up the last hill too exhausted to speak. One dropped in his tracks, out cold. The rest turned to and with the knowledge that there was no time to lose commenced to prepare a perimeter along the lines marked out by Colonel McGee and his senior officers against the onslaught they knew could not be long delayed.

The Japanese were, in fact, coming up fast. Shortly after noon, behind their continuing artillery barrage, they struck in overwhelming numbers against the Marauders' rear guard at Kauri, a mile south of Nhpum Ga. By four o'clock the rear guard had got out under cover of its automatic weapons and rejoined the battalion and the Japanese had commenced the shelling of Nhpum Ga and launched the first of their infantry attacks on its defenses. The siege of Nhpum Ga had begun.

Nhpum Ga, where for eleven days 2nd Battalion was to endure continual attack behind a perimeter 400 yards long and from 100 to 250 wide, sat in a saddle of high ground at an elevation of 2,800 feet. It commanded the trail to the north and watersheds to east and west that led on both sides to rivers paralleling the trail. From Nhpum Ga the trail to the north descended to a flat valley communicating with the Tanai, the easterly of the two rivers. This valley was the site of Hsamsingyang, where Colonel Hunter's command post and 3rd Battalion were located. As long as the Americans held Hsamsingyang, with its airstrip, the Japanese could be prevented from moving north to outflank the Chinese either by the ridge-crest trail or the low river routes on either side of it.

Efforts were made to maintain communications between the widely separated battalions by running two patrols a day from 3rd Battalion at Hsamsingyang up to the 2nd at Nhpum Ga, but on the third day after a sharp fight in which several Marauders were killed and twelve wounded, control of the trail was lost to the Japanese, who had bypassed Nhpum Ga, via the Tanai, and 2nd Battalion was cut off. That same day General Merrill suffered a heart attack and was incapacitated. The news of 2nd Battalions plight was kept from him. Although he refused to be evacuated as long as there were any wounded left —and there were many—Colonel Hunter was now in effect in command.

During the first few days of that pitiless struggle, while the dazed and exhausted Americans recovered some of their strength and got a grip on things, the initiative clearly lay with the Japanese. The 3rd Battalion had all it could do to keep them from extending their gains on the trail from Nhpum Ga and to patrol the other trails around Hsamsingyang and deal with the groups of the enemy trying to open a route of advance to the north. In Nhpum Ga virtually everyone but the overworked medics—headquarters personnel, radio operators, photographers—was pressed into service on the perimeter. The Japanese were attacking successively or in co-ordinated thrusts from every quarter, although it was their artillery and mortars that were doing the most damage. As at Shaduzup, they had both high-trajectory howitzers and 77-millimeter mountain guns that slammed their fire in with only a quick, demented shriek between the report of the gun and the explosion of the shell. One of these had a frightful effectiveness, morally even more than physically. It came close to shooting the top off of a hill behind which 2nd Battalion had its best mortar position; the mortars had to be moved.

Within hours of cutting the trail to Hsamsingyang the Japanese also captured the water hole the 2nd Battalion had been depending on; the hole lay too far out to be held. The defenders were then reduced to the muddy, nearly stagnant water that filtered into some holes they dug in a patch of swampy ground. This water, of which the ration was half a canteen cup a day, was so foul that even men desperate with thirst could scarcely get it down, for 25 feet up the drainage basin lay the remains of a number of horses and mules. Within a few days 75 animals had been killed by machine-gun, artillery and mortar fire and were rotting in the perimeter, and in time the number rose to 112. The stench from these carcasses, from the inadequately buried excrement of the men, and from the decomposing bodies of the Japanese killed in attacks all around the perimeter, which amounted to perhaps 200 before it was over, would have been utterly unbearable had there been any alternative to bearing it. The Japanese could not recover the bodies of their dead and the Americans could not bury the slaughtered horses and mules— for one reason because they lacked the strength to dig deep enough holes in the hard ground of the hilltop and for another because every time a shovel struck the gravelly soil it brought a sniper's bullet, a burst from a Nambu, or a mortar shell down on it.

The two forces were at close quarters. One night a groggy, mumbling Japanese wandered into the American perimeter apparently looking for his foxhole, much like a roomer in a strange hotel trying to find the bathroom down the hall. A Marauder, mumbling reassuringly to cover his own movements, got his rifle to his shoulder and shot him through the head. The episode explains how it was possible for an American lieutenant, Brendan Lynch, in similar circumstances to be shot dead by a member of his own platoon when returning from a reconnaissance.

The rain which had kept the battalion soaked on the march to Inkangatawng and back now held up. There were only a few showers to supplement the seepage into the potholes. The doctors had no water for plaster casts and sulfadiazine had to be taken dry. The consequences of the shortage became so serious that Colonel McGee had to request an emergency airdrop of water. Base complied, and 500 gallons in heavy plastic bags were parachuted in. The first bag recovered was rushed to the aid station and the wounded were allowed to drink their fill. Those hurt badly enough to be incapacitated numbered 25 by this time, in addition to whom 7 had been killed. Trenches to shelter the wounded had been prepared at the start, Major Rogoff having had the perspicacity to set the psychoneurotics to digging as soon as they had reported in after the flight from Auche. The work had its therapeutic as well as concrete results. Six of those who had suffered breakdowns were able to return to the line and only two had had to be sent down for evacuation. One, who confidentially reported having espied a large plane landing nearby, was completely out of his head.

Only the fact that 2nd Battalion was able to take supply drops made its position tenable. It was not easy for the planes to run the gamut of small-arms fire, however, and some of the food and ammunition was lost to the Japanese. Much of the time planes could not fly owing to the overcast of the gathering rainy monsoon. When they could, fighters came in to strafe and bomb the Japanese positions on the hill.

The water drop and the appearance of American planes did a great deal for morale, and so did two other events which occurred at the same time, although the expectations aroused by these latter were to be disappointed. One was a message to McGee on April 1 from Colonel Hunter, who had just got word of 1st Battalion's successful action on the road. "Nips running like hell from Shaduzup," it read. "Too many dead to be counted." It was thought by Hunter and others that with the reverse they had suffered across the hills on the Mogaung the Japanese would abandon the attempt to outflank the Chinese and the force beleaguering Nhpum Ga would make for the rear. Nothing of the sort took place.

The other event was an upshot of General Merrill's evacuation. His first act on arriving at Ledo had been to ask that two pack howitzers be flown into Hsamsingyang. Even before the pieces arrived two crews had been formed of volunteers formerly with a pack artillery outfit in New Guinea—one of the volunteers being "Little Chief" Ross, a Cherokee from North Carolina—under Sergeant John A. Acker. They had been drilled in dry runs and were in a fever of anticipation. On the morning of April 2 the guns were dropped in sections over the field at Hsamsingyang, each section under two parachutes. The drop could be seen by the exultant men on the hill at Nhpum Ga. At 11:30, two hours after the first section tumbled out of the plane, the first round went winging audibly over their heads. It soared 800 yards over the Japanese line, halfway to Kauri. But within an hour both pieces had registered on the Japanese positions fronting the Marauders on the hill.

Thoroughly aware as they were of the effect the enemy's artillery was having on them, they expected the enemy's hold on the hill to be relaxed once the howitzers had made their presence felt. They failed to draw the inference that if they could hold on under shelling so could the Japanese. The two howitzers proved to be an enormous boon, but when they turned to counterbattery fire that seemed indecisive to the men on the hill morale sagged again.

Another blow at morale, but one soon remedied, was struck by a rumor that the battalion had been ordered to withdraw. Undoubtedly most of the men could have made their way out in small parties. A patrol from 3rd Battalion which had been caught at Nhpum Ga when the Japanese cut the trail managed to get back to Hsamsingyang by descending a steep ravine in two separate groups, but the escape route was passable only by unencumbered men. Had the battalion attempted to follow them, all the wounded as well as the animals and heavy equipment would have had to be abandoned. Colonel McGee made it plain that nothing of the kind was in prospect. Surrounded as it was on an unheard-of hill in the midst of a remote wilderness into which the mighty antagonists of the war had been hard put to it to advance less than 2,000 men each, the 2nd Battalion of the 5307th was nonetheless fulfilling its mission, which was to block a Japanese force taking part in a general offensive against India, and there the battalion was going to remain come what might.

The prospect from day to day was only for more attacks, more shelling, more casualties, more sickness, more thirst. The 3rd Battalion had managed to wrest the initiative away from the enemy but was making slight headway in its efforts to push back up the trail. The Americans on the hill had little to give them confidence but the knowledge that they were holding their ground and giving back as good as they got, or better. For the most dramatic of the blows they succeeded in striking primary credit was due to Roy Matsumoto, the Japanese-American sergeant who had intercepted traffic on the 18th Division's telephone line at Walawbum.

Whenever the sound of the Japanese talking and shouting gave warning of an attack, Matsumoto and his fellow Nisei would be moved to the adjacent sector of the perimeter where they could hear what was said and perhaps give some idea of what was coming. In addition, Matsumoto would crawl out in front of the perimeter at night, close to the Japanese positions, to overhear their conversations. From one of these risky expeditions he returned to report that the enemy planned an attack the next morning on the forward slope of a hill which the American perimeter had been extended to include to prevent the Japanese from having the advantage of the defilade it offered. To meet the imminent attack, Lieutenant Edward Mc-Logan, whose platoon held the salient, decided to pull his men back to a less-vulnerable position and one from which greater damage could be done. After booby-trapping their foxholes, the Americans withdrew to the top of the rise and placed their automatic weapons to command the slope—and waited.

At dawn cries of *"Banzai!"* and "Death to the Americans!" broke from the woods down the slope, followed by a barrage of hand grenades arching onto the area the Marauders had evacuated. Immediately afterward 50 or 60 men in khaki uniforms with wrap leggings and pot helmets charged into view. They dashed upon the empty positions, bayoneting the foxholes, firing wildly, and throwing more grenades at the recent gun emplacements. Startled but not long delayed by the absence of opposition, they rushed on up the hill behind a sword-waving officer. The Americans let them come on to within 15 yards before opening up. The simultaneous discharge of 40-odd weapons at that range was devastating. The Japanese went down as if blasted from heaven. A secondary wave that had swept forward in support of the first hit the ground and dove for the booby-trapped foxholes. Then Matsumoto worked his masterpiece. "Charge! Charge!" he screamed. And they scrambled to their feet and charged—into the machine guns, into the Browning automatics at the crest of the ridge. When the action was over, 54 Japanese bodies, including those of two officers, were counted on the slope.

All of us, I suppose, when we are moved to reflect upon what human beings are capable of, find that certain images come to mind as illustrations of surpassing achievement. One that will always leap to mine is a composite recollection of Nhpum Ga, and of no part of it more than the heroism, moral as well as physical, of those Nisei, Matsumoto, of 2nd Battalion, and in the 3rd, Edward Mitsukado and Grant J. Hirabayashi, decorated for—among other services—their persistent volunteering to go forward to intercept the commands of the enemy when the lead units were engaged by trailblocks. What was unspeakably hard for the others can only have been harder still for them. Some had close relatives living in Japan, all had acquaintances if not relatives held in concentration camps in the United States on the grounds that persons of Japanese descent and feature must be presumed disloyal. To help justify the unhappiness we were enduring most of us could tell ourselves that the survival of our people and of the country our forefathers had fought and died for was worthy of a sacrifice; for them there was only the value of an idea. Most of the citizens of the nation for which they were fighting the country of their origin would have considered them enemy aliens, as they well knew. What were their thoughts in the solitude of soul that jungle warfare enforces? I have no way of knowing. But in the case of Sergeant Roy A. Matsumoto, whose mother was living in Japan, we may perhaps justifiably surmise that he took some comfort from the reflection that she was not in one of the major cities but in a smaller one less likely to attract attack by American bombers—Hiroshima.

Further reports now came in to Hunter's headquarters of strong Japanese forces moving north along the Tanai which, if they outflanked him, could create a desperate situation. While 1st Battalion had received orders to rejoin the unit, we were still unaware of the urgency with which help was needed; a message informing us of it had been held up by a failure of communications and we did not receive it until April 3. It would be four or five days before we could be expected to arrive. John B. George with two companions had been sent to Pabum, some 50 miles to the north, to ask the support of a battalion of the Chinese 38th Division which was located there under orders to move south, but they found it could not be expected to arrive until after the 5307th's other battalion.

There was an ominous atmosphere at Hsamsingyang. John, before he took off for Pabum, had confided his anxiety to Colonel Hunter. "Aren't you worried for fear we'll be trapped by the Japs coming up on the east?" he asked. "Don't you ever get scared?" Hunter, who was to include in his later report on the lessons of the campaign the principle that an officer should keep his fears in his foxhole, contemplated the 3rd Battalion S-2 impassively. "Wait," he said, "till you've had twins."

At a staff meeting he called on April 3, Hunter analyzed the situation in straightforward terms. After completing the analysis, he said, "Gentlemen, in the morning we start an attack that will drive through to the 2nd Battalion. It may take two or three days, but we *will* get through." All troops except the sick and the mule-handlers, he stated, would be withdrawn from Hsamsingyang and all large patrols be called in and replaced as far as possible by Kachins. The battalion would move down the trail to within 400 yards of the Japanese, then while one combat team pushed forward on the trail the other would turn off down the mountain and attack the Japanese on their flank. The two howitzers would be moved up to where they could fire at point-blank range on the Japanese bunkers and pillboxes; volunteers among the gunners had been called for and every one of them had come forward.

"Ruses, feints, and anything else you can do to fool the Japs are in order. A fake message will be dropped from a plane so as to fall in the Jap lines. This message will be to the 2nd Battalion and will say that a battalion of parachutists will be dropped between Kauri and Auche at 1700 hours tomorrow. If possible, we will have a dummy drop in that area to fool them."

The attack got under way the following afternoon after Mustang fighters had bombed and strafed the Japanese positions on the trail only 150 yards ahead. Shortly before 4:00 P.M., the battalion command net on the SCR 300's went into operation. The exchanges give an idea of how the unfolding action seemed to the participants:

Colonel Beach, commanding 3rd Battalion, to Major Lew, commanding the combat team on the trail: "The fatboys [the two howitzers] will open at 1600, your mortars at 1605 and the jump-off your decision."

Major Lew to Colonel Beach: "The fatboys are raising hell with the pillboxes on the right slope of the hill. A direct hit on one. Japs ran from another. Have the fatboys hit that machine gun firing 200 yards to the west of their present target, then swing their barrage up the slope of the hill. We are preparing to push off."

Major Lew to Captain Clarence O. Burch, commanding the company making the assault: "Shove off, boy, and good luck!"

Captain Burch to Lieutenant Theodore T. Chamelas, commanding the platoon on the right flank: "Shove off, Tom, and be sure to cover that little draw on your right with at least one squad."

Lieutenant Chamelas to Captain Burch: "Roger on that. The Japs are running from that pillbox to my front. Our snipers got one sure and we lobbed a 60-millimeter or two on them. Believe we got some more."

Captain Burch to Lieutenant Victor Weingartner, commanding the platoon on the left flank: "Did you hear my message to Tom? Same applies to you, Abie. Shove off and keep your eyes open for each other."

Lieutenant Weingartner to Captain Burch: "Roger. I understand you."

Captain Burch to Major Lew: "Have shoved off. Am now moving my command post forward with center platoon. No enemy firing yet."

Major Lew to Captain Burch: "Roger on that—and close in fast."

Major Edwin J. Briggs, commanding the combat team down the mountainside, to Colonel Beach: "Have Luke [Colonel George A. McGee, Jr., commanding 2nd Battalion at Nhpum Ga] fire three rounds of 60-millimeter 200 yards due west of his perimeter. I am close but can't locate him."

Colonel McGee to Colonel Beach: "I heard Boston [Major Briggs]. Will fire in three minutes. Japs are pressing us from the north. Ask the bombers to drop a few and strafe 400 yards north of Nhpum Ga on that little ridge."

Colonel Beach to Colonel McGee: "Roger on that."

Captain Burch to Lieutenant Chamelas: "The Japs are rolling hand grenades down on the squad near the trail. Can you throw some rifle grenades on them?"

Lieutenant Chamelas to Captain Burch: "We just threw three grenades on them. I don't believe these Japs are throwing them.

I'll tell Bill [squad leader] to watch out. We're almost to the crest of the hill so don't fire on us."

Captain Burch to Lieutenant Chamelas: "Roger, old boy."

Major Lew to Captain Burch: "Your left flank is too far down the hill. The Japs are moving out so move that flank up fast."

Captain Burch to Major Lew: "Roger on that."

Major Lew to Colonel Beach: "How about that mortar ammunition? We need some 81 badly."

Colonel Beach to Major Lew: "The supply train is passing my command post now. Will be with you in a minute."

Major Lew to Colonel Beach: "Roger on that. *Rogerrrr.*"

Lieutenant Chamelas to Captain Burch: "We're over the top of the ridge on the way down. Three pillboxes are blown to hell. Bloody Jap uniforms all over the place and one Nambu machine gun blown up. Looks as if the Japs are in strength on next hill. We're drawing inaccurate small-arms fire and a little knee-mortar. Put some fatboys on that hill for us, but be damn sure it's on the hill."

Colonel Beach to Lieutenant Chamelas: "Roger on those fatboys. Good work, fellow. Keep going."

Major Lew to Captain Burch: "Are you on the trail yet?"

Captain Burch to Major Lew: "We are 100 yards past the trail. There are no Japs on the east side of the trail. Japs have moved out of their positions. Will be at top of hill in five minutes."

Colonel Beach to Major Lew: "Have you moved anything up to occupy the ground you have taken?"

Major Lew to Colonel Beach: "I am moving a platoon up now. How about the ground we are leaving?"

Colonel Beach to Major Lew; "I'll occupy it with muleskinners."

Colonel Beach to Major Briggs: "Have you contacted Luke [Colonel McGee] yet?"

Major Briggs to Colonel Beach: "We've hit Jap perimeter. They have machine gun covering this area. Can't get at them with mortars. Am trying rifle grenades now. Looks like I may be held up here."

Colonel Beach to Major Briggs: "Tell Luke to put pressure on that spot. If necessary try farther south."

209

Major Briggs to Colonel Beach: "Roger on that. It's getting dark down here. We'll start digging in soon."

Lieutenant Chamelas to Captain Burch: "I am pinned down by heavy machine-gun fire from west side of hill. Artillery is hitting too high on hill to do any good. My flame-thrower is way round on my right flank trying to knock out that gun, but doubt if he can get close enough. Am going to pull up a little knoll ahead and dig in as it's almost dark."

Captain Burch to Lieutenant Chamelas: "Good work. We may be able to help you when we get our mortars set up. I see that machine gun. Roger on digging in."

Captain Burch to Major Lew: "I am held up by a position on the next hill, like the position we just took. Believe we'll have to have those fatboys in close again. It's almost dark, I am reorganizing and digging in."

Major Lew to Captain Burch: "Fine work. I am going up with the supply train now."

Captain Burch to Colonel Beach: "Have one and one [one killed and one wounded] that I know of."

Colonel Beach to Captain Burch: "Send him right back. We'll notify a plane to stand by."

Captain Burch to Colonel Beach: "[Major] Lew hit by Jap sniper. Suggest you come down at once. Our perimeter is set up and we're digging in." *

The attack by 3rd Battalion did a great deal for the morale of 2nd Battalion, which needed it. April 4 had not been a good day at Nhpum Ga. Said the report for the day:

Three wounded men died during the night and one man lay to the southeast just outside the perimeter with his entire frontal lobe exposed. The medics tried to get at him all night but the Japs threw up flares and opened fire whenever there was a sound in that vicinity. This morning we did get him out, but he died a few hours later.

There are only 70 usable animals left. The others are dead or wounded. We won't shoot the wounded because they stink when

___
* The foregoing transcript, which, remarkably enough, was made of the transmissions, is taken from the official diary of the 5307th, compiled by Major John Jones, with procedural talk omitted.

they're dead, and they may stop some of the lead from getting to the muleskinners' foxholes. One animal had 26 bullet holes in him where he got in the line of fire of a Jap machine gun.

Blood plasma is nearly out.

This morning we found that the Japs had grenaded one of our machine-gun positions at dawn and taken the machine gun. They were firing it at us for an hour this morning. We know because they don't use tracers and the gun they were firing had a lot of tracers in it. Our mortars concentrated on knocking it out and got a direct hit on the 14th round. It has not fired since. Some of the men on our southwest flank captured a Jap machine gun this morning and fired all the ammunition they had for it.

The Japs attacked this morning from the northwest without success. Again at 1700 hours they made a heavy rush attack on a part of the perimeter which had been manned by some muleskinners who had got out of their holes while things were quiet. The Japs broke through the perimeter in one place but were wiped out a few minutes later by a two-man assault force throwing hand grenades. The hole in the perimeter was plugged, but a chill swept through the battalion as the story got around about how close the Japs came to really getting in.

After April 4 there was April 5, and 6, and 7. Nothing diminished the will of the Japanese to hold fast where they were—the threat of a paratroop drop at their rear, the casualties they were suffering, the spectacle of a machine gunner hanging from the limb of a tree into which a 500-pound bomb had blown him. It is not possible to tell the story of 3rd Battalion's tortured struggle toward Nhpum Ga, of men groping through thickets of bamboo, making desperate dashes from a fallen tree to a concavity in the hillside, hugging the ground with throbbing veins, inching forward, nerves assaulted by the exultant, blasphemous, terrifying chatter of the automatic weapons and the stifling stillness of stagnant air as the jungle held its breath, by the moans of the wounded and the sight of friends transformed by death into impassive and appalling strangers, by the imminence in every instant of the sentence from which there is no appeal.

211

No doubt it is hard enough to endure what has to be endured in combat when your country is the battlefield, when your home is threatened, when you have witnessed the brutalities of the enemy against your own people, but it can only be harder still to have to endure it on the other side of the earth in a land as alien as a temple of weird gods, where your death, having no relevance to your own world that you can perceive, would seem as futile as it would be unbearable. Among the men who fought at Nhpum Ga there were some who could take no more. Cases were whispered about of youngsters who simply cowered in their foxholes, heads in their arms, when the Japanese charged and were bayoneted in the back. One can only hope it was not true. There was certainly one such case on the other side. Logan Weston, whose platoon bore a disproportionate share of the brunt of the advance, was rushing forward up the trail on the heels of an artillery barrage when he came upon a foxhole with a sack drawn over it. Beneath were two Japanese paralyzed and shaking with shock. In the heat of the action, and before he could think what he was doing, Weston shot them both with his carbine.

The Japanese, for safety's sake, had formed the habit of withdrawing from their positions at the outset of the barrage which our planes and guns leveled in on them in preparation for the infantry assault. They would wait farther up the trail or down the slope in the jungle for it to be over and then quickly reoccupy the positions. If the advance toward Nhpum Ga was to be pressed at less than prohibitive cost, this stratagem had to be defeated. On April 6 the Marauders took up positions on the very fringe of the impact area. The instant the barrage was lifted they rushed forward. The race for the foxholes was a dramatic and spectacular one—which the Americans won. That day several hundred yards were gained. Woomer the Boomer gave an added lift to spirits with the directions he sent back to a mortar crew on his voice radio after working his way up a hillside to within 25 yards of two Japanese machine-gun positions. With his first instructions he had succeeded in bringing the bursts down directly behind the enemy. "Deflection correct," he said. "Bring it in 25 yards, and if you don't hear from me, you'll know you came this way too far. Then shift it back just a little and you'll be right on it."

On the hilltop, there was not much cheer. "We have 100 wounded, 17 dead and 4 missing to date in Nhpum Ga," said the report. "The stink of the dead horses and men grows worse though it doesn't seem possible that it could get worse. Water was dropped again today and the planes seemed to draw unusually heavy ground fire. Four of the 28 aid men in the battalion have been wounded. Three men that were wounded and were sent back to the perimeter after having their wounds dressed here have been killed. Many of the wounded refuse to stay in the aid station and insist on returning to the perimeter where they know they are sorely needed."

On the morning of April 7, 3rd Battalion still had 500 yards of uphill ground ahead of it, and the few yards that were gained that day in bitter, close-in fighting at a cost of three killed and eight wounded had to be given up when the position was consolidated in the evening. The date, however, marked an important event. At five o'clock in the afternoon 1st Battalion arrived.

The previous afternoon, while awaiting a supply drop, we received a message saying that the other two battalions were in desperate need of support. We canceled the drop and at dark, with empty stomachs and light packs, moved out again and did not halt until after midnight. Night marches were always difficult and seldom justified except in extreme circumstances. Unless the moon was better than half full, the darkness of the trail was impenetrable, as if you were walking with your eyes closed. The guides had to grope their way, and in order to keep the column intact, the rest of us had to hang our compasses on the pack of the man or the mule in front and follow close enough to keep the feeble glow of the dial in view. Those without compasses substituted pieces of decaying, phosphorescent wood picked up from the ground. Bivouacking in total darkness, with lights prohibited, required adaptability, especially when it was raining too. As a PFC in the platoon remarked after being awakened at first light by a gusher from a mule towering above him from which he was protected by the fortuitous interposition of a log, "How's that for woodsmanship, Lieutenant? If I don't make corporal out of this campaign, I sure as hell ought to come out an Eagle Scout."

We had five days of marching to reach Hsamsingyang. The best we could do was five or six miles a day, for it was all up and down, and time and again the trail ahead would be pockmarked with Japanese bootprints and we would have to put out scouts or wait while a line of skirmishers combed a deserted village.

As we neared Hsamsingyang we began to realize what our arrival would mean. We were the relief force! There swam before us visions of cavalry troopers cut off at Dry Forks Gulch, Foreign Legionnaires besieged in the fort at Makum el-Aresh straining their eyes in the direction from which help must come, and for one of the few times since we had left the Ledo Road the business we were engaged in seemed slightly other than wholly dreary and abhorrent. Most of us carried large handkerchiefs cut from the rayon parachutes used for our supply drops, and where possible we tended to pick a color corresponding to our combat team. (The combat teams into which the battalion was divided were designated by colors, and four of the six were represented in the parachutes.) Now, all down the line, the cloths were broken out and tied around the neck as scarves, red in one half of the column, white in the other. The last stage of the march was over fairly level ground and we were able to pick up a little speed. No command was given, but as we wound out of the woods onto the fields of Hsamsingyang we stepped out smartly, as if a racing pace of three miles an hour were habitual with us. In our mud-and-blood-encrusted uniforms, our faces drained, we must have resembled the remnants of a Confederate force before Appomattox. A third of our number now had dysentery and were only dragging along. Still, we had had 30

214

miles of unrelenting mountains to cross, and now, by God, we were here!

Eight hundred men make a long line, and our column as it stretched the length of the field looked imposing even to us, which gave us an idea how it must have looked to those who watched it arrive, standing motionless where they had been arrested when the lead elements came into view. The morale of 3rd Battalion was much higher than we had expected to find it. The men were strained but keyed up and determined. Nothing better than present circumstances could be hoped for so long as the Japanese still clung to the trail, and their only thought was to beat them back—not that they were not glad to have help. It was a happy reunion. We brought reinforcements and they had food. A sergeant at the command post brought out ten packs of K-ration biscuits and told me I could eat my fill. I went at them with trembling hands. These were the biscuits that, we read in a press account that reached us in a batch of reading matter a couple of weeks later, tank crews in Italy managed actually to eat when in the last extremity of hunger.

It was decided that, while one of our combat teams would take over the defense of Hsamsingyang, as many men in the other as were still capable of exertion would be mustered and sent on a flanking move to the west around Nhpum Ga to hit the besieging force at its rear—in the style to which the 5307th was accustomed. About 250 were found fit for this exercise and at dawn the next day moved out under Tom Senff, who had recently succeeded to the command of the combat team. Such was the condition of the outfit by then, however, that before the morning was over five of the picked men had collapsed from exhaustion and had to be sent back along with another man seriously injured from a fall over a 20-foot embankment.

The main hope of a quick rescue of 2nd Battalion lay, it became apparent, in the success of this maneuver in causing the Japanese to fall back from the trail. As it was, the last steep slope and the dense growth of bamboo covering it continued to defeat the efforts of 3rd Battalion. Five agonizing assaults were

215

made upon it, each after heavy preliminary shelling, but none gained more than a few yards, and the platoons making the attack lost twenty men killed or wounded.

In the meantime, Captain Senff's force, fighting several scraps as it threaded its way through forest and occasional overgrown clearings, had by nightfall gone beyond Nhpum Ga. Bivouacking half a mile southwest of the battlefield, it found the stench of death even at that distance almost overpowering. The end, although there was no sign of it yet, was at hand.

The next day was Easter Sunday. It was a day of tense, sporadic fighting for Senff's combat team, but what counted for more than the number of enemy they killed was the fact that they were now in a position to cut the Japanese escape route to Kauri, and that the Japanese knew it. While Father Stuart said Mass beneath a homemade church flag beside the field at Hsamsingyang, the forward platoons of 3rd Battalion felt their way up the trail. By noon, encountering only sniper fire and finding "dead Japs everywhere," the lead scouts reported that they thought they were near 2nd Battalion's perimeter. On his voice radio, Colonel Beach asked Colonel McGee in Nhpum Ga to have three spaced shots fired from the north end of his perimeter. They sounded close by. A few minutes later the 3rd Battalion scouts with Major Briggs behind them walked into Nhpum Ga.

Colonel McGee held out his hand with a smile. "Sure am glad to see you, Ed," he said.

Back at Hsamsingyang we were waiting to rush up with litters as soon as we got the word. There were 103 wounded to be brought out. I went up with several others from the platoon to look over the route for a telephone line. One of our combat teams, together with 3rd Battalion, was to relieve the 2nd at Nhpum Ga and I had found to my delight that enough field wire had been dropped at Hsamsingyang to connect the two places.

The bamboo forest cloaking the last half-mile rise to Nhpum Ga resembled a wheat field over which a herd of cattle had stampeded. Where there were trees, a tornado seemed to have struck. The stripped remains still standing were macerated with bullet holes. All around dead Japanese were sprawled as if they had dropped haphazard from the sky, and along the trail were limbs and torsos thrust helter-skelter out of smashed-in bunkers. It was impossible not to have a sickening sense of what it must have been like for them, too, and not to wonder with what emotions an omnipotent deity would look down upon the scene.

Nearing the crest of the hill we passed a draw in which horses and mules had been picketed. So bloated were the carcasses that to our unbelieving eyes the vista was that of a field of giant melons.

The defenders looked at us out of red-rimmed eyes that were unnaturally round and dark, with death in them and also that incredulous light we could read from our own experience. *I am alive,* it meant.

"Lew, for Christ's sake!"

"Well, it's over now."

Tom Senff, taking a patrol along a trail near the perimeter, came to a trailblock the Japanese had just abandoned, leaving it strewn with dead. One of the corpses, spread-eagled face up, had a second right arm protruding from beneath at just about the juncture of the first. (A Japanese, if he could not take out the entire body of a fallen comrade for cremation would try to take an arm, so that some ashes of the deceased could be sent to Yasukuni.)

"Now there," said Dick Dolan, Tom's radio operator, "was a real handshaking son-of-a-bitch! I'll bet he made corporal the day they drafted him!"

With nerves as taut as they were, jokes that in other circumstances would seem pointless were unbearably funny to us; it seemed as if the universe must collapse in paroxysms of mirth.

Details were formed to tumble the corpses of the Japanese into foxholes and cover them over. A few of our own men had been killed so far out that Japanese fire made it impossible to reach them, and their bodies had to be buried where they lay. To get rid of the hordes of flies whose drone was that of an approaching air armada the carcasses of the animals were hosed with flame throwers. Later they were dowsed with chloride of lime, of which Colonel Hunter had ordered 500 pounds dropped to us, and eventually, at great labor, interred.

In time it was possible to reflect how extraordinary it was that many more men had not been killed. Throughout the campaign our battle fatalities ran far lower than had been expected when the organization was planned—and casualties from disease considerably higher. As the medical historian of the India-Burma Theater was to write: "For in the end, amoebas, bacteria, ricketsiae and viruses rather than Japanese soldiers and guns, vanquished the most aggressive, bravest and toughest outfit that fought in the Far East in the Second World War." [2] The actions between Inkangatawng and Hsamsingyang cost the 5307th 50 killed and 314 wounded. About 400 Japanese dead were counted around Nhpum Ga alone, and these did not include those their compatriots had buried.

General Stilwell had issued orders that no advance south of Nhpum Ga was to be attempted (and, as far as we were concerned, none was intended), but fighting on a small scale continued anyway. There were the inevitable patrol clashes; security depends upon keeping track of the enemy and that means sending out patrols. Above all others, Burma was the country of interminable patrolling. In the south the British soldiers used to quote an imagined military communiqué of the future: "Today the fifth anniversary of the end of World War II was celebrated. On the Arakan front, normal patrol activity continued."

The Mustang fighters came in whenever the skies were open to strafe the Japanese down the trail. Afterwards they would buzz the hill at Nhpum Ga. The idiots would make a bee-line for anyone who happened to be standing on the skyline, and a distinct sensation it was to have one of those things roaring straight in at you at just under 400 miles an hour with the muzzles of the six bore-sighted machine guns in its wings staring at you. If it was supposed to be a test of nerves, they made their point with me; I ducked.

Exchanges of mortar and artillery fire went on intermittently, too. One afternoon when I was walking down the trail from Nhpum Ga savoring the unheard-of luxury of being alone, Japanese shells started whanging overhead and bursting somewhere ahead of me. I deduced—wrongly—that the enemy was leveling in on Hsamsingyang for a counter-offensive, but what impressed the occasion on me almost as much as those forebodings was a fruit pigeon, leaf green but for a sharply defined raspberry patch on its underside, that kept rising from the trail ahead of me and settling down again around the next bend. In that forest where few birds were to be seen its presence seemed remarkable and in an inexplicable way connected with the hammer blows of the shellbursts up front. Sometimes there are occurrences in life that seem to hint at relationships—but what you do not know. Presently a whistling as of ducks flying by signified that our pack howitzers were replying, the Japanese guns fell silent, and the fruit pigeon disappeared.

Mostly we ate, bathed, and went unhurriedly through the day's routine. Ten-in-one rations were flown in to us, and these provided feasts and material for minute analysis and endless discussion. Complete new outfits of clothing were issued. We had our first delivery of mail in two months and could imagine the plight of our correspondents who did not know where we were, imagined the worst, wondered what possible interest the details of their tepid lives could have for us, but had to write something anyway. We were allowed to send two V-mail letters in reply in which we could say nothing of a military nature but that we were in Burma fighting beside the Chinese. That we had been granted these indulgences and a rest, as it was called, did not arouse our suspicions. We accepted them as our due. As we knew, we were waiting to be relieved by a regiment of the Chinese 38th Division. When it arrived, we would go into rainy-monsoon quarters somewhere to recuperate and reorganize for the next season. With the prospect of having a roof over our heads in a settled situation, with no marching, and a chance to read a little, we were in good spirits. I actually enjoyed the eight-mile round trip between Hsamsingyang and Nhpum Ga which I had to make frequently to check the telephone line for any taps the Japanese might have put in on it. Walking without a pack and at your own pace was like floating over the ground in a balloon.

Then a grotesque rumor began to be heard, passed along in deprecating tones, pretty much as a joke. The substance of the rumor was the possibility of our being sent against Myitkyina. It was entirely incredible, of course. We did not know how far anyone would have to walk to get to Myitkyina—actually about 90 miles from Hsamsingyang, including 20 miles of backtracking north to reach a trail across the intervening ranges—but we knew it was a damned long way over mountains higher and steeper than any we had crossed so far and we knew it was the main Japanese supply base in northern Burma, with all that that implied.

But incredible as the rumor was it persisted, like a mosquito whining around your head. You wanted to bat it away from your ears.

"For Christ's sake, will you lay off that story!" someone would explode. "Are you *asking* for it?"

It was like a tale of the supernatural in which from a mere suggestion of something abnormal a phenomenon of monstrous vitality and malignancy burgeons.

A couple of high-ranking officers from the Northern Combat Area Command back at Ledo came to investigate our condition. They visited Phil Weld's platoon among others and asked searching questions like "How are you feeling, Lieutenant? Men O.K.?" Phil was much struck by the appearance of the fatigue uniforms they wore, which obviously had never been worn before and were dark green without the bloom of red dust that made all of us and everything else at Nhpum Ga rusty-looking. It was like a slumming party, Phil said.

We learned that Colonel Hunter had sent a small party

headed by his intelligence officer, Captain Laffin (a former official of the Ford Motor Company in Japan of mixed American and Japanese parentage), to survey the trail leading eastward from Naubum over the Kumon Ranges. Shortly thereafter we also heard that Hunter had informed a small staff meeting that General Merrill would probably be back in a few days to take command of a special force to be formed of the 5307th and two Chinese regiments.

The objective of the task force would, of course, be Myitkyina.

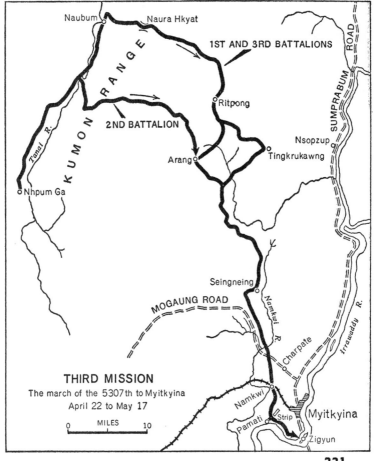

THIRD MISSION
The march of the 5307th to Myitkyina
April 22 to May 17

0   MILES   10

VIII Modern armies had never fought under such conditions as those that prevail in Burma during late spring and summer, when an inch of rain is falling daily and rising rivers inundate the lowlands. But in April, 1944, as downpours grew more frequent, the tapering off of operations that could have been expected did not take place. Instead, both sides summoned up their reserves of strength to win what each hoped would be a crucial decision. Before the climax was reached in midsummer, the combatants would have been tried to their limit, and the example of troops dragging themselves over rain-beaten mountain trails and gutted roads knee-deep in mud, never knowing from what quarter to expect attack, cut down by machine-gun fire from an ambush, blasted by artillery, but more often overcome by fever and exhaustion, was common to all. In the similarity of their ordeal and the pitiful sense of duty or—equally pitiful—acceptance of the lack of an alternative that drove them on there was little to distinguish among the nationalities assembled in that unlikely theater, Japanese, Indians, Gurkhas, British, East and West Africans, Chinese and Americans. The reasons why the military forces of both sides were so agonizingly extended and the hills of Burma, north, west, and south stood witness to such spectacles of human depletion lay in two strategic decisions, one on the part of the Japanese to seize

222

easternmost India and one on the part of the Americans to seize the Mogaung-Myitkyina area, and in the illusion on both sides that a swift and sweeping victory could be pulled off on a low down payment.

At the time the battle was joined at Nhpum Ga, General Stilwell was chiefly concerned not to lose what he had already got. The Japanese, driving through the Chin Hills into Manipur state, had surrounded the British IV Corps in Imphal and the British garrison in Kohima, both of which were having to be sustained by air supply at the cost of reducing shipments to China over the Hump. The awful possibility in Stilwell's mind was that the Japanese would sweep on into the Brahmaputra valley and force him to withdraw his forces from the territory they had won at such bitter price in the north. To help meet the danger, he was prepared to take the Chinese 38th Division from the northern front and move it to the threatened area. However, at a meeting on April 3 which he had requested with Admiral Mountbatten and General Slim, commanding the British Fourteenth Army, he was greatly relieved to learn that Slim believed he could handle the Japanese offensive. Mountbatten as well as Slim was in favor of Stilwell's proceeding with the project on which he had set his heart—the drive on Mogaung and Myitkyina. At the same time Mountbatten remained convinced that the Allies' "ability to capture and hold Myitkyina would depend on the decisive defeat of the main Japanese forces on the central front, and on the advance of at least part of the Chinese Expeditionary Force from Yunnan." [1]

In Washington the Joint Chiefs of Staff took the view that "Myitkyina had to be seized and a buffer zone created to the south so that Hump tonnage could be increased. The build-up of Hump tonnage to 20,000 tons a month and completion of a two-way, all-weather road and a 4-inch pipeline to China seemed necessary and timely to Marshall so that the maximum possible aid to projected U.S. operations in the Pacific might be given by China-based air power early in 1945." [2] Taking Myitkyina was not only essential to the eventual reopening of surface communications with China but would in itself make possible an increase in the tonnage that could be flown to China. It would deprive Japanese fighter planes of the use of the Myitkyina airstrip and would enable cargo planes flying the Hump to take a lower, more southerly route and to refuel en route when the pipeline had reached Myitkyina.

Apart from what might develop at Imphal, Stilwell seemed to have the odds strongly in his favor. He and Mountbatten had induced Chiang Kai-shek to part with two more of his 316 divisions for employment in north Burma—the 14th and 50th—and parts of these had been flown in over the Hump. This gave Stilwell five Chinese divisions, together with the 5307th, with which to attack the three understrength regiments of the Japanese 18th Division, soon to be reinforced by three additional battalions. Weighing heavily in the scales was also the new Chindit force, known as the 3rd Indian Division, though it contained few Indians. Since March it had been operating in central Burma, deep in Japanese-held territory, under Major General Lentaigne, Wingate's successor, with the mission of disrupting communications with the Japanese force in Imphal and the Japanese 18th Division in the north. In April it was ordered to devote its main effort to helping Stilwell.

Against what would seem to have been overwhelming advantages on Stilwell's side certain other factors had to be set. The Japanese in north Burma still had the terrain in their favor; if they could hold a little longer they could confidently expect the Chinese and Americans to bog down in deepening quagmires and rising floods. The Japanese were still on the offensive in India, General Tanaka, opposing Stilwell, had been promised an additional division when that offensive should have gained its objectives. The newly arrived Chinese divisions were ill-trained and poorly prepared. The Generalissimo was in direct communication behind Stilwell's back with the commanding generals of the Chinese divisions in Burma counseling caution, so that Stilwell's main drive, down the Mogaung valley from Shaduzup toward Kamaing, was stalled. The 30 Chinese divisions in Yunnan, which Mountbatten and Stilwell both urged advance into Burma, were to make only limited progress, although the Japanese opposing them amounted at one time during May to less than a division. The Chindits were due for evacuation early in June on the basis of the experience of General Wingate (not a leader to coddle his men) that troops after three months behind the enemy's lines were finished. Lastly there was the condition of the 5307th, which was not the force it had been. Upon receipt of a report from a colonel newly assigned to the unit, Stilwell wrote in his diary: "Galahad is OK. Hard fight at Nhpum. Cleaned out Japs and hooked up. No worry there." This was an illusion. As the U.S. Army history observes, "The consequences of Nhpum Ga were hidden by the veil of the future; at the time, the engagement was seen from the point of view of a commander whose theater stretched from the Indian Ocean to the Yellow Sea. . . . Though one of the hardest-fought American engagements in Burma, it was from the perspective of China-Burma-India Theater headquarters a battle between a few battalions. Farther south, around Imphal, whole divisions were grappling for a prize that might change the course of the war in Asia." It notes, "The most serious result of Nhpum Ga was the exhaustion of troops. The fighting edge of the most mobile and most obedient force that Stilwell had was worn dull. From this fact were to flow consequences of great magnitude."

What the 5307th felt was that while Myitkyina was doubtless important, so was Shanghai, and there was about as much chance of its being able to take one as the other. Most of us believed the Northern Combat Area Command was either ignorant of the shape we were in or indifferent to it—or out of its mind. The large force of Chinese we were to have with us did not reassure us.

The Chinese in our experience had an admirable fortitude, endurance and cheerfulness but little drive or aggressiveness. Our explanation was that they had been at war for years, probably ever since they were children, and in addition saw no end of it ahead; after the Japanese had been defeated the Chinese civil war would remain to be fought. Campaigning was a way of life to them. They ate their rice and drank their tea, bred their horses on the march, put up bashas in their camps, carried on their housekeeping, and took time to boil all their drinking water. All this was in contrast to the attitude of the Americans, to whom the war was a highly abnormal state of affairs and an invasion of their personal liberties; the thing to do was to get in there, throw a million tons of high explosives at the enemy, burn up the equipment, and have it over with. In the meantime—the hell with shaving and water discipline; far from boiling what they drank, many of the Marauders could not even be bothered to await the action of the halazone tablets in their canteens but would pop the tablets in their mouths like aspirin and wash them down with a pint of water dipped out of a trailside stream.

Itself unsold on the Chinese, the 5307th entertained as one of its articles of faith that Stilwell's headquarters or Stilwell himself was promoting the Chinese and determined to make a record for them, if necessary at the expense of the one American infantry unit in the theater. Another article was that as an outsider to the theater the 5307th was in the position of a stepchild with no one of any influence but Merrill to raise a voice in its behalf at Stilwell's headquarters. And now Merrill was incapacitated. Actually, Stilwell was in consultation with Merrill all during the planning of the operation, the plans adopted having been largely those that Colonel Hunter and his staff had already worked out in order to give the operation the best chance of success should it be called for. There is no evidence that Merrill sought to dissuade Stilwell from sending the 5307th to Myitkyina, and equally there is no reason for believing that it would have done any good if he had. Stilwell had told him that he knew he was calling on the unit for more effort than could fairly be expected but that he felt he had no option.[2]

We knew, as Colonel Hunter was later to testify, that relations between our officers and the Northern Combat Area Command were unpleasant. The resentment we seemed to have aroused perhaps reflected in part the defensive attitude of headquarters officers toward combat soldiers and in part the resentment that must have been aroused by the independent relationship with Stilwell enjoyed by Merrill, who two years before had been an obscure major and was now a well-publicized general. We had heard that a list of recommended promotions Colonel Hunter sent in had been rejected with the rejoinder that we interest ourselves less in advancement and more in fighting. This was not forgotten by those of us who had come from overstrength units where young Bonaparte himself could not have made first lieutenant and had been in grade so long that Colonel Osborne proposed issuing oak-leaf clusters for our bars.

Wondering if we would be able to make it to Myitkyina even if there were no Japanese in the way, we were convinced that someone had blundered. Unlike the Light Brigade, we did not scruple to reason why. We reasoned why with volubility and bitterness but also wearily, aware of the futility of it.

There was one compensation. We probably would not reach Myitkyina, but if we did we would wind up with glory and honor and a fling that would make history. This was positively to be the last effort asked of us. We had it from Gerenal Merrill himself that when we had gained our objective we would be returned at once to India, given a party to cause taxpayers a shudder, installed in a well-appointed rest camp, and given furloughs. It was this prospect more than anything else that gave the 5307th the resolution to surmount the obstacles that lay before it on the trail to Myitkyina. The understanding it had been given was to play a decisive role in its history.

Relieved by a Chinese battalion which arrived on April 22 to take over the defense of Nhpum Ga, we marched the 20 miles back north along the Tanai, less a third of our original strength, to Naubum for a rendezvous with the two Chinese regiments with which we were to be combined. General Merrill arrived a couple of days later to take command of the operation which, with no irony intended, had been christened End Run. He informed us that our objective would be the airstrip at Myitkyina. We were to be organized in three forces. Colonel Hunter would command one, composed of 1st Battalion and the Chinese 150th Infantry Regiment (50th Division). Another, composed of 3rd Battalion and the Chinese 88th Infantry Regiment (30th Division), would be commanded by Colonel Kinnison. It was Colonel Kinnison who, flown in to Hsamsingyang, had reassured Stilwell as to the condition of the 5307th. And indeed it was generally better than his own; he was in such ill-health he should probably not have been allowed to take the assignment. Colonel McGee would command the third, quite small force, composed of the survivors of 2nd Battalion (half the original number) and 300 Kachin irregulars.

At Naubum everything was on a bigger scale than we were used to. It was like moving from a village to a town; you kept seeing officers you did not know. General Merrill had with him the equivalent of a divisional headquarters and with our Chinese allies we seemed to be spread out all over creation. He and this headquarters, incidentally, were not to march with the troops but to remain where they were until we had got where we were going. Impressed by our being, in a manner of speaking, in public, Colonel Osborne ordered his officers and men to clean up, shave, get their hair cut somehow, and try to look presentable. The shaving part of it was deeply resented by some, and Caifson Johnson held out against parting with his red beard to the point of insubordination and scandal.

Shortly after our arrival at Naubum, some of my platoon mates came back from a tour of the 150th Regiment's bivouac with a sober mien. "Those Chinese are nothing but kids," they reported. After taking a turn around the area, I had the same impression myself.

There was a critical moment for me at Naubum. I was summoned by Colonel Hunter to the lean-to serving at his headquarters, where he was sitting with the commander of the 150th

Regiment. I was reminded for some reason of the meeting of Marco Polo and Kublai Khan, though not for long.

"The walkie-talkies the colonel has received don't work," said Colonel Hunter. "See if you can fix them."

I had a horrible feeling that for the first and doubtless the last time in my life the national honor was in my keeping, not to mention my commanding officer's face, and I could not imagine a worse repository. If heaven had any further use for me, I thought, now would be the time to show it. There was only one thing I knew about SCR 536's: if you inserted the two batteries head-and-head and tail-and-tail—which would seem the natural thing to do—the set would not work; head-and-tail was the prescribed arrangement. I opened the first set . . . and the American eagle, or Bird of Washington, was saved, and I with it. They were in the wrong way. Nothing else was the matter.

On May 1 Colonel Hunter's force, the 1st Battalion with the 150th Chinese in train, set out on the long march, preceded by Colonel Kinnison's force with 3rd Battalion in the lead. It rained all that day, not unexpectedly; for the past ten days it had rained off and on every day. Said General Stilwell's diary:

May 1. Rain. (Depression days, commander's worries: I start them off for Myitkyina, it rains. The resistance grows here [in the Mogaung valley]. Why didn't I use them on our front [again, in the Mogaung]? Is the gap too big? Will they meet a reinforced garrison [at Myitkyina]? Does it mean we'll fail on both sides, instead of only one? Can I get them out? Are the Japs being sucked toward Mogaung or is the new [Japanese] unit staying in Mitch? Etc., etc., and nothing can be done about it. The die is cast, and it's sink or swim. But the nervous wear and tear is terrible. Pity the poor commanding officer.)

We set off with that what-the-hell-did-you-expect-anyway spirit that served the 5307th in place of morale, and I dare say served it better. Mere morale would never have carried us through the country we now had to cross. We had fought with mountains before, but none like those of the Kumon Ranges

229

under the monsoon rains. The trail that went over them, connecting the valleys of the Tanai and the upper Irrawaddy, had not been used for ten years. The detail that had gone ahead under Captain Laffin, with Lieutenant Paul Dunlap in charge of engineering work, included 30 coolies as well as a bodyguard of 30 Kachins, and it did what it could to repair the worst stretches, redigging the trail out of the slopes. Even so, it was a question whether the column with its equipment would ever be able to make it. The saw-toothed ridges would have been difficult enough to traverse when dry. Greased with mud, the trail that went over them was all but impossible. On the steeper descents the mules simply sat down, sliding 50 yards at a stretch on their haunches. Going up, we hacked steps out of the steeper slopes to give them a foothold. Time to do this was sometimes lacking, though, and in that case the fatalistic animals, recognizing that momentum gave them their only hope, would take it at a run, bounding up the grade like monster rabbits. Or they would when the muleteers had made it clear there was no choice but to go up. The battle of the mules was unending and, I think, took more out of the men than anything else, more even than fighting the enemy and fighting disease. When the mules slipped and fell, which they did continually under their heavy loads, there was, as always, the man-killing labor of getting them unloaded, staggering up the hills with the components of the cargo, and reloading them. The mule leaders became virtually dehumanized.

"Try not to let the set get any wetter than it already is," you would call down to a couple of men trying to get up the slope with a disassembled pack; an officer is supposed to give orders. Rain is pouring off their helmets. Their rifles are hanging in front of them and tripping them up. They are too done in even to curse you.

"Major Johnson says to keep closed up!" shouts a voice from the next hilltop.

"You tell him to halt the goddam column!" you yell back in a fury. "What the hell does he think we are?"

The worst of it was when the mules, losing their footing, would topple off the trail altogether and go head over heels down the mountainside, breaking their necks or stabbing themselves with bamboo. If the latter, they could sometimes be rescued and pushed and prodded back up the hill. Sometimes they could not be and unless already dead had to be shot. Then, after the 200 pounds of supplies and equipment the beast had carried had been inched up the nearly vertical flank of the ridge, there would have to be a reapportionment of loads among the surviving animals, and some hard decisions about what to throw away. One day, in a stretch of only a few miles, 3rd Battalion lost twenty of its mules—which meant not only the mules themselves but about two tons of equipment.

We were scarcely ever dry. When the rain stopped and the sun came out, evaporation would begin. The land steamed. The combination of heat and moisture was smothering. You had to fight through it. For those most weakened by disease, it was too much. For the first time you began to pass men fallen out beside the trail, men who were not just complying with the demands of dysentery—we were used to that—but were sitting bent over their weapons, waiting for enough strength to return to take them another mile. During the worst times heretofore we could always count on one thing to keep us going—and that was the process of keeping going itself. As long as the column was on the march, men somehow seemed to be able to keep up, and it was only when we laid up for a day that the sufferers would collapse. But it did not work any longer. We had stragglers. Whenever we bivouacked, men who had been incapable of keeping up with the column, slowly as it moved, and were too tired to worry about the danger from any Japanese there might be lurking about, would be plodding in for hours afterward, unsmiling and clammy with sweat. There was a feeling in the organization that it was coming apart. And Myitkyina was still 60 miles away.

The plaintive refrain that sounded from a few yards down the trail during the halts and from beside me when we had strung up our ponchos for the night had less conviction and was growing more intermittent:

> I'm going to buy a paper doll that I can call my own,
> A doll that other fellows cannot steal. . . .

During one of the six days we spent crawling over the Kumon mountains the rain came down so hard that the column had to halt where it was. It simply could not move. We camped where we happened to be caught. For the communications platoon, this was on a steep hillside. The trail was a slide grooved with the hoofmarks of mules that had shot the length of it like otters. Bill Bright and I got our ponchos up and soon had a fire going for tea. The beauty of campaigning in northern Burma is that the dead stems of bamboo will ignite readily even when they have been rained on, although a fire of bamboo requires constant replenishing. We were steaming off in front of the fire when a French-Canadian noncom came by to make a report of some kind and remained surveying the hopeless scene from under his rakishly tilted helmet, his hand on his hip, his shoulder raised in a shrug. He was clad in filthy, sodden fatigues and was wasted by fever, but his mustache twitched with an irrepressible insouciance, like a mouse's whiskers, and he had all the style and jauntiness of a Parisian boulevardier as he twirled the stick he carried and then, leaning back upon it theatrically, lifted his voice against the drumming of the monsoon shower in the tune of the song "Pennies from Heaven":

> Every time it rains,
> It rains little drops of water. . . .

Well, I thought, there was the 5307th. Or perhaps that was what I thought when I told him good-by a week or so later. He was being evacuated with the customary tag reading FUO, meaning Fever of Unknown Origin, though as often as not it might as well have read AOE, or Accumulation of Everything. It was my task to relieve him of the 17-jewel wrist watch he had been issued and was preparing to take with him. A fudging of the line between what is rightfully one's own and what is not is common enough in the service, but I like to think that only a member of the 5307th would have been capable of quite the astonished indignation with which our French-Canadian confronted me as I insisted upon his turning in the watch, just as if I were one of *them*—that horde of bastards comprising everyone outside the organization.

Ahead of us loomed the Naura Hkyat, the 6,100-foot pass over the backbone of the Kumon. It looked insurmountable and very nearly was so. It strengthened our feeling that we had become detached from the rational world, like the Russian regiment that was forgotten about after the Czar sent it marching off in a direction that happened to be that of Siberia. All the way up we had to spend as much time resting and giving our hearts and lungs a chance to catch up as we did climbing. One thing that helped keep you going was the thought that this was the worst there could be. It was so bad it was preposterous. At times it was possible to drop to your hands almost without bending over, and we did so, scrambling up on all fours. We were unable to reach the top the same day we began the ascent and had to camp halfway up.

That night was one of those rare times when we were able to pick up a program of good music from a U.S. Army station in Australia. It included Marian Anderson singing "My Heart at Thy Sweet Voice," the spiritual "Heaven," and the Largo from *Xerxes*. On an earlier occasion, on the way to Walawbum, we had heard portions of *Aïda*.

Among the things we learned about ourselves in Burma was that, even in times of hunger for food, a hunger for music and books persisted. Winnie Steinfield had brought along a paperback collection of five of Shakespeare's plays and had split it up into its constituent parts which, after binding them with adhesive tape from a K-ration carton, he circulated among a few friends. They were considered priceless. I had had the foresight to bring a copy of *Hamlet* of my own, one about three inches high, and I read it all through the campaign, dipping into it

233

during halts on the march. However pressing the reality, it never seemed more real than Shakespeare and never dimmed his force and appeal or, for that matter, Kipling's or Conrad's—those two especially weathered the ordeal of that period—though in their case I had only my recollections to go on.

Art, you might think, would do little for a faint heart. It holds out no promise of a happy resolution in this world or a next, it has nothing to say about any higher purpose that life is serving—life being to art an end in itself. Yet when you read the poetry of *Hamlet* or hear the music of Handel's Largo or Verdi's "Su del Nilo" amid the wild, dark hills, you find that it transcends hunger and sickness and fear. If art cannot fulfill our yearnings and aspirations, it can voice them with an eloquence that ennobles our cause. A great expression of literature, painting or music is like the sun when it breaks through the clouds to transfigure a wearisome landscape in a golden light. Bringing a heightened awareness of the realm of experience, it brings also a sense of the triumph of the human spirit, and perhaps because of the harmony of its own vision seems to testify, like the cosmology of science, to the underlying oneness of all things, in which is our immortality.

In the morning we recommenced the slow ascent. We felt we were climbing right out of Burma, and in effect we were. It was another world on top—another climate certainly. There was a biting wind, and chilled in our wet fatigues we looked around wonderingly at the thin, ghostly cloud forest of under-sized trees furred with mosses and lichens that clothed the summit of the pass.

The hills on the far side of the Naura Hkyat were worse than the nearer ones—still sheerer in their ups and downs. In the course of a few days we managed to get across even the tumultuous eastern ridges and with that we had put behind the most formidable natural barrier between us and Myitkyina. But the toll from disease and exhaustion continued to mount. A new enemy had attacked, and in a way it did more damage than any other, for it was mysterious and unforeseen, a fever

234

no one could identify. It struck without warning, felling its victims virtually where they stood. Before it finished with us, 149 men succumbed and had to be evacuated. Many of them died later in the hospitals of Assam, where the fever was ultimately identified as mite-borne typhus. Before we knew how serious it was, Bill Bright came down with it, and then one of our best radio men. They were sent to the rear to be litter-carried by Chinese coolies until it should be possible to fly them out, which was not to be very soon.

The Paper Doll song was heard no more. There was still the bird that went "*Whee-oo,* WHEE-*oo*," however.

We also heard jungle cocks crowing in the distance. It always took an instant to realize that they were not domestic fowl, and the realization when it came made the wilderness seem all the wilder.

Having terrain as difficult as the Kumon mountains to fight had one great compensation: we did not have to fight the Japanese while we were in it, for with every reason to feel safe about it they had left it alone. Once we had come through the worst of it, however, we were soon reminded that we were back where the enemy was. Captain Laffin's party, when 3rd Battalion overtook it, had information that the Japanese were entrenched in the village of Ritpong, up ahead, about 150 strong.

The 3rd Battalion reached Ritpong on May 7, ten days after its departure from Naubum. Leaving a battalion of the Chinese 88th Regiment to attack the village from the north, it cut a trail through the jungle to catch the garrison from the rear. Not having dreamed that such things still went on, we were fascinated to learn that the Chinese assault was made to a bugle call. Chinese casualties were heavy, but two thirds of the defenders were killed on the spot, and of the rest only four were believed to have escaped our patrols.

The clash at Ritpong meant that our advent in the upper Irrawaddy must now be known to the enemy. The consequences could be serious for Colonel Hunter's force, which, having now caught up with Colonel Kinnison's, was ready for what the

235

newspapers were to call a dash for Myitkyina, 35 miles away; it was our battalion that had been picked to take the lead and seize the Myitkyina airstrip. In order both to protect our flank and to deceive the Japanese, Colonel Kinnison's force was sent on a feint 20 miles to the east, to a village called Tingkrukawng where a sizable body of Japanese was holding up a British-led force of Kachins and Gurkhas. This force had come down the Irrawaddy from the tiny, air-supplied base in the northern tip of Burma that was the one foothold the British had managed to retain in the country.

The 3rd Battalion reached Tingkrukawng only after losing an ominous number of men to prostration; at the lower altitudes the heat had become overpowering. Attacking what it thought to be a platoon of Japanese, it quickly found itself pinned down by a reinforced battalion. A Chinese company was sent around to attack from the flank. For the next two days both Americans and Chinese maneuvered around the village, hacking trails through bamboo and clawing their way up steep slopes under heavy fire trying to find a weak spot in the formidable Japanese positions. They made no headway. It was bitter, heartbreaking work for the now dazed and wholly spent Marauders. They suffered casualties of 8 killed and 21 wounded in the fruitless attacks, and the Chinese considerably more. In view of the fact that 3rd Battalion had largely run out of ammunition and that Colonel Hunter's force was now well launched on the last lap of what had become the race for Myitkyina, Colonel Kinnison decided to break contact and pull back—an exercise sounding neat and expeditious but in reality quite different for men stumbling blindly in the dark, burdened with the wounded and famished for food, of which they had had none since the day before.

For me, time had finally run out. One night before we reached Ritpong we had camped in an abandoned village on an open elevation. Colonel Hunter had his command post in a basha raised on posts five feet above the ground on the highest point of all. Because Colonel Osborne was there too, so was I, as one of his staff officers. A fire had been started on the dirt hearth and was blazing away merrily. We were making coffee over it when a machine gun broke forth with shattering abruptness on the hill down below us. I felt that clutch at the stomach and sudden taste of brass in the mouth that to my exceeding annoyance I could never control. Then the perimeter let loose in an uproar of firing. Bullets began to crack overhead and whine all around. We sat there and let the battle rage, surmising that most of the shooting was being done by the Chinese. The thought dawned on me, however, that with the fire in it the basha must stand out like a jack-o'-lantern for miles in every direction. The thought must have struck one of the captains at the same time, and when he went out one door, I went out the other, unfortunately not stopping to put on my shoes, which I had taken off on coming in to avoid tracking up the floor with mud. After hitting the ground, I trotted around the basha to round up the platoon and get the men, myself included, off the crest of the hill and I came down on an empty cheese can, edge up. The cut, when I had a chance to see it, looked as if someone had nearly succeeded in cutting an inch-thick biscuit out of my heel. I stumbled on out of the circle of light and hit the ground. Lying there in the dark with the bullets flying overhead, with the machine guns stuttering away on the perimeter, the ground soggy and a drizzle of rain falling and the blood flowing all over my hand while I held the heel together as best I could, I observed to myself with a distinctness I still remember that this was unquestionably the low point of my life so far.

When in time the firing let up, I hobbled back to the foot of the basha and sent for one of the medics. After one of them finally got there—it was Captain Closuit, the chief of the section—the firing began again.

"Get down, man," I said. "Never mind about me now. You can take care of me later."

He paid no attention and with the bullets whining and cracking on every side went ahead and dressed the cut, keeping as low as he could. I was tremendously impressed, and had he been

237

aware of it he would have felt inundated as by warm syrup from the flood of gratitude that went out from me. I kept apologizing and pleading with him to take cover, but to no effect.

At length the battle subsided for good. Almost all, if not all, the firing had been from the Chinese. The Japanese, if there had ever been any, had been dispersed. The mortar shells that had been landing among us all over the hilltop had been fired exclusively by the Chinese. They had apparently simply let fly in every direction. Fortunately, there were no half measures in their incompetence. If one must be mortared by one's friends, it is nice to have them neglect to pull the pins and thus fail to arm the shells. Most of those that hit around us buried themselves harmlessly in the ground.

The Chinese regimental commander felt humiliated by the episode, as well he might. The order he issued to his troops was a model of its kind: any further attack upon the perimeter that night, however massive, was to be repelled with bayonets, and if anyone fired a shot, no matter what the provocation, he would be taken out at dawn and put to death. The remainder of the night passed quietly.

In my case it was too late. The indulgence accorded to invalids of having their packs put on a mule was granted to me. I was even deemed horse-worthy and provided with one of the few remaining mounts. This proved to offer only a partial solution of my difficulty, however. Having continually to jump off to lead the beast down into rain-washed gullies and up the muddy banks without being able to put my heel to the ground was brutal work. Harder still was being flailed and smacked by bamboo and the branches of trees when we marched at night and I could not see what was ahead. At times I gave up and hobbled along on an improvised crutch. I went on like this for three days, until we reached a village in a valley where a small paddy field looked as if it might be made serviceable for liaison planes. Between the Chinese and us, we were accumulating casualties at the rate of a score a day and were always ready to

238

try to convert almost anything into a landing strip. (At Arang, where General Merrill flew in for a last council with Colonel Hunter, we had left 120 for evacuation.) I had expected to plug on to the end, hoping the foot would heal, but the medics found it infected and getting worse, and since there seemed to be no purpose in my tagging along with the column in that condition, it was decided to send me on back. Never had my world been so transformed with such suddenness.

I suppose I felt shame-faced. Certainly I felt it ironic that after coming through without a day's illness or even indisposition—an almost unique record—I should have come to this. I cannot recall putting up an argument, though. At that time the whole structure of the enterprise was manifestly so rickety that, regardless of the outcome of the march, the evacuation of everyone in a matter of days appeared to be inevitable.

It had no connection with anything, but I remember that while I was in the aid station Winnie Steinfield was preparing to treat Phil Weld, who had discovered a tick fastened on him where even a person as tolerant of animal life as a Jain would be ill-content to have it remain. Winnie, who still carried a Tommy gun minus its stock and reputedly so clogged with mud it would have exploded if fired, took out his forceps, wiped them on the seat of his GI shorts—his sole attire for office hours —and blew on them. "Must have ab's'lute sterility for this op'ration."

The field we had cleared for the landing strip was so bad that the planes when they ran down it reminded you of a Model T Ford bouncing over an old pasture and when at the end they lifted off the ground it seemed as improbable as a cow jumping over the moon. As the day progressed, the cool of the forest created a downdraft and one of the planes pancaked into the trees just after the take-off. The pilot, though not badly hurt, was put in the next plane. And before our astonished eyes it crashed too. This time the pilot of the first plane was bloodied up about the face and hands; he must have been one of the few persons in the history of aviation to have had two crack-ups in the space of half an hour. They managed to get him away on the third attempt, but there were no more flights that day.

We completed the evacuation the next morning after a report that a band of Japanese had blundered into our camp and had created a little excitement. (We did not find them.) The only other time I had ever been in an airplane had been thirteen years before, and that made it seem all the more dreamlike to be crossing in an hour or so the country we had toiled through ever since leaving the Ledo Road, three months ago. We put down at Maingkwan, which the Chinese had captured after we had hit the Japanese at Walawbum. There, where I was to transfer to a Dakota for the trip to Ledo, I blinked uncomprehendingly at everything I saw, for everything was fantastic to me—the sight of trucks and a road, the mugs of coffee in seemingly inexhaustible supply, the robust and solid appearance of everyone, the casual, relaxed manner everyone had, the loud voices. I felt vacant and empty. What I was told to do, I did. This was to wait in a tent with half a dozen other evacuees—glinting eyed, unshaven scarecrows making you think of criminals who had at last been run down, cornered and captured.

While I was waiting, they brought in a litter case. It was Bill Bright. They had been all this time carrying him down out of the Kumon hills, before finally reaching a spot from which they could fly him out. His eyes were like gems and physical wastage had brought out the slightly foxyish lines of his flushed face, but he spoke with his inveterate cheerfulness when he saw me. "What the . . . hell are you doing here?" I explained in a few words what had happened. "Who's got the platoon?" he asked. There was no platoon any more, just some men trying to work the sets when they had a chance, but I could not go into this, and his consciousness was slipping even before they carried him off to the hospital plane. He had a temperature of 104 degrees. Soon afterward two enlisted men of the local complement staggered in with a loaded blanket slung between them in the manner of a hammock, a pair of feet protruding from the front end. Nothing else of the occupant of the blanket could be seen,

240

but from the bulge at the bottom blood was dripping freely. It was explained that he and a friend of his had been great collectors of unexploded artillery shells, of which Maingkwan afforded quite a number. "So one of the duds goes off when he picks it up, and that's the end of him. And you know what this other fellow says? He says, 'He picked up the wrong one that time.' That's all. How d'ya like that?" I suppose it was especially because of having just seen Bill Bright that I was so angry.

A few hours later I was in the hospital at Margherita, with the war seeming inconceivably remote, as remote as Shiloh. Nine o'clock that morning I had been limping up a hill in Burma in the direction of the firing and by evening I was lying in a real bed after having eaten a real meal and listening to almost the loveliest sound I could imagine—the drumming of rain on a *roof!* I was almost out of my mind with the luxury of it. All that was needed—and it was a lot—was the promised mass return of the Marauders. As it developed, the beginning was not far off.

On May 13, the day I was evacuated, 3rd Battalion was still tied up at Tingkrukawng, while 2nd had not yet got over the worst of the Kumon Ranges; it had taken a more southerly and even more difficult route than the rest. But by that evening Hunter's force, with 1st Battalion in the lead, had reached the watershed of the Namkwi River, which flowed past its destination, and from his headquarters at Naubum Merrill sent a message to Stilwell saying, "Can stop this show up till noon tomorrow, when die will be cast, if you think it too much of a gamble. Personal opinion is that we have a fair chance and that we should try." On May 14 Stilwell wrote in his diary, "Hunter expected to give us the 48-hour signal tonight. I told Merrill to roll on in and swing on 'em." Later, when 1st Battalion had come down out of the mountains at Seingneing and had less than twenty miles of level country between it and its goal, he added: "48 HOUR NOTICE."

On the 15th the column marched by night. At ten o'clock a halt was called because the Kachin guide who was conducting the column by unfrequented trails, off those the Japanese might be watching, had been bitten by a poisonous snake. For two hours Captain Laffin and Lieutenant Dunlap took turns sucking poisoned blood from his swollen foot. By 2:30 in the morning he was well enough to go on, mounted on Colonel Hunter's horse, and the march resumed. On the morning of the 16th the force crossed the Mogaung-Myitkyina dry-weather motor road and a little later the railroad of which Myitkyina was the terminus. Shortly afterward it entered Namkwi. The expectation had been that a fight for the village might be in store, but it turned out that no Japanese were there. Nevertheless, the battalion rounded up and confined the native population to forestall the possibility of a tip-off. It was now in country where the Burmans were numerous, and the Burmans, in contrast to the Kachins, had been helping the Japanese.

The Myitkyina airstrip was now only four miles off. Hunter decided to hold off hitting it until the next morning to take advantage of the reported habit of the Japanese of pulling back off it into the woods during the daytime when American bombers were likely to come over. The force went into bivouac on the Namkwi River, one of the idyllic streams of that beautiful country (where, I was afterward very proud to hear, Colonel Osborne had observed while sitting on its bank, "Oggie would have enjoyed this. I wish he were here"). However, a patrol was sent out to the airstrip under Sam Wilson's platoon guide, Sergeant Branscomb. (Sam himself, whose face betrayed his physical condition, and who had also been overextending his luck, was forbidden to go by Osborne.) Branscomb, "cool and unassuming as always," as Sam put it, "handled the job with marvelous skill, getting on the strip and returning without being spotted to report the locations of the Japanese fortifications covering the strip from the east and providing us with an azimuth of advance to follow the next day." The platoon also reported having seen nothing to indicate that any very large body of Japanese was in occupation. As a precautionary measure, the Chinese pack artillery troop was ordered to set up its weapons and

242

train them on the strip, but Osborne upon checking on them found them somewhat more than 90 degrees off their target.

That night, while trying to get some sleep, their minds full of the attack they expected to have to make on the Japanese garrison the next day, the Americans heard a train clicking and lumbering, the engine panting, on the tracks behind them, receding in the direction of Mogaung. It was a spooky experience, Meredith Caldwell said, but a comforting one in that it demonstrated that the Japanese were still unaware of their presence.

In the country that the column had now entered geography is mostly the Irrawaddy River. After coming down from the north, the Irrawaddy flows on southward past Myitkyina and then past a village called Zigyun, located on an island between its banks, turns through almost half a circle and flows northwest for a few miles before resuming its course to the sea. Thus in the area in question, the Irrawaddy has the shape of the letter U. At the top of the right-hand stem of the U is Myitkyina. About five miles to the west, at the top of the left-hand stem, is the village of Pamati. The airstrip is between the two, closer to Pamati and directly south of Namkwi.

Marching out of their bivouac on the Namkwi together on the morning of the 17th, 1st Battalion under Colonel Osborne and the Chinese 150th Regiment soon separated, the Chinese turning east toward the airstrip, the Americans west to Pamati. On the approach to Pamati the country lay open to view on all sides. The invaders had, for the first time since the campaign began, come altogether out of the woods, and the impression of dizzy spaces, the low-grade fever most of them were running, and the even keener than usual feeling of uncertainty and isolation combined to give the men the sensation of having moved into a surrealist world of exaggerated but insubstantial perspectives and values and echoing voids. Evidently there were Japanese around Pamati, for a sniper kept firing at them. A few months before, the whole battalion would have hit the ground at the crack of the bullets, but now no one paid any attention.

243

Leaving a platoon to hold the village, the battalion took the road that led directly back to the airstrip. On the way some Indians ran up to report excitedly that thirty Japanese were blocking the road up ahead from well-dug-in positions around the base of a big tree. Sam Wilson, whose platoon was leading, went back and gave the information to Caifson Johnson. Johnnie, although as far gone as everyone else, had not lost his wistful appetite for action. "All right, Sammy, let's take them!" he said. Upon Sam's venturing to question whether it was worth getting into that kind of scrap when there were limitless expanses of open country all around by which the block could be bypassed, the light went from Johnnie's face. It was apparent that doubts about Sam's courage had entered his mind. However, to Sam's relief he at length agreed to forbear from crashing through the opposition and the battalion, skirting the position, reached the airstrip without firing a shot.

The Chinese, thanks to Hunter's timing, had been able to sweep over the strip without difficulty. The Japanese were in positions to the east, and from these the Chinese were now fighting to eject them. The Marauders, falling out on the end of the strip, had the remarkable experience of watching the battle as if it were a football game or a motion picture. Little Chinese figurines would spring up from the ground, waving their disproportionately long weapons—Lee-Enfield rifles with fixed bayonets—and rush forward while the notes of a bugle would drift back to the spectators. Some of the attackers would fall. Among them, but usually some distance wide of the mark, black geysers would erupt where Japanese mortar shells had hit. It was the only time in the campaign when any kind of view of the battlefield was offered, and the Americans, some with binoculars, watched it open-mouthed for an hour.

At 10:30 that morning Stilwell had received the message "In the ring," which meant that Hunter's force was at the airstrip. At 3:30 came the message "Merchant of Venice," which meant that transport planes could land and the process of supply and reinforcement begin.

244

The failure of the Japanese to send a force out from Myitkyina to counterattack at the airfield indicated that they had no troops to spare. In fact, the Japanese garrison at that time, though larger than was realized, numbered only about 700 able-bodied men, almost half from the 114th Regiment of the 18th Division, with which the Marauders were well acquainted from Nhpum Ga. Hunter's aim was to get into Myitkyina with the least possible delay—though he had no orders touching upon the town—while at the same time blocking the main avenues of reinforcement. It was impossible to know how many troops the Japanese might be able to pour into the area from the south if given a chance. Hunter sent urgent requests for assistance to Colonel Kinnison and Colonel McGee, whose forces were far back up the trail, the one five miles the other side of Seingneing, the other at Arang. He had been promised that ammunition and food would be in the air as soon as the attack on the strip was made, and he relied upon their quick arrival. The crucial phase was at hand.

Transports loaded with Chinese troops, but without the supplies Hunter had counted on, began arriving from Ledo at once. By late afternoon a battalion of the 89th Regiment had arrived and the movement continued on into the night. From its bivouac on the road to Zigyun, 1st Battalion watched the Dakotas come in behind their landing lights—a wonderful sight, as Caldwell said.

Says *The U.S. Army in World War II*:

Back at his headquarters Stilwell was exultant. Again and again he had been told that Myitkyina could not be taken, if taken could not be held, and if held was not worth holding. Now his transports were landing on Myitkyina airstrip, flying in the Chinese who would take the principal center of north Burma and go on to lift the blockade of China. In six months his forces had driven 500 miles into Burma and won engagements against seven Japanese regiments, among them the victors of Singapore. The brilliant seizure of the Myitkyina airstrip was the height of Stilwell's career and the grand climax of the North Burma campaign.

It is interesting to note what facet of his exploit most excited General Stilwell, or at least which one he reserved capital letters for in his diary: "WILL THIS BURN UP THE LIMEYS."

The British were certainly astonished, at any rate. They knew that Myitkyina was Stilwell's dream but had not known that he had any plans to take it other than as an ultimate objective of the Chinese Army in India's drive down the Mogaung valley, which so far had not progressed 15 miles beyond Shaduzup. Only General Slim had been apprised by Stilwell of End Run and he only on condition that he divulge the information to absolutely no one. Stilwell's contention was that British security was not completely reliable and he feared that word of his plan would reach the Japanese. Knowing that Stilwell was already under orders to take Myitkyina and could be expected to do so at the first opportunity, Slim accepted Stilwell's condition. The consequence of Stilwell's caginess was that when Prime Minister Churchill asked Admiral Mountbatten by telegram if he had expected the attack on Myitkyina, the Supreme Commander Southeast Asia had to reply that he had heard only incidentally of what his deputy was up to—an extraordinary, almost incredible circumstance.

Stilwell was not given long to enjoy his triumph unalloyed. Within two days he was to confess his anxiety in his diary and within four to write "BAD NEWS."

There were ominous developments almost from the start. The plans Merrill and Hunter had made for supply and reinforcement were not carried out. What was needed was ammunition and food, then fighting troops, but the supplies did not arrive, and even before the first infantry appeared (the battalion of the 89th) an engineer aviation company had been sent in by glider and an antiaircraft battery flown in. Then, when the weather opened up enough on the 18th to permit flights to Myitkyina to be resumed, Hunter was further dismayed to find the transports bringing British antiaircraft troops which General Stratemeyer, commanding the U.S. Army Air Forces in the theater, had ordered in on his own initiative. It was another instance of the confusion that attended so much of the higher-level planning where the 5307th was concerned. Hunter did not know it at the time but later heard that the 5307th no longer controlled its own supply.

On the afternoon of the 17th, on instructions from General Merrill's deputy, Hunter had sent two battalions of the Chinese 150th against the town. Losing their way and running into Japanese rifle fire, they became confused and fell to shooting each other, and the attack was a failure. The next day two battalions of the 150th were again sent forward against the town and incredibly enough the blunder was repeated but on a bloodier scale. As we heard the appalling story from an evacuee back in the hospital at Margherita, the two battalions, entering the town from different sides, had each mistaken the other for the enemy and had driven each other back out and into the arms of the 150th's third battalion, which, thinking they were both Japanese, had opened up on them. Two days later the 150th made a third attempt against the town. This time it managed to push far enough to set up its command post in the railroad station, leading Stilwell to believe that the Japanese were in confusion and trying to pull out and that "we are reasonably sure of the place." But thereafter the regiment panicked under heavy Japanese fire and, having so far suffered 671 casualties, had to be taken out.

At the outset the 150th was all Hunter had at Myitkyina except the failing 1st Battalion of Marauders under Osborne. On the 18th, in an effort to concentrate what effective forces he had against the Japanese as quickly as possible, he sent a company of the 150th to Zigyun to relieve 1st Battalion, which had occupied the village to block an access route to Myitkyina. Osborne was to have brought his battalion back at once, but the Chinese took 48 hours to reach Zigyun, having dug in nine times in a stretch of five miles. Supposedly this was their reaction to their meeting up with groups of Japanese stragglers, but the American liaison officer with the 150th made a somewhat different report of their attitude to Colonel Hunter: "No

247

food, no ammo—no move." (The liaison officer, Lieutenant Colonel William H. Combs, was a favorite of the 1st Battalion officers, and among them Meredith Caldwell who, on the long march to Myitkyina, had found him able to discuss cotton futures on a professional level. A month later, shortly after his son was killed, Colonel Combs died of wounds he received while trying to warn a green American unit of a Japanese ambush.)

While 1st Battalion was at Zigyun, a patrol under Caifson Johnson brought back from a clash with the Japanese a man shot in the chest and Captain John J. McLaughlin, the battalion surgeon, stayed up all night with him with his mouth against the hole, forcing air into the lungs or sucking blood out; Osborne, on whom the incident made an impression as illustrative of Doc Mac's selfless dedication, was not sure which. In any ordinary military situation the thin, soft-spoken, gentle medical officer, who for months had worked with the sick and wounded night after night, would long since have been evacuated himself.

The Marauders, as General Merrill wrote after a brief visit to the airstrip, "were pitiful but still a splendid sight." Such as they were—and one platoon had cut open the seats of its trousers so as to be handicapped as little as possible by dysentery in any combat emergency—the six hundred or so troops of 1st Battalion were the only ones at Myitkyina of any demonstrated reliability. And the Japanese were coming up fast.

Hunter had sent an urgent summons to the only quarter where he could be sure it would produce results—to the remnants of the other two battalions of the 5307th, which were making their painful way down from the north. In response, they called upon their last reserves of will to quicken their pace, 3rd Battalion, although without food, foregoing a supply drop. They arrived in the area on the 19th. The 3rd, which was coming in by the Mogaung road, was ordered to take Charpate, a town on the road four or five miles north of Myitkyina. The 2nd Battalion, which was in desperate condition, came in by

248

the route the 1st had followed and was ordered to occupy and outpost Namkwi, north of the airstrip.

American and Chinese troops now held the villages and routes of access on the south, west and northwest of Myitkyina. The ring was more than half closed, but Japanese reinforcements could still be brought in from the north (down the road from the upper Irrawaddy) and from the east across the Irrawaddy. The enemy made the most of the opportunity. The influx had already begun by the afternoon of the 17th, the day the airstrip was taken, and it gathered momentum. Stilwell headed the entry in his diary for May 22 BLACK MONDAY and wrote: "Bad news from Mitch. Now they saw 800 Japs go into Charpate last night. And 200 crossed the river from the east. McCammon [Merrill's deputy] says, 'situation is critical.' Not a thing I can do. It has rained heavily all morning. We can't get troops in, also the field is in bad shape at Mitch. . . ." That day 3rd Battalion, having pushed on south toward Myitkyina and run into strong Japanese positions, had to pull back to Charpate to face a Japanese force coming in behind it by the Mogaung road. By the next day the Japanese at Myitkyina were going over to the offensive. The opportunity to take Myitkyina at low cost and achieve a brilliant success, which Hunter believed could with adequate planning and support have been done in the first two days, had been lost.

Hunter had led the march to Myitkyina with no knowledge of what his superiors had in mind beyond the capture of the airfield. Having accomplished that, he did not know whether he was to attack the town, cross the river, or what. Indeed, he was never ordered to take Myitkyina, and when on the 18th Stilwell visited the airstrip and Hunter told him he was going to take the town, Stilwell only grunted. Perhaps the matter was considered outside Hunter's competence. When at the start he had endeavored to find out from Merrill what the plan was, Merrill had simply told him not to worry since he would be on hand the moment the strip was taken. Merrill had, it is true, arrived shortly thereafter, but he was far from fully recovered from his heart attack and had barely had time to regroup the units in the area under his command as the Myitkyina Task Force, with Hunter placed again in command of the now re-united three battalions of the 5307th, when he suffered another attack. That was on the 19th. On the 20th he was evacuated. Command of the Task Force passed to Colonel McCammon, who was already a sick man and was to last only ten days. Why Colonel Hunter was not put in command we could never understand. Hunter had as much commissioned service behind him as Merrill himself, had had far more experience than Merrill with tactical units, knew intimately the tools he would be working with, and was an outstanding soldier.

So far as Hunter was aware there had never at any time been any formal written directive in the theater governing the employment of the 5307th. At the start of the campaign, Hunter was to recall, Stilwell had issued his orders by simply clapping Merrill on the back and saying, "You know what I want, Frank, so go in there and get it for me." There had never been any disagreements between Merrill and Hunter and Merrill had always been receptive to advice given by his next-in-command. The problem was in Merrill's relations with Stilwell. Stilwell in his published diary seldom has anything favorable to say of anyone, but he must have had considerable regard for his intelligent, accomplished, dynamic lieutenant, who had marched beside him in the Exodus in 1942. Merrill's very rapid rise in the China-Burma-India Theater indicated that he had. As commander of the 5307th, Merrill dealt directly and exclusively with Stilwell. So far as Hunter was concerned, the effect of Merrill's practice was to place him in an awkward and ill-defined position with respect to the command structure of the theater when Merrill was not present.

Phil Weld's term for Myitkyina was "our little Gallipoli." To those on the spot, he said, it was obvious from the fumbling orders and incompetent direction that adequate plans had not been prepared. A visit to headquarters at the airstrip made it plain, he added, that the command had been thrown off balance by the ease with which the strip had been taken and had no strategy with which to follow up that initial success.

An important factor in the confusion and air of improvisation that prevailed during the critical phase at Myitkyina, one is forced to believe, was Stilwell's practice of running the theater from his field bag and leaving his headquarters (of which it is to be remembered that he had several) to its (or their) own devices while he busied himself at the front. The explanation of this, in turn, is probably to be found partly in Stilwell's character and partly in the exigencies of the situation, which required him to rely largely upon Chinese divisions under the command of generals who, while officially taking orders from him, had to look for their future preferment to Chiang Kai-shek, whose purposes and those of the United States were far from congruent. The wonder is, moreover, that American military headquarters are as well attended as they are in view of the tradition in our democratic country by which a general is judged less by the quality of his generalship than by the frequency with which he appears up front, showing that he does not consider his life more valuable than anyone else's and providing material for photographs and stories.

The 5307th had been depended upon with such gratifying results in the past that now it was regarded as the answer to every need. The day after the Marauders had reassembled in the environs of Myitkyina, Stilwell recorded in his diary that "they are to finish the job." Of this expectation, which revealed a far-reaching ignorance of reality, Stilwell was soon to be disabused.

When the Japanese, on May 23, began to take the initiative, it was 3rd Battalion at Charpate that took the first blows. One assault carried the Japanese into the battalion's position, and it was only by a desperate effort and at the cost of heavy casualties that they were driven back. They attacked again the next day and the fighting was going badly for the Marauders, now reeling from exhaustion, when Hunter ordered them to break contact and pull back toward the strip. Two days later the Japanese

251

turned on 2nd Battalion at Namkwi and after a heavy attack succeeded in wresting from it the control of the town. It too fell back toward the strip.

Fortunately, a considerable force of Chinese was now present, some fresh, some less so. In addition to the battered remainder of the 150th, now dug in around the airstrip, there was the 88th Regiment, which had come down with 3rd Battalion and fought at Ritpong and Tingkrukawng, and its sister regiment, the 89th, which had been flown in from Ledo, and the first elements of another regiment, the 42nd, which was in process of being flown in. The 5307th, for its part, was simply melting away. Evacuation of the 1,310 who had reached Myitkyina—less than half the original force—was running at between 75 and 100 a day.

Caldwell, when I saw him next, said his platoon had come back to the strip after a week at Zigyun and he was sitting around near the aid station when he noticed Phil Weld regarding him curiously. "You look funny, Meredith," he said. "Why don't you get out?" Meredith thought it over that night. His wife was due to have had her baby by now and since it was their first-born he was pretty eager for news. The next day he reported to the aid station. "How about taking my temperature, Winnie?" he asked Steinfield. It was 101 degrees, which for anyone saturated with fever-repressant Atabrine was fairly high. "Winnie gave me a ticket, I threw all my belongings in a pile for the Chinese, and got in line."

The wards back at Margherita had begun to fill up within four days of my own arrival. To begin with there had been elation in the hospital as the long stream of white-faced, incredulous-looking refugees swelled. The well-earned, final victory had been achieved, we thought. It was the first elation the unit ever knew and the last, and of course it was short-lived.

When they brought in Tom Senff I did not know him. Tom had injured his back while crossing the Naura Hkyat Pass on May 4. Under the strain of marching the injury had grown progressively worse until, on the 15th, his lower left leg and

252

foot had become paralyzed and he could no longer stand on it. By that time he had also contracted a throat infection which prevented his eating, drinking or talking except with great pain. Accordingly, he was left behind at Seingneing with the 32 other casualties the unit had acquired merely in the two-day, 20-mile march from the last evacuation site. Arrangements were made—or supposedly were made—for the men to be flown out and the battalion scraped up three days' rations for them before leaving. However, by the night of the 18th no planes had arrived. Rations were then at the point of exhaustion, several of the typhus cases were running a dangerously high fever, and the lesions of two of the wounded had become infected. It was imperative that the invalids be evacuated without delay. Tom, who that afternoon had himself suffered a rupture of his infected throat, decided to try to make it to Myitkyina to get help. He set off on the morning of the 19th with one volunteer, Sergeant Frank S. Drolla, whose malaria had subsided sufficiently for him to attempt the trip.

Unable to put his weight on his left foot, Tom had to swing along on a bamboo staff. As much as possible they kept off the trail left by Hunter's force, especially at stream crossings, trail junctions and clearings, where an ambush would have been most likely. By the middle of the afternoon they heard firing ahead of them and to avoid it left the trail and headed across country, guiding on the sound of the firing and the direction in which the American fighter planes were flying. When night fell they were three miles from where they estimated Hunter's headquarters to be and, rather than risk a contact in the dark, remained until dawn in a thicket of bamboo. In the middle of the next morning, after making a wide swing around the smoke of several small fires that they thought might be Japanese, they limped into 1st Battalion's perimeter. A message was put through to base, in response to which rations were dropped at Seingneing and planes sent in to take off the casualties. Tom's condition was such that he had to be flown back to the United States in a litter.

They brought Sam Wilson back the same day Tom came in. Sam was worn down about as much as anyone could be and yet be alive. He had as good as come to the end well before reaching Myitkyina. He had voiced the prayer that was his resort in extremis, "Lord, I've taken it as far as I can. It's up to you from now on," and from then on had not tried to do more than get through the next moment. The last mission for which his platoon had been detached from the battalion had been to cross the Irrawaddy at Zigyun and, while scouting the area for Japanese, forage for meat, rice, or any other food that might produce a feeling of having eaten. He found most of the inhabitants to be Indians and had a friendly reception. There was only a small amount of rice on hand, but the villagers collected enough to make a difference and let Sam have it. Before returning Sam took his platoon up the river to reconnoiter the far bank. While they were doing so, a formation of American fighter planes came roaring in and, as Sam related it, made one run after another over the village and simply strafed it all to hell. The I and R platoon itself had to take cover in irrigation ditches while the slugs ignited tufts of grass around them. The villagers were coming out of their holes when the platoon got back. It was not the same village. A dignitary who seemed to be the headman took Sam by the arm and led him to a dugout from which a sound of sobbing and wailing could be heard. In response to a call from the headman an Indian man came out carrying in his outstretched arms, holding it out to Sam, the body of a two-year-old girl, shot through the back. The father's hands were red with the blood that still flowed from the dead child as he continued to hold her out, waiting, as his expression made only too plain, for the American to tell him why . . . why, while down below, crouched in a heap, the mother wept. An abstract knowledge of the infinitely greater scale on which this sort of thing was taking place in other theaters did not help one confront it face to face. Through Sam's emotions ran the thought of how far the world had come from Sayler's Creek . . . in a mere eighty years!

254

When the battalion was relieved at Zigyun by the Chinese, Sam's platoon returned with it to the airstrip. "We were at the north end of the strip, falling out for a break," Sam said, "and I was looking for something to sit down next to that I could lean against when I spotted a mound of earth. I was just getting ready to drop down beside it when I saw there was a cross at the end of it, with a dog tag hanging over it. I looked at it, and the name was Captain William A. Laffin! God—I'd never heard he'd been killed!" Bill Laffin, for whom Sam had a specially warm feeling, had been flying over Myitkyina in an L-1 examining Japanese defenses when a flight of Zeros put in one of their occasional appearances and shot his plane down.

"Sam," said one of the doctors, "I know for a fact you've been defecating blood for two weeks, and I don't even need to take your temperature. You've had it, boy. Out you go."

"Sammy, can I have your Tommy gun?" one of the men asked.

There was never much ceremony when the end came for another Marauder.

They had to take Sam out of the plane at Ledo on a litter. After an examination, he was taken to the typhus ward. "Don't worry," said a nurse just outside the circle of light, patting him on the head. "You'll be all right." It had not occurred to Sam, whose only thought was that this was heaven, that he would not be. He had, however, no right to take it for granted. He had all of the three worst scourges of the organization, in combination: mite typhus, amoebic dysentery and malaria. He also had youth, without which he would never have lived. Others were not so fortunate. Sam found in the morning that Bill Bright was in the bed next to his. Bill was hardly conscious, though, and the next night Sam was aroused to half awareness by people with flashlights stirring beside him, and when he awoke he found Bill's bed empty. Billy Lepore, with whom he had buried the two men on the hilltop the second day of the march to Shaduzup, also died in a bed near his. So did Colonel

255

Kinnison. So did Sergeant Herbert Nelson, a mainstay of my platoon.

On May 25, in response to a gloomy report from McCammon, Stilwell flew into Myitkyina for his second visit. There a jolt from an unexpected quarter awaited him. Colonel Hunter had held his peace a long time but what required saying could be held back no longer.

Hunter can be pictured writing his statement, sitting beside his foxhole stripped to a pair of baggy-pocketed fatigue trousers, the sinews of his arms and trunk unnaturally prominent, the black gap in his teeth where two incisors were missing—left embedded in a dried-out fruit bar—giving him somewhat the appearance of a boyish witch.

He wrote, citing instances to support the assertion, that Galahad had from the start been treated as a visiting unit for which Theater Headquarters felt no responsibility. He recalled, among other things, having taken up several times with the authorities in New Delhi without apparent result the consequences of Galahad's organization as a provisional composite unit, which were such as to deprive it of colors, insignia and other emblems that military units are normally provided with as important contributions to their morale. Recalling also a statement by General Merrill that no officers would be promoted until the end of the operation, he pointed out that, although the unit had been in continual contact with the Japanese for over three months and had performed capably, no award or decoration, no citation or indication of appreciation other than the routine award of the Purple Heart to those who were wounded had, so far as he could determine, been made to any member of the organization. The morale of Galahad had been sustained, he pointed out, only because of promises that it would not be used as a spearhead for Chinese troops and that immediately upon its arrival at Myitkyina and the capture of the airfield its personnel would be flown out for rest and reorganization—neither of which had been carried out. Repeatedly, he said, adverse reports on the health of the organization had been submitted

256

but no effort had been made by the theater to satisfy itself about the facts, and Galahad was now practically unfit for combat, with the consequence that the sense of security afforded by its presence at Myitkyina was false. Concluding, he recommended, first, that promotions be awarded to officers of the unit who deserved them and that until that was done no other personnel in the theater be promoted, second, that on the termination of present operations Galahad be disbanded and its personnel assigned to other units, and, finally, that in the future American infantry units assigned to the theater be treated in such a manner as to instill in them a pride of organization, a desire to fight, and a feeling of being part of a united effort.

Charles N. Hunter had a belief in the Army, a belief in discipline, and a deep aversion to prima donnas. (I can hear him addressing us at Deolali: "I don't want to see anyone taking sun baths. I don't know why it should be, but I've found that people who take sun baths are difficult to get along with.") A soldier less like the moody, intuitive, intractable Orde C. Wingate (who, if he never took sun baths, liked to deliver disquisitions stretched out stark naked on his bed, munching a raw onion) could scarcely be found. It was illustrative of the difference between them that, while Wingate publicized his methods as a radical departure from the conventional, Hunter, when he came to write up the lessons learned from Galahad, emphasized that they chiefly confirmed the hard lessons learned in the past and embodied in Army doctrine. It is all the more striking, therefore, that Gideon and Galahad should have ended in the same way, with their commanding officers penning an indictment of the higher headquarters for the indifference it displayed and its neglectfulness. Wingate broadcast 250 copies of his Appreciation, however, while Hunter—which is further indicative of the difference between the two—confined the distribution of his to a single copy, which he handed directly to Stilwell. Suicide, which Wingate attempted in the hotel in Cairo, was the last extremity ever to have had any attraction for Hunter, although it must have at least crossed Hunter's mind

257

that in speaking up as he did he was taking his career if not his life in his hands.

Two days later the last action fought by a battalion of the 5307th, as such, ended with its commanding officer declaring it unfit for further employment and requesting its relief. The 2nd Battalion, or what remained of it, had been ordered to push south of Charpate. The Japanese force it met was not very strong, but during the action several men fell asleep from sheer exhaustion while Colonel McGee lost consciousness three times while directing it. By that time a man had to run a fever of 102 degrees or better for three consecutive days and be certified as unfit by a board of medical authorities before being tagged for evacuation. All the same, at the end of May only 200 of the 3,000 men with which the 5307th had started—a remnant of 1st Battalion—were considered fit to remain at Myitkyina. The point was now clear. "Galahad," wrote Stilwell in his diary, "is just shot."

IX During the last week of May, while the commanding officer was coming down with pleurisy, there was alarm in Task Force Headquarters at Myitkyina. The 5307th was collapsing. An element of the Chindits called Morris Force, which had come up from central Burma, was on the other side of the Irrawaddy with the mission of blocking Japanese communications on the east, but this mission it was proving incapable of carrying out, for it was suffering the same acute deterioration as the 5307th and for the same reasons. The Chinese 150th Regiment was down to 600 men. The rest of the available forces were quite unable to prevent the Japanese from receiving supplies and reinforcements. At the same time reserves of food and ammunition on the Allied side were perilously low and replenishment was difficult; the nine grim-looking, wrecked transports on the strip were a reminder of the difficulties. Great as was the anxiety at the strip, it would have been greater still had the size of the Japanese garrison been known. It was, in fact, grossly underestimated. Not until after the war was it learned that 4,600 Japanese had been at Myitkyina, as many as 3,500 at one time. Oddly enough, the Japanese made just as gross a miscalculation of Allied strength, but in the other direction. Instead of the 30,000 the Japanese believed were besieging them, Stilwell was never able to muster much more than 12,000 until near the end of July. At the period of the emergency there were no more than half that number, and those that were there were dependent upon an attenuated, unreliable line of communications which a few days of rain, in a season of heavy rainfall, could totally disrupt.

Stilwell had made several gambles that had not panned out and now the bills were due. The question was, who was going to pay them?

Through the wards and convalescent camp at Margherita raced a piece of stunning news: orders had been issued that any of those in the 5307th who were able to walk were to be rushed back to Myitkyina. As the *U.S. Army in World War II* observes, "This order was in sharp contrast to the men's expectation that after reaching Myitkyina they would have a long period of recuperation." It was indeed.

On the heels of the order the convalescent camp was combed and 200 were adjudged sufficiently recovered to be sent back in. (One reason why we had so few recovered convalescents was that back in April the earlier evacuees to the number of 250 had been collected and sent back to Burma to be combined with a force of Chinese for what proved to be a wild-goose chase in the Mogaung valley.) Upon arrival, many were found quite unfit and some had to be immediately re-evacuated.

Then began a time when the Marauders, who had done so much fighting, were themselves fought over. On one side was Stilwell's headquarters, which was placing "extremely heavy moral pressure, just short of outright orders . . . on medical officers to return to duty or keep in the line every American who could pull a trigger." [1] On the other were the medical officers themselves—the unit's own and the local hospital authorities—who were loath to certify as fit for combat men who were broken physically and mentally.

General Stilwell was later reported in *Time* to have been appalled at the overzealous interpretation given his instructions by his subordinates. On that point I cannot testify. On one occasion when these subordinates had several hundred of us loaded in trucks, the medical officers took after the convoy in jeeps, intercepted it, and forced it to return. In the end the doctors were to win—but not before the damage had been done.

During the crisis at Myitkyina, Stilwell thought of asking that the British 36th Division be rushed in to take the town, but quickly dropped the idea, doubtless because, having burned the Limeys up, it would have been a little awkward to ask them to bail him out. He desired, as he wrote General Marshall, to "keep an American flavor in the fight." Accordingly, "American reinforcements of any men who could hold a rifle were rushed in from every possible source." [1] In addition to the convalescent Marauders, these included two engineer battalions from the Ledo Road which "had not seen a rifle since their basic training days and had simply been taken from their bulldozers and power generators to fight as infantry combat teams." [1] They also included 2,600 men who had just arrived in Bombay and were to have provided the personnel for a new Galahad which, after organization and training, would have gone in the next season. However, after an average stay of about a week at Ramgarh they were flown to Myitkyina. There, with the chalked numbers giving the order of their disembarkation from their transport still visible on their helmets, they were formed into three battalions under Colonel Hunter, each battalion being starched with veterans from the 5307th. (A month later the engineer battalions as well were placed under Hunter's command.)

Pathetic and harrowing accounts of the fate of the green American troops came back to us in the hospital wards. New evacuees told of men receiving instruction in their weapons in the planes taking them to Myitkyina—the "Cassino on a shoe-string," as the official history was to call it—and of how they were unnerved at the start by having to dive for cover on disembarking because the airfield was under Japanese artillery fire. The officers and men of the new battalions had never seen one another until three days before leaving the United States; there had been no chance whatever to develop teamwork. Captain

261

Robert P. Maxon testified that of the 200 men in his infantry company there were 53 who had never before been in any branch but the field artillery. "There were M.P.'s, tankdrivers, one laundry machine operator, and various other branches, all classified as infantry—riflemen. Other company commanders told me that they had the same situation in their outfits too." Lieutenant Lewis B. Mitchell testified that the weapons platoon (which is to say mortar and machine-gun platoon) that he organized at the Myitkyina airstrip on June 3 contained exactly two experienced mortar men and three experienced machine gunners. They had received none of their weapons when they moved out that same day to assume responsibility for the defense of Colonel Hunter's command post on the railroad. "When we arrived at the C.P. perimeter we took over five 50-caliber machine guns from the Engineers. The rest of the day was spent in organizing the position. I had one man in the platoon who knew 50-caliber machine guns. He went around to each gun and explained how to load, aim and fire the weapon. The night was spent in this position. On the afternoon of June 4 we were given two 60-milimeter mortars and two heavy 30-caliber machine guns. We spent the rest of the day training the inexperienced men on these weapons. On the morning of June 5 we were notified that we would move out and attack at 1300. . . ."

Instruction in weapons continued for the new units; on one sector of the front it was sometimes difficult to be sure whether a rattle of firing meant a Japanese attack on the perimeter or a practice session of the improvised range by a group of newly arrived Americans. More realistic practice was provided by taking the newcomers to Namkwi, where they could be pitted against a Japanese force and disengaged if the situation became too hot.

The occurrence that brought home to us most tellingly the peculiar horror of the Myitkyina fighting was one that involved a company of the replacements for Galahad. On its way to join a battalion of Chinese which had pushed deep into Japanese defenses, it met a patrol of Asians whose Chinese uniforms seemed to warrant the assumption that it had been sent out to guide the American company forward. Indeed, the officer in command beckoned smilingly. It was only when the two units had come together and the ostensibly Chinese patrol leader asked the company to lay down its arms that the inexperienced American commander realized that he had fallen into an ambush. A dreadful toll was taken of the Americans by Japanese machine gunners before the remainder could scatter and escape. The company was never reconstituted.

By June 7 the 89th and 150th Chinese Regiments mustered between them only 1,000 men, while the 88th and 42nd could put up only one battalion each for an attack.[1] Some of the Chinese units, moreover, were causing almost as much consternation among their allies as they may have among the enemy. At a time when supply was particularly tight and the number of disabled planes on the strip had risen to thirteen, we heard of Chinese recklessly firing off by night all the ammunition that could be flown in by day.

"They lie back in their foxholes and turn their machine guns loose like hoses," one of the Marauders told us. "You'd think it was a damned amusement park, to see the tracers." The disgust of the Americans was surpassed, however, by the anger of the adjoining Chinese regiment, the 89th, which threatened to attack the offenders unless they behaved.

An American lieutenant colonel, Franklin T. Orth, attached to the unhappy Chinese 150th as a liaison officer found out the first night the sort of thing he was in for when the regiment pulled out quietly under cover of darkness and left him asleep in no man's land. The tables were turned, in a manner of speaking, shortly afterward when twenty American planes bombed the 150th in error and killed 6 and wounded 15.

The British in Morris Force, east of the river, as their commander pointed out in reply to demands by Task Force Headquarters that the unit launch prompt attacks upon the Japanese, were wasting away at the rate of a third of a platoon a day and

were so exhausted they were falling asleep under Japanese fire.[1]
A bitter controversy developed between Stilwell and Mountbatten's headquarters over the question of the evacuation of the
3rd Indian Division, the Chindits, of which Morris Force was
a detachment. The bulk of the division was in central Burma,
blocking Japanese rail communications. The British wished to
withdraw it in accordance with Wingate's doctrine that three
months behind enemy lines was enough for any unit. Mountbatten and Stilwell had had fierce personal arguments over
this point, and Mountbatten had angered Stilwell, who believed
his troops to be more rugged than Wingate's, by maintaining
that overstraining his forces in long-range penetration operations could lead to their disintegration and even to mutiny. Stilwell, who particularly did not wish to have the 3rd Indian Division retire toward his lines "bringing with it all the Japanese it
had attracted," [1] was strongly opposed to its withdrawal. His
headquarters, even as late as mid-July, insisted that Morris
Force was still capable of launching attacks, although it had
been reduced to three platoons from its original 1,310 men.
Stilwell's position seemed to be that he could not permit the
British to withdraw without permitting the Americans to do so,
or vice versa, or permit either to withdraw while the Chinese
22nd and 38th Divisions, which had been in Burma since November, were required to remain—which begged the question
of whether the cases of the British and Americans, on the one
hand, and the Chinese, on the other, were really comparable.

Against the depleted Chinese and British units and the unready Americans, braced by a few hundred battle-worn Marauders, was ranged a numerically smaller Japanese force but
one made up of some of the toughest and most experienced
fighters in Asia confident of success in the expectation that reinforcements were on their way and prepared, whatever the event,
to fight to the last for the God-Emperor. "There were days in
which a *banzai* charge by General Mizukami's garrison or a
determined push by the [Japanese] 53rd Division (which had
once been ordered to send a regiment and lift the siege) would

in all probability have swept right over the airstrip," in the view of the Army historians.[1]

The defenders had, moreover, every advantage of terrain: trenches to fight from and trenches to fall back upon, houses and railroad cars for shelter and concealment, roads built up as high as twelve feet above the level of the flooded paddy fields, forming natural breastworks, and, on one side of the town, low-lying ground that had been turned into a lake by the rains. The prospect confronting Morris Force, whose commander pointed out that except for a few avenues of approach, well covered by Japanese machine guns, the country was flooded chest-high,[1] was similar to that faced by many of the Allied units.

The situation was one that must be unusual in war; the besieging force was itself surrounded by enemy-held territory. Allied forces could not hope to forge any "ring of steel." Far from it. They held a series of strong points stretching from Pamati, on the river, northeast to Charpate, but there were Japanese in strength behind the line, at Namkwi, as well as in front, and between the strong points were generous gaps. This made for a peculiarly desperate kind of combat. There was infiltration and counterinfiltration, uncertainty as to the whereabouts of both friendly and hostile forces, and the ever-present threat of being cut off. From time to time units were in fact cut off and were either relieved with great difficulty or forced to break up and infiltrate back at heavy cost. It was no wonder that the inexperienced American troops sometimes went to pieces. Many were simply terrified, and there were instances in which engineer units broke and ran under fire, abandoning their wounded. Fifty individual cases were recognized as "psychopathic." One lieutenant of whom we heard suddenly discovered, upon being ordered to take a patrol out, that he was a conscientious objector—which did not spare him a court-martial. His was not the only court-martial or the only case in which an officer was found unfit and relieved. One of the battalions of the so-called New Galahad, says the official history laconically, "reported trouble in effecting reorganization and enforcing orders." [1]

But every case of panic could be matched with one of heroism. After suffering casualties as heavy as those of any American unit in any theater [1] the engineers became first-rate combat soldiers, as did the replacements for Galahad. The Chinese fought and died as courageously as the Americans. Within a few weeks the Allied effort, backed by increasing troop strength, a swelling flow of supplies, and the support of fighter planes based on the Myitkyina airstrip, began to tell even against the furious determination and unsurpassed courage of the Japanese. Before June was over, though the end at Myitkyina was six weeks distant, the end could no longer be in doubt.

On the 22nd of June I had a good look at the airstrip at Myitkyina. With its deeply dug-in and sandbagged headquarters installations, its vistas of trenches, foxholes and mounds of raw earth—for it was still within Japanese artillery range—it was as dreary and dispiriting as one had expected, its atmosphere as sour. Having fighter planes right there at hand, perched fastidiously on the field like brightly colored hornets, was a novelty, and the effect of the brilliant-hued parachutes strung up as tents was an odd one, giving the scene the appearance of a fair grounds—one in hell, attended by an army of the condemned. The slow-moving oxcarts that carried supplies out over the muddy roads and brought back the sick and wounded were altogether in character. Anyone expecting the front to be a place of frenzied activity would have been greatly surprised. Combat leaves men no feeling or energy to squander, and the lethargy of war hung over Myitkyina. I am afraid that I did not have to be urged when Colonel Osborne, who seemed very surprised to see me, told me to go on back.

What had happened to account for my appearance there was that while supposedly convalescent I had found myself with a strange debility that sometimes made me feel I could not stand up. It was like being drugged. It could not be explained by the

266

cut in my heel, which was just about cured, or by the malaria from which I had just recovered, and I concluded that it must be mental, the result of the fear of Myitkyina, which brooded over that camp like the literal figure of Death. The only thing to do—for I seemed to be getting worse—was to take the bull by the horns. All I had to do was bring myself to do it. William Beebe wrote that once when suffering a collapse of morale he had been restored by reading a pile of dime novels, and I remembered how, shortly after I had volunteered for what turned out to be the 5307th and had got an inkling of what it was about, I had been cured of the funk into which it had thrown me by the hero's performance in a run-of-the-mill war movie. In the collection of books at the Red Cross canteen I found one on developing will power, and the effect of reading it was all I could have hoped for. Flooded with resolution, I went down the line to Dinjan, presented myself for repatriation, and was put on a plane. By that time, however, the emergency had passed, and Osborne said the idea now was to get the 5307th out of Myitkyina, not reassembled there. John George, who had been so sick at the end of his 50-mile hike to Pabum in quest of Chinese support at Nhpum Ga that he had been sent straight on out of Burma, had the same experience when he reported to Colonel Hunter at Myitkyina. By that time few of the Marauders who had been there continuously still remained. Among them was Phil Weld, whose cheerful and self-deprecating conscientiousness somehow kept him going into July. On the morning of the 6th, his son's sixth birthday, it came to him that he was finished. He looked at his Atabrine pills and said the hell with them, whereupon his temperature shot up to 105 degrees.

Among the contributions to progress at Myitkyina were the successes of the Chinese and British on other fronts. Two days after the capture of the Myitkyina airstrip the generals commanding the Chinese divisions in the Mogaung valley apparently received authorization from Chiang Kai-shek to advance, for the next morning General Sun Li-jen of the 38th Division astonished the American liaison officer by stating, "We go on

267

to take Kamaing now." [1] A few days later, having executed a Marauder-style envelopment, one of Sun's regiments burst in upon a major supply depot of General Tanaka's below Kamaing, capturing relatively enormous booty and cutting off the 18th Division. Although subjected to terrible punishment, the Chinese succeeded in holding the block. With his communications far to the south already blocked by the Chindits, unable to dislodge the Chinese from the road below Kamaing, pounded by Chinese artillery and American planes, the rations of his men reduced from 860 to 100 grams of rice a day, and greatly outnumbered, Tanaka was faced with the destruction of his division. A report by the commander of the 56th Regiment, which had fought the 5307th at Walawbum, gives a picture of the straits to which the Japanese had been reduced. It is difficult to read without emotion:

The advance attack of the enemy from the north is unexpectedly swift; the enemy is advancing southward, threading through the gaps in our lines by wading chest-high through marshy zones. I am unable to get in touch with 1st and 3rd Battalions, which are under my command, and their situation is unknown. The platoon occupying the vicinity of Nanyaseik received an enemy onslaught and all troops were annihilated. The enemy stormed into our main artillery position, and with our motor trucks, artillery and other vehicles crowded together in the vicinity of the narrow, forked road, there is much confusion. The transfer of most of the patients has been completed. The regiment will cover the withdrawal of the main body of the division at the sacrifice of our lives. I believe this will be our final parting. Please give my best regards to the division commander.[1]

Of the 18th Division and the two additional regiments under Tanaka's command only 5,000 men succeeded in escaping.

Following the fall of Kamaing, British Chindits who had pushed up from the south made contact with the Chinese and Stilwell ordered a Chindit brigade to attack Mogaung. In the hospitals of Assam and at the airstrip of Myitkyina spirits were buoyed by news of the sweeping British onslaught upon Mogaung and by the news of the town's fall on June 26 to simultaneous British and Chinese thrusts. With that the road from Mogaung to Myitkyina was open and the Allied Task Force was no longer an island but was joined with the main British and Chinese Armies.

Farther to the south, the Japanese invasion of India had been checked in April and by early May the Japanese had begun to weaken. By the end of the month the British were counterattacking, and on June 22, four days before the fall of Mogaung, they succeeded in reopening the Imphal-Kohima road.

The total of enemy casualties in the battles of the Imphal plain [Admiral Mountbatten reported] is not known, even to the Japanese themselves; but the three Japanese divisions and the Indian National Army Division [which fought on the Japanese side] all suffered very severely. 13,500 dead were counted on the battlefields; these included neither losses by air actions, nor the wounded (of whom the greater part must have died), nor those who died of disease and hunger. At a conservative estimate, it may be said that the enemy lost 30,000 men between mid-March and mid-June; and among a large amount of equipment we captured were nearly 100 guns. The defeat of the Fifteenth Japanese Army was resulting in a disorderly withdrawal under monsoon conditions—a contingency for which the Japanese had made no allowance.[2]

The Japanese retreat from Imphal over the Chin Hills under the torrents of the monsoon rains was one of the horrors of the war in Asia; no one will ever know how many thousands of Japanese died of wounds, starvation and exhaustion on those trails which two years before had provided the avenue of escape for the defeated British and for the Americans in Stilwell's party.

In following the fortunes of an American infantry outfit in Burma it is easy to form an exaggerated idea of the part that American troops played in the victories by which the country was painfully, and in the end completely, retaken. In the full picture of the ground war in Burma, extending over three years

269

and some 150,000 square miles, the American part made up only a small fragment. American Lend-Lease and the U.S. Army Air Force played essential roles, but the bitter task of winning the country back mile by mile, hill by hill, house by house, sometimes yard by yard, was—to borrow a British expression—a British show primarily, and secondarily, in the north, a Chinese show. And a magnificent show it was in the performances the soldiers of the two armies gave against the varied backdrops of that cruel theater—for the Chinese, Bhamo's entrenchments and the gorges of the Salween, the "Mad River," for the troops of the British Empire, the 9,000-foot heights of the Tamu road, the pestilential Kabaw valley, the dry plains across the Irrawaddy, the fortress of Dufferin in Mandalay, the ceaseless downpours of the Arakan. "I called on the troops . . . for the impossible," said General Sir William Slim, commanding the largest single army in the world, as it was termed, "and I got it." It was a fair appraisal of all those who gave and achieved the ultimate in Burma.

At Myitkyina by mid-July, as it is now known, 790 of the Japanese garrison had been killed and 1,180 wounded. At the end of the month the weakening of Japanese resistance was apparent to the Allies. On August 3 all units of the Task Force closed in and quickly overcoming the resistance of the rear guard entered the town. They learned that at the end 600 survivors of the 114th Regiment had succeeded in getting away. General Mizukami, after having granted their commander's request for permission to withdraw the regiment, had committed suicide.

As for the 5307th, its wreckage was by now complete. An investigation prompted by Colonel Hunter's letter to General Stilwell found that by about June 1 there had been an "almost complete breakdown of morale in the major portion of the unit." The testimony taken by the Inspector General is still today being withheld from the public on the grounds that it was given by men speaking in the heat of feeling under assurances that what they said would be kept confidential. The report itself did not delve very deep. According to *The U.S. Army in World War II*, it ascribed the breakdown of morale to "plans and assumptions of the War Department plus unauthorized statements [that] reached the enlisted men and junior officers of Galahad as promises . . . [and] never materialized . . . coupled with the physical deterioration of the unit, after months of arduous jungle combat, and culminating in a rapidly growing feeling that hospitalization procedures were not being carried out."

The "plans and assumptions" of the War Department as set forth in a telegram from General Marshall to General Stilwell of September 30, 1943, were "that Galahad is provided for one major operation of approximately three months duration and that the termination of this operation may result in . . . physical and mental fatigue of survivors necessitating three months hospitalization and rest with probably well-deserved furloughs in U.S. for some personnel who have been in tropics, with some participating in combat, for as much as two and a half years and who waived earned furloughs to volunteer for this operation." An OPD memorandum of the same date noted that "the original personnel for this operation were highly qualified volunteers who tacitly understood they are to take part in one particularly hazardous, self-sacrificing operation." In the 5307th the belief that three months in the field would be the most demanded of the unit, supported by assurances from General Merrill with respect to its withdrawal, was firmly held (as it was among the Chindits) and was the basis upon which the men put forth what they did.

During the month before I went to Myitkyina I was—when on my feet—one of a handful of officers trying to run the rest camp at Margherita. At Myitkyina Colonel Hunter assigned me to the job of adjutant of the Staging Area Detachment at Dinjan, 50 miles south of Margherita. Accordingly, when Caifson Johnson, taking over as senior officer when he was released from the hospital late in July, saw what conditions were he turned to me for the preparation of a report describing them and explaining how they had come about. Having subsequently

271

forgotten the report and remembering only that I had had to write a similar analysis for representatives of the Army's morale division, I did not recognize it when I came upon it recently among other papers on the 5307th I had obtained. What I read made me blink. Whoever wrote this, I thought, was certainly aroused—and made no bones about it. I had gone halfway through it before a dawning suspicion led me to turn to the end to see whose name was on it.

Reading it, my mind went back to a remark Tom Senff had muttered huskily through his infected throat while we were watching the column trudging into a bivouac one evening on the way to Myitkyina, the appearance of the men that of gaunt, fanatic-eyed, and for the most part bearded Indian holy men. "They look as if it were the end of the war for them, don't they?" he said. "But you know, all they need is a pat on the back, a little recognition of what they've done—maybe a parade —and they'd be back in here next season ready to do it all over again."

That was what they had not had. Instead, they had been made to feel that what they had done was not enough.

There were, it is true, other issues. Far from being relieved after three months, the 5307th had still not been relieved when I came to write my report, after five months. In addition, individuals were kept in combat beyond the point at which they could no longer take it. Stories, apparently authentic, came back to us of sick men passed for evacuation by the doctors at Myitkyina having the tags snatched off them at Task Force Headquarters. Moreover, the standing order that any convalescents able to carry a rifle be immediately returned to combat made recovery almost impossible for men still suffering nervous and physical exhaustion—as I knew from my own experience.

Despite assurances that a comfortable rest camp awaited the unit, the area to which the convalescents were released from the hospital "bore no evidence of preparation for the reception of battle-worn men," said the report, and was "a pest-hole." It was a pasture surrounded by bashas in which cows would not have been stalled at home. The shower baths we had been told to expect consisted of a couple of old oil drums and some lengths of rusty pipe kicked off the back of a truck one morning with the information that they were all ours. No one suggested that the base-area troops who had never spent a night away from their comfortable quarters and concrete shower stalls a few miles up the road might move over for us. Then when some of our early evacuees returned from leave they brought back stories of electric fans and refrigerators that rear-echelon officers at New Delhi had abstracted from the supply line for their offices or even private use—while our sick and wounded were in some cases sweltering in stifling wards with only tepid drinks to cool them. Later I was myself put up in one of the barracks in New Delhi and was reminded, as I wrote in a letter, of the dormitory of an expensive university. "I have a room about 25 feet square all to myself, with rugs on the floor, an electric fan, a lamp as well as overhead lights, a bed, two closets, a bureau, a hearth, a writing-table and upholstered easy chairs. This is the first room I've lived in since I came to India. And mind you, *this is how 2nd lieutenants live here!"*

But even more than unfulfilled promises, what destroyed the 5307th was the imputation of inadequacy. The Marauders were made to feel that it was lack of courage and stamina on their part that necessitated sending unprepared troops into combat. What made the imputation all the more galling was the knowledge that it was their own hard-won successes, as much as anything, that had led Stilwell to attempt far more than he had originally planned and that they could have warned, had they been asked, that he was biting off more than he could well chew in launching the drive on Myitkyina. There were 30 Chinese divisions in Yunnan doing practically nothing. In India and Burma Stilwell had perhaps 60,000 Chinese divisional troops. He also had about 40,000 American troops. The Marauders had had the experience, common in all armies but characteristic above all of the United States Army, of finding that the farther back you went from the thinly tenanted front lines the more soldiers you met until, a thousand miles to the rear, you could hardly shoulder your way through the press of them. In the circumstances to have theater demanding more even of them than they had already given made the Marauders feel cheated of that for which they had struggled harder than for anything else in their lives.

Most of the men swallowed their bitterness and anger, but not all—and because of the minority the rest camp, as it filled up, was little better than a shambles. At night it was enlivened by gunfire from the side arms a number of the men had retained. The basha where our private belongings were stored was ransacked and the contents either stolen or destroyed in sheer wanton violence; the place looked as if an elephant had gone berserk in it. Administration and control were frustrated by lack of officers. "While the bulk of the unit has been in India," the report I wrote pointed out, "its commanding officer [Colonel Hunter] and the commanding officer of 1st Battalion [Colonel Osborne] have been retained at Myitkyina. The commanding officers of 2nd and 3rd Battalions went straight from the hospital to the United States. The present battalion commanders (each battalion consisting of about 400 men on duty status, with a like number in the hospitals to be administered and supervised) are, respectively, a captain, a first lieutenant and a second lieutenant, with the only field-grade line-officer present —a major—in command of both the rear echelon and the Staging Area." The policy of the local MPs seemed to be to keep out of our camp, and I could not say I blamed them. "Nurses in the hospital," the account went on, "report that in cases of disorder in the wards, the MPs are useless, being afraid to interfere." Back pay and the proceeds of theft went for beer or, which was much worse, a product of the Assam Distilleries labeled "Bull-Fight Brandy," which had been proscribed—but not effectively —by the military authorities because it turned men into maniacs ready to assault anyone interfering with them. ("This beverage," said the report, "has been found by the medical officers

274

of the 14th Evacuation Hospital to contain marijuana, and it renders those under its influence completely irresponsible.")

Once, receiving an urgent summons, I rushed to the little Red Cross canteen to find two enlisted men, evidently Bull-Fight addicts, well on the way to demolishing the place. Two horrified Red Cross girls were backed against the far end while the two drunks hurled plates and shouted obscenities as extreme as I had ever heard even in the 5307th. My intervention merely provided a new target for them and I had to swing a chair to get them out of the place. "It is significant," said my report, "that of the many enlisted men who were present, none would lift a finger to quell the disorder or, subsequently, agree to testify against the offenders."

The report went on: "On two separate occasions within the past ten days men have had to be spirited away to protect them from mob violence. . . . The relief of the Motor Transport Officer, Staging Area Detachment, by the Commanding Officer resulted in gang action by the drivers against an enlisted clerk whom they accused of being responsible for the officer's relief." I do not remember those cases. The motor transport officer, I suppose, had been letting the drivers get away with anything— unlimited time off, use of the vehicles for their own pleasure, and so forth.

Heretofore the worst tendencies latent in the 5307th had been held in check by discipline, lack of opportunity, the ardors of training, marching and combat, and the 5307th's curious and inverted but nonetheless genuine *esprit de corps*. These restraints were now removed. And, as the report said, the unit contained far more than its share of drunkards, derelicts, guardhouse graduates, men of low intelligence, and out-and-out badmen of the traditional kind.

While he was still at Myitkyina, Phil Weld heard a shot inside the perimeter just after his platoon had received half a dozen replacements, men who had been evacuated from earlier actions and now had been sent from the hospital back to combat. He found that one of them, a staff sergeant, had put a

275

bullet through the middle toe of his right foot, leaving a clean puncture in his leather boot. Said the sergeant in an even voice, "There'll be a lot more doing the same, Lieutenant, if you don't get us the hell out of here." Phil spoke his mind to the others and the epidemic did not develop. As a matter of fact, the two hundred who were flown back to the unit from the hospital helped save the day and shared in the six Dis ͏ ͏ ͏ ͏ ͏ d Service Crosses earned at Myitkyina by the 5307th.

At the rest camp, the report went on, "thievery within the unit has reached the proportions of a major preoccupation. . . . Nothing in the area can be considered safe. Sentries, owing to their indifference and untrustworthiness, are of scant value."

Lew Kolodny and I would share our dismal reflections. At the time when the pressure was on to herd the convalescents back to combat—the source of so much of the trouble—he had been working tirelessly with the local hospital authorities to prevent it. "By God," I would say, "anyone who wants to be an officer should go try his bloody command presence on those sullen, arrogant bastards out there!" Orders were all but impossible to enforce and work details were not worth the effort of trying to assemble. There was nothing with which to threaten the rebellious but the guardhouse, and this would have appealed to most of them as a luxurious alternative to Burma. AWOLs were wholesale, and as furloughs began to be granted the MPs in Calcutta had their hands full. In the rest camp there were men living like bands of pirates—still sick, most of them —gambling and pitching empty beer cans out the windows; in some cases junior officers were gambling and getting drunk with them.

Such was the camp around which it fell to me to conduct an inspecting officer from the Northern Combat Area Command. We made the tour in silence, and I wondered what form of dressing-down I would receive from Colonel Easterbrook. What invective adequate to the enormity would he find? Had I known that he was General Stilwell's son-in-law I should have stood in even greater expectation of incineration. At the end—and I shall always remember him with gratitude and admiration for it—he simply held out his hand, allowed our eyes to meet for an instant of understanding, and got back in his jeep.

The end of it was that we were left to our own devices, and I cannot believe there was any alternative. The 5307th was beyond being cajoled, and I should rather not consider what the consequences would have been had another military unit been brought in to police the camp. What gave the situation a peculiar twist was that at the time of its degradation the organization's reputation for proficiency and valor shone throughout the theater. We heard with amusement of a group of rear-echelon types in New Delhi who, one day on a street corner, desisted from their congenital pastime of deriding the British to bait a Japanese-American enlisted man standing by himself. The object of this attention merely made a quarter turn, bringing into view the 5307th's well-known shoulder patch. And that was that.

Our insignia, which was colorful and dramatic, with a bolt of red lightning cutting through a field of green between the Star of Burma and the Kuomintang Sun of China, was one by which, having designed it ourselves and knowing it be unauthorized, we set particular store. In the hope of combating the thievery and other delinquencies rampant in the organization by promoting its pride, I spent two days reproducing its insignia in oil paints on a two-foot-square piece of sheet metal and hung it from a telephone pole outside the orderly room. All day, as word of the ornament spread, groups of soldiers came to gaze up at it and stop by to express their admiration. By evening I had about decided that I might be a success as a regimental adjutant after all . . . and by morning the sign had been stolen, never to be seen again.

I had better luck when, in the spell of moral weakness that follows malaria, I composed a 10-stanza poem on the 5307th's exploits which General Merrill, to whom I had sent it in the hospital in the spirit of an offering, passed on to the *C.B.I.*

277

Roundup, which printed it. Unit censors told me that half the letters coming out of the 5307th contained copies of it—which seemed to confirm what I had suspected, that what the Marauders chiefly wanted was what we all want: a little praise before it is too late.

In a memorandum of June 30 to General Marshall, Major General Handy of OPD made the statement that no general of modern times had faced and overcome the obstacles that General Stilwell had. "Beset by a terrific struggle with the jungle, the monsoons, the Japanese, logistics, to say nothing of mite typhus complications, he has staged a campaign that history will call brilliant." On the basis of Handy's memorandum, Stilwell on August 1 was promoted from Lieutenant General to full General. "We read that Stilwell's promotion is perhaps an indication of big things to come," I wrote home. "We interpret that as meaning that maybe poor old 5307th will be reinforced. We also hope Stilwell's ascension to four-starhood may persuade him to promote some of us second lieutenants."

Far gone as it was in disintegration, we never doubted that Colonel Hunter could pull the 5307th together again in short order; the officer who had dumfounded the entire organization a few days after the fall of Nhpum Ga by sending the ragged victors up and down the field at Hsamsingyang in close-order drill would, we knew, have waded in with a will. But it was not to be.

On August 3, the day Myitkyina fell, and two days after Stilwell's promotion, Colonel Hunter was abruptly relieved. Shortly thereafter he received the orders sending him back to the United States by ship, which could be expected to keep him en route for a month at least. With him when he left he took a letter from General Merrill, which read:

Dear Chuck:

I feel like hell about what you have been up against and want you to know that I have greatly appreciated and recognize all that you have done. I'm sorry that our ending is bound to be rather unpleasant for most of us. I have talked with the boss and have done all I could to get many things squared away but am afraid not much except getting him to recognize that we weren't so far wrong in many things, resulted.

Sincerely,
Frank

If Stilwell was troubled by what had happened to the soldier who had done more than any other to give him the taste of triumph, the recollection must have added a wry twist to the bitterness that he could not have failed to feel over his own fate; for his rewards were, ironically, much like Charles N. Hunter's. He too had had to suffer from maneuverings behind the arras but little related to the winning of the war. ("The Japs continue to be the least of my troubles.") He too was suddenly relieved of command—in October, 1944—at a time when he had finally fought through to an important victory and in the process had worn himself out. He too was sent home under wraps, as it were; the situation with respect to China, he was told, was "dynamite," not to be discussed with anyone, and when his plane stopped at Dallas he found that he was forbidden to leave the airfield and that an MP had been posted by his door to make sure no one got in to interview him.

Given the state of feeling about Stilwell in the 5307th, it could be supposed that a knowledge of his impending recall would have afforded us considerable satisfaction, and I am sure it would. In July, in answer to a question of my father's as to what impression I had of Stilwell, I wrote that to everyone I knew in the 5307th his name was as a red flag to a bull. ("I had him in my rifle sights," said an enlisted man regretfully, speaking of a time at Myitkyina when Stilwell during an inspection had withdrawn to relieve himself. "I coulda squeezed one off and no one woulda known it wasn't a Jap that got the son-of-a-bitch.") I said that, while I had seen him only once, "he impressed me as a small man in a big job . . . bloodless and utterly cold-hearted, without a drop of human kindness." I added, though, that I thought "probably the main trouble was

279

not with the old bird himself but with the stuffed baboons with whom he surrounded himself."

Yet had we known the circumstances in which he was to be recalled, the sympathy we should have felt for him might have caused us to forgive him, in part anyway, for what had happened under his headquarters to our organization and the commander of whom we were so proud. At bottom was the issue between Stilwell and Chiang Kai-shek as to how much China was to exert itself in the war against Japan, and Stilwell's recall was a victory for Chiang—though Chiang's insistence upon winning it was to cost him much of his remaining prestige with the Administration in Washington. On that issue there could be no question as to which side we were on. The preference of the governing regime in China for letting the United States bear the burden of the war, of which we were convinced by its evident military passivity and the reports that kept coming back of its practice of storing away for its future use in perpetuating itself in power vast quantities of military supplies flown over the Hump at the sacrifice of American lives, could not have been expected to appeal to American soldiers, and it did not.

On another, related issue—this one between Stilwell and his own government—we should also have been on Stilwell's side. Like many American soldiers, Stilwell had to fight the notion that there is a cheap and easy way to win wars. In the China-Burma-India Theater this notion took the form of the Chennault plan for winning the battle of China with 150 airplanes. Because Roosevelt was attracted to the plan, as—unfortunately for his own future—was Chiang Kai-shek, the bulk of the supplies flown over the Hump went to Chennault's Fourteenth Air Force rather than to the Chinese Army, with the results that Stilwell had foreseen. In April, 1944, at the time End Run against Myitkyina was being prepared, Japan's China Expeditionary Army commenced to move in the direction of the Fourteenth Air Force's bases in Eastern China. The United States Chiefs of Staff warned President Roosevelt that the Chinese ground forces were "impotent" to meet the threat and that Chennault's air force could do "little more than slightly delay the Japanese advances." They went on to say that "our experience against both the Germans and Japanese in theaters where we have had immensely superior air power has demonstrated the inability of air forces alone to prevent the movement of trained and determined ground armies." Had Stilwell's advice been followed, the Chiefs of Staff observed, "the Chinese ground forces east of the Hump would have been far better equipped and prepared." Terming Stilwell "the one man who has been able to get the Chinese forces to fight against the Japanese in an effective way," they recommended that the Generalissimo be urged to place General Stilwell in command of all Chinese armed forces.[1] The upshot was that while Chiang accepted the idea of an American commander, he would not accept Stilwell and succeeded in bringing about his withdrawal. Meanwhile, the Japanese forces, "moving virtually at will," had captured all the American bases east of Kunming, leaving, as Stilwell pointed out, "nothing to show for all the effort and expense involved."

In writing of Stilwell as bloodless and cold-hearted I was giving vent to an opinion admittedly based on scant acquaintance in circumstances not conducive to objectivity. Dean Rusk, who as Deputy G-3 of the theater saw a good deal of Stilwell and is a man of singular astuteness, says that "underneath the shell which earned for General Stilwell the sobriquet 'Vinegar Joe' was a warm-hearted, cultured human being—a personality he went to considerable lengths to conceal. He was not, in fact, nearly so ruthless as other commanders who had a more agreeable and social exterior." That the complications of a theater command were beyond the range of Stilwell's competence and that his responsibilities took him into waters in which he was out of his depth seems clear. Yet it is difficult to follow his career in the China-Burma-India Theater, with all he was up against, and to read his published diary without feeling his appeal as a soldier and a vital human being. At least I find it so. And no one, certainly, would accuse him of not having strived to the limit of his ability and endurance. It was in the spirit of a man who did not spare himself that he made a remark in a letter to Mrs. Stilwell which, to those of us who also know what it is to be beyond our depth, offers as good a phrase to live by as any we are apt to come upon: "I can only do my best. And the hell with it."

The 5307th Composite Unit (Provisional) was deactivated on August 10, a week after the capture of Myitkyina. By that time a new regulation had been issued by the Army authorizing the return to the United States of all those with over two years of foreign duty. This applied to the entire roster of 2nd and 3rd Battalions, which were now shipped home, some of their members to die in the Battle of the Bulge. Logan Weston was one of those who were sent across India by train and thence flown home, passing over the Holy Land, and he went pursued still by the dichotomy that it was his fate to suffer, exulting, on the one hand, in the number of Japanese his platoon had killed —which he reckoned at over 260—and, on the other, anguished by a sense of guilt at "shedding innocent blood," telling himself that "our hands were smeared with blood, our hearts were hardened to it."

The 5307th was never more than a provisional unit. According to an OPD memorandum dated just after the unit had left San Francisco, the Ground Forces were "not enthusiastic about this type of organization and its special employment," and because it was provided for one major mission, which was expected to finish it more or less, it was "not considered feasible" to make up for losses "by individual replacements."

Yet the end had not been reached after all! As in death the spirit of the Dalai Lama passes to an infant born that very moment, so the 5307th was reincarnated as ("consolidated with," in official terminology) the 475th Infantry Regiment, activated also on August 10. Those of the Marauders in 1st Battalion who were still fit were incorporated in the new regiment under Colonel William Lloyd Osborne's command along with the survivors of New Galahad. The 475th Infantry combined with the 124th Cavalry Regiment (of the Texas National Guard) in the "Mars Force" completed the next year, in co-operation with the Chinese, the task the Marauders had helped carry so far and reached the Burma Road.

The 475th was itself inactivated in China a month before the end of the war—and that surely, one would have thought, was the finish. But no! Nine years later, in 1954, the 475th Infantry was reactivated as the 75th Infantry, Regular Army, with antecedents which could not be in doubt: the 75th was declared entitled to campaign streamers for India-Burma and Central Burma and a Distinguished Unit streamer embroidered "Myitkyina," while for its insignia it was granted a shield on which are two elephant tusks in the form of an arch representing Burma as the gateway to India and two crossed kukris (Gurkha knives) within the arch representing the regiment's victories in jungle combat and also completing the form of an "M"—for "Marauders"! So you see . . . !

All this was in the unforeseeable future, however, when the 5307th Composite Unit (Provisional) came to an end. Its end was characteristic. There was not even a final formation. The outfit had simply trickled away. But before the end we finally had our moment. The day after the battle of Myitkyina was concluded the War Department bestowed upon the 5307th the Distinguished Unit Citation. The order read:

After a series of successful engagements in the Hukawng and Mogaung Valleys of North Burma in March and April 1944, the unit was called on to lead a march over jungle trails through extremely difficult mountain terrain against stubborn resistance in a surprise attack on Myitkyina. The unit proved equal to its task and after a brilliant operation of 17 May 1944 seized the airfield at Myitkyina, an objective of great tactical importance in the campaign, and assisted in the capture of the town of Myitkyina on 3 August 1944.

On top of that our long-recommended promotions were approved. I was one of those who became first lieutenants! That was a surprise that awaited me when I returned from three weeks' leave in New Delhi and Kashmir (plus a week's travel time), but it was not the only one; orders had been received while I was away transferring me to the Military Intelligence Service in Washington.

That was reason enough for bliss. I had everything to look forward to, everything that offered in the country of American girls and vanilla milk shakes, and what I was leaving I could leave with rejoicing. I was sick of Assam, of its raw and ugly military installations and flooded latrines, of the mud and streaming eaves and moldy-smelling clothes when it was raining and, when it was not, of the heat so oppressive that you could hardly inflate your lungs. I was sick of soldiers, of there being nothing but soldiers, of never being able to get away from them. I wanted to put the memory of Walawbum and Shaduzup behind me. I wanted to forget the abyss over which we are held suspended on a three-day supply of food, a shelter against rain and cold, and that fragile state of being known as health. I wanted to forget what fear could do to one.

It was still fresh in my mind how I had told myself once when my part of the column was caught in a volley of firing in a rocky ravine that I would never forget what I knew now, that war was the worst calamity that could befall; anything else would be better. Sometime after that we had come into possession of a few copies of the paper-bound, pocket-sized books printed for servicemen by the Army—the good old Army, as it really was after all. I had one on the history of the Arabs. It was an excellent book, and its accounts of the battles the Arabs fought were doubtless instructive—only I could not read them. They made me ill. The same thing happened when my thoughts turned to the War Between the States. The engagements that once had stirred me with their demonstration of Confederate prowess now meant nothing to me but the terror and agony of the men helplessly caught up in them. I did not want to read about them any more. Perhaps all this was one reason why, when I heard some of those around me avow that once the war was over they were going to write the story of the Marauders, I said in a letter that it almost seemed as if I were the only member of the organization who could definitely be counted upon not to attempt anything of the kind.

Yet, despite all I was getting away from, I did not feel quite as gay about it as I had expected to when I left the site of the 5307th's last assembly, such as it had been, carrying in a suitcase what remained unfilched of my possessions. Just walking away without finding anyone to say good-by to was not much of a way for it all to finish, though it was typical enough. Then . . . there was the organism we had worked so hard to create, now dissipated. There were the comrades now to be scattered around the earth, Sam Wilson to school in the United States, Phil Weld into OSS for a season with the Kachins behind Japanese lines, Meredith Caldwell and Winnie Steinfield into the 475th. . . . Perhaps, too, I had a premonition that the experience I was so eager to put out of mind, the one I characterized in a letter home as incomparably the worst I had ever been through, would in the end stand out in my mind as the experience I would more deeply regret having been deprived of than almost any other I had had.

If I did have such a premonition, it could well have been inspired by a remark another lieutenant had made earlier that day. I believe it was Meredith. At least I seem to recall that the wave of the hand accompanying the remark, bringing the area of the largely deserted camp at Dinjan within its compass, was languid and majestic, in the Caldwellian manner. "The time will come," he observed, "when you will realize that you were with the Green Mountain Boys and Mad Anthony Wayne's Indian fighters and Morgan's Raiders. And being as big an idiot as I am, you will wonder how anyone as fearful and unworthy as you could have been included in such a glorious company."

The years that have passed since then have made the speaker's prescience ever more evident. It has been brought home to me with growing force—if it needed to be brought home—that above everything courage is what counts. With experience we begin to know in our hearts, however we may resist accepting the painful knowledge, that we are alive not in so far as we are having things as we like them but in so far as we are overcoming obstacles. It is courage beyond all else, wherever it is displayed, that quickens the pulse of life. Almost, perhaps, the two are synonymous. "The secret of happiness is freedom," said Pericles, "and the secret of freedom is a brave heart."

Courage is not easy to come by, but I have told myself that if men could find it in them to lead the columns of the 5307th blindly through those hundreds of miles of menacing trails it should be possible for others of us to go on, also blindly but with brave hearts, in the face of the adversities and hazards of existence even though in the end we must prove unequal to them. Such being the case, I credit myself with a foresight equal to Meredith's in my having asked Sam Wilson, while it was still fresh in his mind, how such courage was achieved. Sam was one who, I reasoned, had the insight as well as the experience to tell me if anyone could. He had at that time just sufficiently recovered from his dysentery, typhus and malaria to be released from the hospital.

How, I asked him, were he and the others like him able to keep on going when they knew that sooner or later they were bound to get it, if not around the next bend, then the one after that, when indeed they repeatedly *had* got it, when they had no reason to expect there would be divine intervention on their behalf any more than there had been on behalf of the men we had lost the day before and the day before that—brave men, who prayed, who longed to live as much as he and I and could have had ahead of them as full a measure of life's delicious rewards? How had he been able to face it and keep going—all those miles, all those weeks, those months?

"I can only speak for myself," said Sam. "But as far as I was concerned, it wasn't possible. At least it wasn't when once you had got over the idea you were different from the rest and nothing could touch you. You couldn't face it. Maybe that kind of courage is made. But I haven't got it. There was one ability I found I did have, though. It was a very modest one, to be sure—

but it had to serve. I could command one foot to move out in front of the other one. There's no great trick in that, is there? A matter of elementary muscular control! You can tell your leg what to do, certainly. What's a step? A child can take one! You advance one foot, so . . . and then the other . . . and now the first again. And that is all you have to do, except wipe your hands off from time to time so they won't be too slippery to hold your gun. That's all that is required of you. You just have to take the next step."

Everyone must have wondered at times what it would be like to go back to some period in his past and, in an undefined way, to try to bring it to life again, or relive it. Of course it cannot be done in any but the most limited and figurative sense. The past is gone beyond recovery, and nothing so brings home that truth as an effort to reconstruct a part of it. As you try to establish "how it really was," you discover that the world you have gone back to, though its atmosphere will occasionally flash upon your senses, and you feel for an instant that you are there again, is so shifting and indeterminate, like a vapor, that you almost wonder if it ever existed, if it ever actually happened at all. This gives a peculiar quality to the objects that, bridging the chasm of time, try to assure us that it did. Here among some odds and ends is one of the leaflets addressed to the people of Myitkyina *(Myitkyina Mare Masha Ni!)* which, dropped on the town, warned against trying to come over to Allied lines *(Hpyen ma ni n htet yang gaw)* because of the danger of being accidentally shot. Here in the files from the Army's Record Center in Kansas City is a penciled memorandum dashed off by Frank Orth to protest the bombing of his Chinese regiment by American planes. Here is the small map envelope of khaki duck I carried, still with the maps in it, still stained with the dirt and rains of Burma. Here is the cheap, inch-tall gilded Buddha that spilled out of the pocket of the dead

288

Japanese litter bearer at Lagang Ga. It is as if you awoke from a dream to find before you some of the objects you dreamed about. But they seem, like the flotsam of a shipwreck, to connote not so much the survival as the transience of what has been. However painful the period to which you have turned back may have been, you are filled with a sense of irremediable loss.

Perhaps what you feel you have lost is primarily yourself. You keep coming face to face with the figure of yourself as you were. You know you were not superior then to what you are now. You had more hair, more physical endurance and a smoother face, but on balance you would find it harder to put up with the earlier version of yourself than with the later. You were more foolish and ill-organized then and had more affectations. But what you cannot conceal from yourself is that as you were then your range of possibilities was so much greater than it is now. There are some few possibilities you have realized since then, but they have been paid for at the cost of many more others relinquished to the realm of the forever unrealizable.

If you are drawn to research into lost times, it is almost preferable, I think, to go back to events with which you had no personal association. Almost, but not quite; for there is one wonderful reward in going back to your own past, which is going back also to the friendships that circumstances—particularly the circumstance of geographical separation—have interrupted. Friendship, like love, transcending the law of the conservation of energy by generating warmth where nothing was before, is among the few specifics against the cold that descends upon the earth from empty space, of which there is such a great deal all around us. To be back after thirteen or fourteen years with those with whom one shared a life-and-death experience, in the full sense of that overworked expression, and for whom one felt an affection based on more than a community of fate, is to discover that time is not necessarily all-consuming after all.

289

In having, as I had, an ulterior justification for seeking out those friends, I felt as if I were cheating, almost. I also had a sense—a pleasurable and exciting one—of having beaten the game when I found myself sitting across a table from Lloyd Osborne in the Officers Club of the National War College, walking along a rocky cliff above the harbor of Gloucester with Phil Weld and his wife, Anne, meeting Lew Kolodny in a drugstore in Pimlico, driving to Atlantic City with John George and Sam Wilson to attend a reunion of the Merrill's Marauders Association; I kept wanting to laugh. (The effect of the reunion itself was somewhat different. You could not expect to have known a large proportion of an organization of 3,000 individuals, but to recognize so few among the 70 or 80 who, with their wives, made up the decorous assemblage in the banquet hall gave me the sensation, when I looked around, of having come to the wrong place, and one very unlike Hsamsingyang, perhaps to a meeting of the Chamber of Commerce.) I was still dubious about the book and should not have undertaken it had they not encouraged me to go ahead and promised to help all they could. They were as good as their word. They helped a great deal indeed. Without their contribution there could have been no book.

Two of those I should have gone to straight off for assistance were no longer accessible. Major General Frank D. Merrill, after having served as State Highway Commissioner in his native New Hampshire after the war, corresponding with many ex-Marauders and helping them in their difficulties as well as he could, had died in Florida in December, 1955, overtaken at last by the weakness of the heart he had so overtaxed in Burma. (He was not the only high-ranking officer we had lost. Lieutenant Colonel Charles E. Beach, commander of 3rd Battalion, after facing unperturbed the worst the enemy could do, had killed himself after several years of civilian life in the office of police chief to which his admiring fellow townsmen had elevated him.)

I still found it hard to believe that Winton Steinfield, who had stood at the beginning of an exceptionally promising career in medicine the last time I had seen him, was no longer alive. You would think that if a man were held in as much affection by so many as Winnie was it would protect him, but it is not so. Several years before I had been shocked to read in the newspaper that he and his lovely young wife had disappeared during a squall in a small boat they were sailing off the coast of Maine. I remembered so vividly how Winnie used to swim up and down the Betwa River by the hour with a peculiar wallowing stroke he used, giving you the look of a benign, blue-eyed porpoise when you swam near him; the water had been his second element, and that made his death in such circumstances all the more difficult to adjust to, and the more chilling in its hint of inexorable purposes.

Colonel Charles N. Hunter had become Deputy Chief of Staff for Operations of Fourth Army. It was a great disappointment to me that I did not have a chance to see him; he had no reason for coming east, and I could not afford to go all the way to Fort Sam Houston in Texas. He was good enough to let me see a selection of his papers from the period and to spell out patiently answers to the questions which, in my extensive ignorance, I raised with him in our correspondence, but the residue of his feelings about the campaign and its outcome, whatever they are, remain in his private possession. As for the feelings of the rest of us, we make no bones about them. Ask any of us what they are and the reply will be an expression of loyalty to Colonel Hunter and esteem for him such as few commanders arouse, and one also of distress that he has had so little of the recognition that was his due.

Colonel William Lloyd Osborne, when I first saw him again, turned out to have returned only recently from a tour of duty with what I believe is called EUCOM in Germany. After finishing the course at the National War College he was assigned to work on tactics in a future war at the Pentagon, where, thank goodness, he was available to be telephoned continually. We had to eat several meals together before I could get it into my head that Lloyd, whom, by virtue of the disparity in rank between us, I had regarded as a patriarch in Burma, was actually my junior. This recognition was assisted by his looking no older than he had then—and indeed a great deal better—a condition he ascribed to his never worrying. Lloyd was one of those who had turned out, to my astonishment, to be living within a few miles of me. Logan Weston and Sam Wilson were others.

Logan Weston, like Lloyd Osborne, had been assigned to the Pentagon after several years in Germany. After the war, and after leaving the Army, he had been denied ordination for an unconscionable time on technicalities (as they seemed to me) and then, after he had received it and had rejoined the Army in the expectation of assignment to the Chaplains Corps, technicalities arose again to bar him from that, and he found himself back in the Infantry, headed for Korea a week after the Communist armies launched their attack. There he had fought through the worst year of the war as a company commander; the account of his experiences he gave me, while delivered calmly enough, even gently, was a harrowing one. Now a major, he is still dividing his time between the Infantry and religious duties in the expectation of giving himself up wholly in time to a rural church in Pennsylvania which he now serves as pastor.

Logan was not our only veteran whose exploits in Korea made him widely known. John P. McElmurray, the lanky, taciturn, cigar-chewing Oklahoman, had also become a legend on that grim front for his iron-tempered skill and courage, I learned from Sam Wilson. Only it had been Mac's fate to be killed. He had faced death, I am sure, with that disdain that was characteristic of him.

Sam Wilson, now also a major, had as a Russian linguist and Soviet specialist been adding to his outstanding record in the Army while serving in the office of the Secretary of Defense. At the end of the period he was designated to attend the Command and General Staff College at Fort Leavenworth. In a letter he wrote me from there he spoke of having "Bounced off of" a solidly-built figure in the Post Exchange and of having opened his mouth to apologize when "there, grinning his sleepy-eyed grin was Caifson Johnson, Lt. Col., AUS, veteran of Korea, now teaching staff subjects at C and GSC. . . . Caifson has changed less in fourteen years than any of us." Sam himself had taken on a little weight, as well as a wife and four children, but had a complexion as fresh and pink as ever. One of the things he told me that struck me most, because it was so characteristic, was that he had taken up parachute jumping, in part as a way of dealing with his fear of heights. Having as bad a case of acrophobia as anyone, I asked him if the treatment had helped—not that I had the slightest intention of resorting to it. "No," he said with the round "o" sound of Virginia he still retains, "every time it's as bad as ever." But of his first jump he said with a smile that, after the jolt of the parachute's opening, when he hung there in space, motionless, as it felt, with the initial deafening roar of the airplane's motors receding and the earth laid out peacefully below, "I felt as if I had conquered the universe."

The detail with which Sam remembered our common experience, which approached total recall, never ceased to amaze me. He explained it on the basis of his having had at the time the uncrowded and receptive memory of youth. Anyway, it was invaluable to me. My special indebtedness to Sam will have been apparent to any reader, as will also my special indebtedness to Phil Weld. Phil had recorded his impressions in a notebook while they were still fresh and had written a narrative account of his experiences at Shaduzup, and I helped myself to both of them even more liberally than it would appear from the parts in quotation marks.

I had seen Phil when he came home near the end of the war after serving in the adventurous and hazardous capacity of a leader of the Kachin Rangers from Bhamo south to Mogok. Then again, several years later he had come down to Washington while trying to raise the money to buy two newspapers in his native Massachusetts. He reported that venture capital in Boston could not be bothered with newspapers; it was too excited about a new kind of lemon crystals. "I told them," said Phil disgustedly, "that I'd seen trails in Burma littered with packets of the stuff that starving men had thrown away." I learned later that Phil had finally managed to borrow enough to buy the papers, but I had not realized what a formidable enterprise the Gloucester *Daily Times* and Newburyport *Daily News* represented until I saw the plant in Gloucester. Phil said any awe he had felt about the press was dissipated when he asked the elderly German who came with it to assemble it, in 1956, if he were not overwhelmed by the prospect of the job facing him. "Dot's noddings bud a liddle sewving machine," Phil said he was told. "Me, John Kohlman, I pood in all de *N'Yawk Dimes* presses ven I vas younger." All the same, the press seemed to me to stretch the length of a city block. But what was even more impressive was that Phil was making a success of the venture in a period of high mortality among newspapers and paying off the loans. He and Anne and I sat on the terrace of their house, which looks upon the sea from a high promontory out beyond the Gloucester Coast Guard station in a setting of spectacular beauty, and talked of Burma and the authorship of the plays of Shakespeare over gin-and-tonics. It was lovely.

Lew Kolodny, as I have said, performed the invaluable service of discovering Major Jones's *War Diary* in the Departmental Records Branch of the Adjutant General's Office, as it then was, in Alexandria, Virginia. He even provided me with a photostatic copy he had had made of it, for Lew was so steamed up over the idea of telling the Marauders' story that he had begun a book on the subject himself, intending to write it in the pitifully slim fragments of leisure his burdensome medical practice in Baltimore leaves him. When he heard that I was considering devoting full time to such an undertaking he turned over to me what he had accumulated, after unleashing on me the full force of his enthusiasm for the project, which would have moved a stone.

Tom Senff had recovered from his multiple injuries but because of his daughter's health had had to leave Kentucky and begin a new life and a new law practice in the warmer, drier climate of Victoria, Texas. I exchanged letters with him and also with Meredith Caldwell, Jr., who had become vice president of the Nashville Stock Yards. Meredith had seen the campaign through to the end, which had come with the establishment of a roadblock on the Burma Road; after that, all that was left of the 5307th, he wrote, had been flown back to India from an airstrip north of Lashio. He himself, when he boarded the plane, he added without elucidation, had nothing in his pack but six bottles of grain alcohol.

It is interesting to see how the patterns of individual lives are formed. A passion for the rifle, in which his proficiency is attested by a cabinetful of medals, had taken John B. George into a National Guard regiment and with it to Guadalcanal, before he joined the 5307th. A book on small arms in Guadalcanal which he wrote helped pay for a college education after the war. His studies in international relations and politics, combined with a still-unquenched thirst for hunting, led to three and a half years in East Africa, followed by two years as Executive Director of the African-American Institute and the launching of a career as a writer of fiction concerned especially, so far, with war, hunting and Africa.

Sometimes the logic is less apparent, and when chance seems to govern the example can be disturbing. You make great plans, you issue pronunciamentos, you take determined stands—and nothing comes of them. It is not in the cards. Then you do something offhand and life—fate, or what you will—takes you up on it and nothing is ever the same again.

The Director of Intelligence, Colonel Alfred McCormack, was having to prepare a special briefing on the Ledo Road the day I reported into the Military Intelligence Service at the Pentagon in October, 1944, bringing with me the still vivid

295

impressions acquired from having walked the road. The coincidence struck him forcefully and so fixed me in his mind that when at the end of the war he went to the Department of State he recommended me for a position in the Division of Southeast Asian Affairs. I worked in the Department of State for eleven years, which included serving a year in Indonesia and meeting in the U.S. Consulate General in Batavia the girl I subsequently married, until, supplied with courage by the girl from the Consulate General, I left to write the story of the 5307th—and all this simply because I had remarked to Lieutenant Lewis of the Adjutant General's Section in the mess line one morning in Mississippi that I wished I could do my fighting in a warm climate.

REFERENCES

TO BEGIN WITH . . .

1. *The U.S. Army in World War II. Stilwell's Command Problems*, by Charles F. Romanus and Riley Sunderland.

CHAPTER I

1. This, and most of the rest of the information about Wingate in this chapter, is from *Gideon Goes to War*, by Leonard Oswald Mosley.
2. *Defeat into Victory*, by Sir William Slim.
3. *Stilwell's Command Problems*, by Charles F. Romanus and Riley Sunderland.
4. This and all other quotations from Stilwell in this chapter are, except where noted, from *The Stilwell Papers*, edited by Theodore H. White.
5. *Closing the Ring*, by Winston Churchill.
6. Biennial Report of the Chief of Staff, June 30, 1945.

CHAPTER II

1. War Diary of the 5307th Composite Unit (Provisional); Appendix 16 to History of the Northern Combat Area Command, China-Burma-India and India-Burma Theaters.
2. *The Stilwell Papers*, Theodore H. White.
3. OPD Memorandum 320.2 Sec 8 November 1943.
4. OPD telegram to CG, USAF, CBI, 13 November 1943.
5. *Defeat into Victory*, Sir William Slim.

CHAPTER III

1. *The Stilwell Papers*, Theodore H. White.
2. *Stilwell's Command Problems*, Romanus and Sunderland.

CHAPTER IV

1. *Stilwell's Command Problems*, Romanus and Sunderland, p. 152.

297

CHAPTER VII

1. War Diary of the 5307th Composite Unit (Provisional).
2. James H. Stone in *The Infantry Journal*, March, 1949.

CHAPTER VIII

1. Report to the Combined Chiefs of Staff by the Supreme Allied Commander Southeast Asia, 1943-1945.
2. *Stilwell's Command Problems*, Romanus and Sunderland.

CHAPTER IX

1. *Stilwell's Command Problems*, Romanus and Sunderland.
2. Report to the Combined Chiefs of Staff by the Supreme Allied Commander Southeast Asia.

INDEX

Acker, Sgt. John A., 203
Addis Ababa, 12
African-American Institute, 295
Agra, intelligence school at, 54
Air Force, U.S., 73, 246, 270; at battle of Shaduzup, 179-180; Tenth, 18; 14th, 18, 20, 280
air supply drops, 87, 119, 124, 146, 191; construction of fields for, 147; strain of, 103; of water, 202
Air Transport Command (U.S.), 17
Allahabad, India, 73
Allen, "Young" and "Old," 183-184
Allied Task Force, 269
ambushes, by Japanese, 93, 108; by U.S. troops, 195
American Forces in Action Series, ix, 134
Ammon, Edward G., 96
Anderson, Brig. Gen., 54
Anderson, Marian, 233
Anderson, T/5, 184
Arakan, Lower Burma, 270
Arang, Burma, 239
Army of the United States, first American combat ground force in Asia, 10; role of in Burma ground war, 269-270; see also Infantry Divisions; Infantry Regiments; 5307th Composite Unit (Provisional); Battalions, 1st, 2nd and 3rd; Signal Corps, U.S.
Army Record Center, Kansas City, 288
Arnold, Gen. H. H. ("Hap"), 15
artillery, exchange of, 219; Japanese, 194, 210; at Nhpum Ga, 200-201; at Shaduzup, 180; U.S., 207, 212

artillery fire, sensations under, 7, 181-182; see also fears, combat
Assam, India, 17, 48, 65, 102, 235, 268, 284
Assam Distillers, 274
Associated Press, 69
Atabrine pills, 45, 267
Auche, Burma, 192, 195-198, 207
Australia, 45-46
awards and citations, absence of, 256; see also promotions
AWOLs, "wholesale," 276

Ballard, Sgt. James C., 130
bamboo forests, cutting of, 141-142, 158, 215-216
Banks, Ernest, 176
Batavia, 296
Battalions of Casual Detachment 1688, later 5307th Composite Unit (Provisional): 1st, 56, 109, 137, 149, 189, 192, 194, 202, 213, 228, 241, 247-248, 253, 258; 2nd, 71, 109, 111, 116-117, 119, 137, 189, 196-198, 201-202, 207-208, 210, 216, 228, 241, 248-249, 252, 258, 282; rescue of at Hsamsingyang, 215; in siege of Nhpum Ga, 199-221; 3rd, 39, 71, 107, 110, 125, 189, 192, 196-197, 200, 203-204, 207, 210, 213, 215-216, 228, 235-236, 241, 248, 251, 282
battlefield emotions, 181-182; see also fears, combat
Battle of the Bulge, Germany, 282
Beach, Lt. Col. Charles E., 56, 207, 216, 290
Beebe, William, 267

299

Bengal & Assam Railway, 73, 75
Betwa R., 52, 57, 68, 291
"Black Monday," 249
blood plasma, 211
Bombay, India, 46
booby traps, 108, 119
books, hunger for, 233
Boxer Rebellion, 10
Brahmaputra R., 73-74, 223
Branscomb, Sgt. Clarence, 164, 184, 242
Briggs, Maj. Edwin J., 208-210, 216
Bright, Lt. William T., 54, 150, 152, 177, 187, 232, 240
Brisbane, Australia, 45
British Army: 14th Army, 13, 223; IV Corps, 223; role of in Burma ground war, 270; surrounded at Imphal, 188
British Indian Army, 23, 46
British rations, 55
Brooke, Field Marshal Sir Alan Francis, 15
Brown, Col. Rothwell H., 88, 118, 124-125
Browning automatic rifle (BAR), 96, 116, 129, 138, 171, 194
"Bull-Fight Brandy," 274
Burch, Capt. Clarence O., 208-210
Burma, 29, 31, 75, 78, 88, 106, 139, 150, 167, 190, 194, 218-219, 224, 233, 260; American part in ground war, 269-270; invasion of, 58; late spring and summer conditions, 222; march through, 2; recapture of, 18, 23-24; Stilwell's defeat in, 16, 251, 260, 279
Burma Road, 78, 295
Burmese forest, 92-93

Cairo Conference, 21
Caldwell, Lt. Meredith, 37, 50, 77, 121, 166, 170-171, 177, 243, 245, 248, 252, 285, 295
Camp Adair, Oregon, 36
Camp Stoneman, San Francisco, 29, 32
Canadian Black Watch Highlanders, 43
Caribbean Defense Command, 9, 24
Casual Detachment 1688 (and 1688B), 33-35, 42, 44, 52
casualties, U.S., Inkangatawng and Hsamsingyang, 216, 218; Nhpum Ga, 210; Myitkyina, 270; Walawbum, 134
Cavalry Regiment, 124th, 282
CBI Roundup, 277-278

CBI Theater, *see* China-Burma-India Theater
Chamelas, Lt. Theodore T., 208-210
Charpate, Burma, 248-249, 258, 265
Chengun R., 157-159, 163, 182, 186, 192; passage along, 161-163
Chennault, Maj. Gen. Claire L., 18, 20
Chennault plan, 280
Chiang Kai-shek, Generalissimo, 18, 21, 27, 58, 194, 224, 267, 280; Stilwell's opinion of, 19
Chicago Daily News, 35, 90
China, blockade of, 245; pipeline to, 223
China-Burma-India Theater, ix, 1, 9, 18, 22, 24, 62, 65, 225, 250, 280-281
Chindits, 13-15, 54, 224-225, 259, 264, 268
Chindwin R., 84, 86
Chinese Army in India, 58, 66, 88, 107, 124, 133-134, 137, 180, 194, 206, 219, 224-225, 246, 252; in battle of Myitkyina airstrip, 244; India training center for, 18; military potential of, 23; mortar shelling of 5307th by, 237-238; pack artillery at Shaduzup, 185; reckless firing of ammunition at Myitkyina, 263; seen as "impotent" to meet Japanese threat, 280-281; Stilwell's problems with, 20; strength of, 17; *see also* Infantry Divisions (Chinese); Infantry Regiments (Chinese); Chinese soldier
Chinese Expeditionary Force, 223
Chinese 1st Provisional Tank Group, 88, 118
Chinese Nationalist Army, 89
Chinese soldier, fortitude and endurance of, 225-226; lack of aggressiveness in, 225; Stilwell's appraisal of, 24
Chin Hills, 223, 269; march over, 64
"Chow Raiders," 56
Chungking, China, 16, 18, 22, 69
Churchill, Sir Winston S., 9-10, 14, 16, 20, 38, 246; on Burma campaign, 23
cigarettes, American, 80, 182
Clark, Sgt., 140
Closuit, Capt. Frederick, 237
Coburn, Harry, 178
Combs, Lt. Col. William H., 248
Commandos, 10
communications platoon, work of, 144

Conrad, Joseph, 234
convalescents, return to duty of, 272
Cosmopolitan magazine, x
courage, analysis of, 286-287
courts-martial, of officers, 265-266
Curl, Capt., 190

Dakota planes, 146, 245
Dalton, W. O. Thomas, 35
Darlington, Capt. Charles Evan, 105-106, 119, 148, 150, 157-158
Dayan, Gen. Moshe, 11, 14
death, on battlefield, 181, 211-212; *see also* fears, combat
Delhi, India, *see* New Delhi
Deogarh, India, 52, 63, 65, 68, 71, 79, 98
Deolali, India, 47, 49-50, 82, 257
dextrose tablets, 154-155
Dinjan, Assam, 102, 144, 157, 271, 285; disorder and violence among enlisted men at, 274-275
Diorio, Cpl. Joseph, 129
disease, casualties from, 218; exhaustion from, 197; *see also* dysentery; fever; typhus
Distinguished Service Crosses, Myitkyina, 276
Distinguished Unit Citation, 2, 283
Dolan, Dick, 217
Douglas, Melvyn, 80
Doyer, M. Sgt. Joseph, 43
Drolla, Sgt. Frank S., 253
Dufferin fortress, Mandalay, 270
Dunlap, Lt. Paul, 230, 241
Durdin, Tillman, 79
dysentery, 141, 143, 214, 231, 248, 286; amoebic, 255

Easterbrook, Col. Ernest F., 276
End Run, operation, 228, 246, 280; *see also* Myitkyina
engineers, as combat soldiers, 265-266
Ethiopia, liberation of, 12
exhaustion, physical, 197

fears, combat, 120, 181, 197, 199, 212; at Myitkyina, 267
fever, 232, 235, 252, 258, 267; *see also* disease
Fightin' Preacher, The, x, 41
fish, as food, 136
5307th Composite Unit (Provisional) ("Merrill's Marauders"), 61-65, 81, 111, 116, 125, 132, 139, 149, 187, 193, 195, 221, 224-225; casualties, 134, 210, 216, 218,

270; collapse of, 259; "coming apart" feeling before Myitkyina, 231; "complete wreckage" of, 270; deactivation of, 282; disintegration of after Myitkyina, 247; inadequacy imputed to, 273-274; insignia of, 277; last action fought by, 258; "melting away" of, 252; morale of, 229-230; name changed to "Merrill's Marauders," 70; as relief force at Hsamsingyang, 214; "worst day in history of," 197; *see also* "Merrill's Marauders"
floods, 224
food, absorption in, 150, 153; *see also* rations; rice
Fort Benning, Ga., 32, 37, 46, 96
Fort Hertz, Putao, 78
Fort Leavenworth, Kansas, 292
14th Air Force, *see* Air Force, U.S.
Fourteenth Evacuation Hospital, 274-275
foxholes, booby trapping of, 205; fear of death in, 181-182; race for, at Nhbum Ga, 212
Freeman, Douglas Southall, 38
Fremantle, Australia, 46

Galahad, operation, ix-x, 44, 48, 225, 261; acquires new CO, 58; control of, 49; dangers and discomforts of, summarized, 4-6; Distinguished Unit Citation, 2, 283; Hunter's criticism of to Stilwell, 256-257; investigation of, 1; morale breakdown in, 1, 229-230, 256, 258, 270-271; organization of, 15; reorganizations of, 60; Stilwell and, 22; thumbnail description of, 7; *see also* 5307th Composite Unit (Provisional); "Merrill's Marauders"; New Galahad
Ganges, R., 71-73
Gauhati, Assam, 75
George, Lt. John B., 4, 39, 41, 45, 127, 206, 267, 290, 295
Gideon (Long Range Penetration Group), 11-12, 257
Gosho, Hank, 115
Grant, Gen. Ulysses S., 38
Great Indian Peninsula Railway, 51
Green Mountain Boys, 285
Greer, Sgt. Alfred, 115
grenade launchers, 128
Grissom, Lt. William C., 91, 95, 100
Grumich, Charles, 69

139; at Mogaung, 165-166; at Shaduzup, 170-180; withdrawal of from Walawbum area, 134

Jewish leaders, Zionist movement and, 11

Johnson, Maj. Caifson, 31, 34, 125, 138, 143, 166, 168-171, 178, 228, 230, 244, 248, 271, 293

Joint Chiefs of Staff (U.S.), 22-24, 223, 280

Jones, Maj. John M., ix, 130, 191, 294

jungle warfare, 45, 48; training in, 9, 28-29

Kabaw valley, 270
Kachin Rangers, 139, 293
Kachins, Indian tribe, 103-105, 148, 158, 190-192, 207, 228, 230, 285
Kamaing, Burma, 85, 195, 224, 268
Kamaing Road, 86, 88, 91, 107, 110, 116, 137, 158, 189, 194
Kandy, Ceylon, 22, 26-27
Katz, Cpl. Werner, 94, 116
Kauri, Burma, 192, 199, 203, 207
Kinnison, Col. Henry L., Jr., 228-229, 235-236, 245, 255-256
Kipling, Rudyard, 234
Kohima, India, 223
Kohlman, John, 294
Kolodny, Dr. A. Lewis, ix, xi, 41, 117, 143, 276, 290, 294
Korean War, 292
K rations, see rations
Kumon Ranges, 221, 229, 233, 241
Kunming, China, 17-18
Kweilin, China, 21

Laffin, Capt. William A., 221, 230, 235, 241, 255
Lagang Ga, Burma, 107-108, 111, 119, 124, 132, 289
Lallitpur, India, 68
Landis, Pvt. Robert W., 95
Lanem Ga, Burma, 95
leadership, quality of, 57
Ledo, India, 71-72, 120, 220, 245, 255
Ledo Road, 23, 58, 65-66, 73, 76-77, 86, 106, 171, 240, 261, 295; construction of, 78-81; deaths on, 83
Lee, Gen. Robert E., 38
leech bites, 143
Leitner, Pete, 116
Lend-Lease, 18, 270
Lentaigne, Maj. Gen. W. D. A., 224
Lepore, Lt. William, 140-141, 255
Lew, Maj. Lawrence L., 207-210

Life magazine, 69
liquor ration, British, 55
literature, hunger for, 234
Long Range Penetration Group, 11-12, 15, 29-30, 46, 62, 71, 90
Lurline, S.S., 30, 43, 45, 48
Lynch, Lt. Brendan, 202
Lyons, Capt. Fred O., x, 116

MacArthur, Gen. Douglas A., 30
McCammon, Col. John Easton, 249, 256
McCormack, Col. Alfred, 295
McDowell, Lt., 140
McElmurray, Lt. John P., 41, 138, 157, 166, 169, 178, 292
McGee, Col. George A., 32, 194, 202-203, 208, 216, 228, 245, 258
McLaughlin, Capt. John J., 248
McLogan, Lt. Edward, 204
Maingkwan, Burma, 85, 106, 117-118, 125
malaria, 255, 266, 277
Malaya, 88
Manipur, India, 223
Manuel, Herman, 179
Marauders, see "Merrill's Marauders"
marches, training, 53, 57-58
marching, combat, 77-78, 86; exhaustion from, 197
Margherita, India, 72, 134, 241, 252, 271; staging area, 75
marijuana, use of, 274-275
Mars Force, 283
Marshall, Gen. George C., 9, 17, 20, 24, 48-49, 59, 223, 261, 271, 278; appraisal of Stilwell's mission, 27
Massachusetts Institute of Technology, 64
Matsumoto, Sgt. Roy A., 117-118, 204-205
Maxon, Capt. Robert P., 262
Mediterranean, Allied offensives in, 22
Men at War, 74
Merrill, Brig. Gen. Frank D., 64-65, 68-70, 87, 91, 98, 100, 117, 123, 125, 134, 137, 143, 157, 189, 192, 194, 203, 221, 226, 228, 239, 241, 246, 256, 271; heart attack, 200; and resentments of 5307th Composite Unit, 227; and confusion at Myitkyina airstrip, 249-250; relations with Stilwell, 250; letter to Col. Hunter, 278-279; death, 290
Merrill's Marauders, 14
"Merrill's Marauders," 1, 190, 212;

adoption of name, 70; dazed and spent at Tingkrukawng, 236; deactivation of, 282-283; defeat of Japanese at Walawbum, 127-132; first man lost in action, 95; "pitiful but splendid sight," 248; *see also* 5307th Composite Unit (Provisional)

Merrill's Marauders—What Really Happened, x

Merrill's Marauders Association, 290

Military Intelligence Service, 284, 295

"Mitch," *see* Myitkyina, Burma

Mitchell, Lt. Lewis B., 262

mite typhus, *see* typhus

Mitsukado, Edward, 205

Mizukami, Gen., 264, 270

Mogaung-Myitkyina area, 223

Mogaung-Myitkyina road, 242

Mogaung R., 59, 85, 137, 157, 163, 169, 189, 194-195, 202, 243, 268-269; attack at, 165

Mogaung road, 248

Mogaung valley, 86, 224, 267

morale, complete breakdown of, 270-271; Hunter's appraisal of, 256

Morgan's Raiders, 285

Morris Force, 259, 263, 265

mortars, 90 mm, 128

Mosley, Leonard O., 11, 26

mountain ranges, 229-230

Mountbatten, Admiral Lord Louis, 10, 15, 21, 25-27, 48, 59-60, 68, 223, 269; controversy with Stilwell, 264

mud, 222; *see also* rainy season

mules, as pack animals, 66, 125-126, 141, 143-144, 162-163, 191, 199, 201, 211, 230-231

music, hunger for, 233

Mustang fighters, 207, 218

Myitkyina, Burma, 59, 78-79, 86, 220, 234, 236, 280, 288; Allied and Japanese strengths at, 259; "Cassino on a shoestring," 261; confusion during critical phase at, 250-251; Japanese casualties at, 270; Japanese counteroffensive at, 248-249; misgivings about march to, 226-227; need for taking, 223-224; ominous developments after capture of, 246-247; weapons instructions at, 262

Myitkyina airstrip, 236, 242; battle of, 243-246

Nagas tribe, 80

Nambu machine gun, 172

Namkwi R., 241-243, 249, 262, 265

Nampama R., 192, 195

Nashville Stock Yards, 295

Nasik, India, 47

National Geographic Magazine, 190

Naubum, India, 190, 221, 235, 241; headquarters at, 228

Naura Hkyat, 233-234

Negro engineers, 80

Nelson, Sgt. Herbert, 256

New Caledonia, 44, 66

New Delhi, India, 16, 18, 22, 69, 273

New Galahad, 282

New Georgia, 40, 128

New York Times, 1, 79

Nhpum Ga, 192, 194, 197-199, 223, 278; bamboo forest at, 216; consequences of, 225; killed and wounded at, 210, 213; siege of, 199-221

Ningam Sakan, 86-87

Ningbyen, 86-87

Nisei, in Casual Detachment 1688, 42, 117, 178, 204-205

Norris, Sgt. Tinsley, 173-174

Northern Combat Area Command, 156-157, 220, 225, 227, 276

Noumea, New Caledonia, 44

Nprawa Ga, 149

Numpyck Hka, 107, 109, 118-119, 128

Nyang Ga, 94, 100

Office of Strategic Services (OSS), 39, 100, 105, 139, 149, 190-191, 285

Officer Candidate School, 40, 50

Ogburn, Lt. Charlton, Jr., volunteers for jungle training, 28-29; commands communications platoon, 1st Bn., 33, 54; impressions of senior officers, 42-43; unfamiliarity with electronics, 43, 49; nostalgia in India, 50-51; experience with pack animals, 67-68; as "information center," 91; cut off by Japanese, 93; in attack at Numpyck River, 119-120; meets Lt. Tilly and Kachin Raiders, 148-149; on fear and prayer in foxholes, 181-182; injury at Ritpong, 236-239; evacuated to Ledo, 240; sees Myitkyina airstrip, 266; as adjutant of Staging Area Detachment, Dinjan, 271; impressions of Stilwell, 279-280; promoted to 1st Lt., 283-284; reminiscences and reflections on campaign, 288-295

OPD (Operations Division), *see* War Department

Operation End Run, *see* End Run

Operation Galahad, *see* Galahad

Orth, Lt. Col. Franklin T., x, 263, 288

Osborne, Maj. (later Lt. Col.) William Lloyd, x, 30, 34, 52, 57, 62-63, 67, 123, 131, 137, 139, 145, 148, 150, 156-158, 163, 165-166, 177-178, 182, 186-188, 228, 236-237, 242, 247-248, 266, 274, 282, 290-292

OSS, *see* Office of Strategic Services

Overby, Sgt. Al, 170, 172-176

Owens, Sgt., 123, 125, 154, 168

Pabum, Burma, 206

Pacific Ocean, fighting in, 10

pack animals, 124, 141, 191, 199, 230-231; abandonment of, 204; at battle of Nhpum Ga, 210, 213; cremation of, 218; dead and rotting, 201; growing weakness of, 162; on Ledo Road, 65; shooting of, 127-128

pack howitzers, *see* howitzers

Page, Pvt. Norman, 172-174

Pamati, Burma, 243

Pandu, India, 73-74

Pangsan Pass, 78, 82

panic, in combat, 198, 265-266

parachute jumping, 293

paratroop drop, Nhpum Ga, 211

Parker, Lt. James, 189

Passanisi, T/5, 42, 82, 131

patrolling, interminable, 218

Pearl Harbor attack, 23, 64

Pick, Col. Lewis A., 79

pipeline, 4-inch, to China, 223

Piper Cubs, 133, 189

Poakum Trail, 195-196

"Poncho Villa," 187

prayer, on battlefield, 181-182, 185

private property, theft of at rest camp, 274

promotions, delayed, 227, 256-257, 283-284

psychoneurosis, following Walawbum, 134

psychopathic cases, among American troops, 265

Puerto Rico, 32

Purple Heart, awards of, 256

Putao, Burma, 78

Quebec Conference, 9-10, 14, 20-21, 28

radio contacts, in jungle, 144-146

rainy season, Burma, 187, 198, 202, 222, 229, 231-232

Ramgarh, India, 18, 58, 66-67, 261

Rangoon, Burma, 24, 64

rations, 65, 81, 91, 136, 154-156, 215; air drop of, 103; D, 150; increase in, 65; K, 150-151, 153-154, 168, 215; regime in preparation and use of, 156; scarcity of, 55; ten-in-one, 87, 219

regiments, *see* Infantry Regiments

rest camp, Dinjam, disorder and violence in, 274-275; as "pest hole," 272-273

rice, as food for 5307th, 136, 153, 254

Richardson, Sgt. Dave, x, 69, 129

Ritpong, Burma, 235

river crossings, pack animals and, 67

Rogoff, Maj. Bernard, 117, 199, 202

Romanus, Charles F., x

Roosevelt, Franklin Delano, 9, 14, 16, 20, 65, 280

Ross, "Little Chief," 203

Russell, Lillian (password), 169

Saigon, Indochina, 78

Salween R., 270

San Francisco, 32, 123

"Saucy" offensive, 20-21

Sayler's Creek, Battle of, 38, 254

Scott, Lt. Charles R., 35, 61, 179

Scott, Lt. William, 71

Seagrave, Col. Gordon S., 186

Seingneing, Burma, 241, 245, 253

Senff, Capt. Tom, 34, 37, 120-121, 150, 183, 215-217, 272, 295; evacuation of, 252-253

sensations under fire, 120-121; *see also* fears, combat

Shaduzup, Burma, 85, 137, 148, 156, 166, 189, 200, 224, 246, 255, 293; battle of, 170-188; march to, 142

Shakespeare, William, 233-234, 294

Shepley, James, 69-70

Shikau Ga, 133, 136, 189

Shingbwiyang, Burma, 78-79, 83, 86

Shytle, Charlie, 161-162

Siever, Lt. Edward, xi

Signal Corps, U.S., x, 33, 43, 80; *see also* communications platoon

Silver Star award, 140

Singapore, Malaya, 88, 109

Slim, Lt. Gen. Sir William, 13, 25, 27, 60, 223, 246, 270
Smith, Lt. Warren R., 195-196
smoking, on battlefield, 182
snakebite, 242
Southeast Asia Command, 21, 47-48
Southwest Pacific Command, 45
State Department (U.S.), 296
Steele, Arch, 90
Steinfield, Dr. Winnie, 42, 61, 63, 65, 73, 122, 233, 239, 285, 290-291
Stilwell, Gen. Joseph W., 1, 9-10, 15, 48, 58, 62, 64, 69, 71, 134, 137, 185-186, 189, 192, 194-195, 218, 223-224, 226, 228, 241, 244-245, 249, 268-270, 276; on apprehensions in war, 6; character, aims and responsibilities of, 16-27; arrival in China, 16; defeat in Burma, 16; appraisal of Chinese Army by, 17; bitterness revealed in diary, 19-20; deputy to Mountbatten, 21; real character of mission, 23; dedication to job, 24; greatest weakness of, 25; motto, 25; lack of self-assurance, 26; praise for Russians, 26; regard for Mountbatten, 27; on Chiang Kai-shek, 58; gains command of Chinese Army in India, 59; irked at Wingate's command of Galahad, 59; absence felt at Ningan Sakan, 86; visits Marauders on Tarung River, 87-88; strategy of, 89; visits Myitkyina airstrip, 249; relations with Merrill, 250; "field-bag" headquarters, 251; second visit to Myitkyina airstrip, 256; losing gambles of, 260; and "American" flavor of Myitkyina fight, 261; controversy with Mountbatten's headquarters, 264; made full general, 278; relieved of command, October, 1944, 279; as "small man in big job," 279; issue with Chiang Kai-shek, 280; responsibilities vs. competence appraised, 281-282
Stilwell's Command Problems, x, 107, 134
Strasbaugh, T/5 Bernard, 129
Stratemeyer, Lt. Gen. George E., 246
Stuart, Father James, 190-192, 216
Sudanese, 12
Sukup, John, 138, 163
Sumprabum, Burma, 191
Sunderland, Riley, x
Sun Li-jen, Gen., 89, 125, 267

surgery, battlefield, 117
Susnjer, Milton, 175-176

Tamu road, 270
Tanai R., 86, 102, 106, 190-191, 194, 200, 227, 229
Tanaka, Gen., 88-89, 106-107, 118, 134, 194, 224, 268
Tanja Ga, Burma, 91-92, 97, 102
Tarung R., 87
Tatbum, Burma, 195-196
Tawang R., 92, 102
tea drinking, 53-54, 72
Texas National Guard, 282
thievery, at Staging Area, 274-276
Thompson submachine gun, 170-171, 196
Tilly, Lt. James L., 139, 148, 157
Time, 1-2, 69, 260
Tingkrukawng, Burma, 236, 241
Tingkrung Hka, 139-141
Tintary, Perlee W., 164
trailblocks, 107, 205
training schedules, 44, 53
Transylvania Bible School, 40-41
Trinidad, B.W.I., 32
typhus, 235, 253, 255, 278, 286

under-fire sensations, 120-121; *see also* fears, combat
United Nations Southeast Asia Command, 10
United Press, 69
United States
Air Force, *see* Air Force, U.S.
Air Transport Command, *see* Air Transport Command
Army, *see* Army of the United States
War Department, *see* War Department
U.S. Army in World War II, The, x, 194, 245, 260, 271

Verdi, Giuseppi, 234
vitamin C, 155
vultures, 73; mistaken for turkeys, 56

Walawbum, Burma, 85, 107, 109, 123, 125, 127, 137, 145, 156, 180, 268; battle of, 127-132
walkie-talkies, repair of, 229
Wanting, China, 79n.
War Department General Staff (U.S.), Operation Division (OPD), 1, 9, 48, 62, 271
War Diary of the 5307th Composite Unit (Provisional), ix, 294

306

Washington Conference, 20
water, shortage of, 201-202; sources of, 76
Wavell, Gen. Sir Archibald P., 12-14, 19
Wayne, Mad Anthony, 285
weapons, instruction in at Myitkyina, 262
Wedemeyer, Gen. Albert C., 48-49
Weingartner, Lt. Victor ("Abe"), 128, 208
Weld, Anne (Mrs. Philip S.), 290
Weld, Lt. Philip S., 35-36, 45, 53, 80, 90, 105, 119, 123, 125, 148, 153, 158-159, 161, 165-173, 175, 182, 186, 220, 239, 250, 267, 275-276, 285, 290, 293
Weston, Lt. (later Capt.) Logan E., x, 39-41, 54, 56-57, 74, 91, 100, 108-109, 130, 195-196, 212, 282, 292; trapped by Japanese, 94
West Point, 64
Wesu Ga, 107, 110, 118, 124-125, 130, 133
Wilder, Paul, x
Wilson, Lt. (later Maj.) Samuel Vaughan, 3-4, 32, 37-39, 56, 74, 91-93, 95, 97-98, 102, 123-124, 137, 140, 148, 163-164, 183-184, 242, 244, 285-286, 290, 292; incident with jungle "cats," 98-99; message to Merrill, 99-101; evacuation of, 254-255
Wingate, Maj. Gen. Orde C., 3-4, 10, 24, 46, 48-49, 54, 58-59, 62, 188, 224-225, 257, 264; character and qualities of, 11-16; attachment to Zionist cause, 11; force organized by, 11-12; attempted suicide, 13, 257; Chindit raid by, 13-14; impressions of, by Allied generals, 13-15; airplane crash, 26; loses command of Galahad, 60
Woomer, Lt. William, 115-116, 212

Yank, x, 69
Young, Harold, 75
Yunnan, China, 19, 58, 223-224, 273

Zazama, Dr., xi
Zigyun, Burma, 243, 245, 247, 252, 254-255
Zionist Movement, 11